The Best of
THE
REFORMED
JOURNAL

The Best of
THE
REFORMED
JOURNAL

Edited by

James D. Bratt & Ronald A. Wells

WILLIAM B. EERDMANS PUBLISHING COMPANY

GRAND RAPIDS, MICHIGAN / CAMBRIDGE, U.K.

© 2011 William B. Eerdmans Publishing Company
All rights reserved

Published 2011 by
Wm. B. Eerdmans Publishing Co.
2140 Oak Industrial Drive N.E., Grand Rapids, Michigan 49505 /
P.O. Box 163, Cambridge CB3 9PU U.K.

Printed in the United States of America

18 17 16 15 14 13 12 11   7 6 5 4 3 2 1

Library of Congress Cataloging-in-Publication Data

The best of The Reformed Journal /
edited by James D. Bratt & Ronald A. Wells.
        p.   cm.
    Includes bibliographical references and index.
    ISBN 978-0-8028-6702-5 (pbk.: alk. paper)
    1. Reformed Church — Doctrines.   I. Bratt, James D., 1949-
II. Wells, Ronald, 1941-   III. Reformed journal (Grand Rapids, Mich.)

    BX9422.5.B47   2011
    285.705 — dc23

                                        2011039465

www.eerdmans.com

Contents

Contents

Contents

On the Church in Society

Race and Rights

Theology

Contents

Contents

Contents

Contents

Contents

Publisher's Note

If my ministerial father was not a charter subscriber to *The Reformed Journal*, he was at least an early one, owing in part, I think, to James Daane, a *Journal* founding editor and an old friend from their student days together at Princeton Seminary. It was Jim who likely got my father going on *Christianity Today* as well, Jim having joined Carl Henry and others on that evangelical masthead. These personal connections interest me because together they embody in a small way the intellectual and cultural ethos that was central to the *Journal* and, beyond, to the Eerdmans Publishing Company, which produced the magazine. Here in the late 50s or early 60s were two ministers firmly rooted in their Dutch-Calvinist tradition but having one eye on the broader mainline Protestant world, as represented by Princeton, and the other eye, however warily, on the evangelical world of Billy Graham, who had founded *Christianity Today*. They were, in fact, undoubtedly wary in both directions, concerned about theological slippage on the one side (my father, while revering Princeton, had sympathies for Machen) and on the other side concerned that, however fervently held the evangelical truths and whatever the clarion intellectual summons of Carl Henry and others, there hadn't been a great deal of theology in the first place from which to slip.

Those wanting a general account of Eerdmans' attempt as a publisher to navigate among these worlds can refer to *An Eerdmans Century*, the company history written by Larry ten Harmsel and Reinder Van Til for this centennial year. *The Reformed Journal*, over the course of its forty years of publication, played an important role in the Eerdmans program, both in its own right as a magazine, and as a supportive adjunct to the book program. The company is pleased now to offer here, as part of its anniversary celebration, a volume of pieces from the magazine's own particular history. We are grateful to Ronald Wells and James Bratt, erstwhile colleagues together in the history department at Calvin College, for making so judicious and well-introduced a compilation. Those wanting a deeply informed and beautifully rendered account of where the *Journal* came from and where it went hardly need look farther than this volume. Wells came to the task as a frequent writer for the magazine and as a former member of the *Journal* editorial board, and Bratt came to it as one of the most astute historians of Dutch Calvinism in its American context.

The *Journal*, over its forty years, had a wonderfully symbiotic relationship with the book program, benefiting from the intellectual and ecumenical expansion of the Eerdmans list and contributing to it through its own growing network of authors and readers. A book idea might first try its wings as a *Journal* article. From the other direction, an article might be drawn from an already published Eerdmans book or from one still in progress. Usually, however, the relationship was indirect and diffuse, simply a matter of books and magazine stirring the same pot. The magazine also, of course, especially through its reviews but also through excerpting, helped to keep the book program alert to what was being produced by other publishers.

Whatever the importance of the articles and reviews, it was the opening "As We See It" section that probably most defined the magazine for its readers. This section also produced some of the *Journal*'s best (and journalistically most awarded) writing, its eclecticism and diversity, in form and substance, reflecting the omnivorous curiosity of its contributors. Akin, to speak a bit grandly, to the *New Yorker*'s fabled "Talk of the Town," the pieces ranged from classic editorials, straight down the middle of the fairway (the selections that follow include at least two references to golf!), to irregular but interesting little mashie niblick shank shots off to some hitherto unexplored patch in the woods or perhaps catching some unsuspecting orthodoxy in the shins, to quietly reflective personal commentary that would sink home in the reader's shared human experience.

Ideally, an issue contained four or five such pieces to provide the desired variety, and editing them and commissioning them, often at the last minute, was a good deal of the challenge and fun of putting the magazine together. Would that piece needed to fill the empty spot come in at the eleventh hour? And, when I was the editor, would my stalwart and exacting in-office colleague in the enterprise, Milton

Essenburg, be able to accommodate yet another change in the layout, along with all the other endless tweakings throughout the magazine that pursued it all the way out the door to the printer? Where "As We See It"s were concerned, what had been submitted as an article might on occasion emerge in print as an editorial, having sacrificed some of its length to a noble journalistic cause. Titles, whether for "As We See It"s or for the other pieces, were particular fun in polishing the magazine, and if we thought of a good one that didn't quite have the proper referent in the piece itself, we'd look for a way to install it there, where, we were sure, God had meant it to be in the first place.

All the last-minute improvisation and extended fussing did not, of course, make the *Journal* the most punctual of magazines, and in a world in which respectable monthlies arrive in the mailbox in the month preceding the month announced on the cover, the *Journal* never, that I can recall from my own experience, achieved this feat. I do recall that we once managed to land our Christmas issue on the doorstep in early January, putting us in the dismal company of *The Wittenburg* [*sic*] *Door,* which at least made a point of such failures.

Editing the *Journal,* which was always a kind of sideline occupation for the editor-in-chief of the Eerdmans book program, produced its own persistent worry but was also more immediately gratifying than book publishing. Books take months to work through the system and the reward for one's labor is long delayed. A monthly magazine, by contrast, provides an almost immediate response, and generally a more spirited one, for better or for worse. Moreover, a magazine quickly gives way to the next issue and the chance to start afresh and do better. A book tends to be a more lingering burden on the editorial conscience, especially as the financial returns come in, these being more specific to a book than to a single issue of a magazine. But, most importantly, books involve many hands in the making, whereas putting together a magazine as modest as the *Journal* gave the editor more control over the project, with more pieces to creatively manipulate. Each issue could feel a little like a work of art.

Whatever the benefits of the *Journal* to the Eerdmans book program, it was also a significant diversion, financially and editorially, and in 1990 the company decided that it needed to throw all its resources behind the books and to end its relationship to the magazine. The *Journal* was combined with *Perspectives* magazine, inevitably resulting in a rather different entity than either magazine had been.

The old *Journal* is still missed by some erstwhile readers and contributors and, over the years, the question has arisen whether it could be revived. Perhaps. But, of course, much has changed in the past two decades. Beyond *Perspectives*, other magazines have come into the picture, most notably the splendid *Books and Culture*, which, whatever the differences in format and outlook, appeals to much of what would have been the *Journal*'s audience, too. *The Christian Century*, in broadening its reach over the years, reflects new ecumenical alliances in religious culture which the *Journal*, too, whatever its residual ecclesiastical and confessional identity, encouraged in its time and would have wanted to encourage today. One must also note here the ongoing presence of *First Things*. And — a challenge to all magazines now — what of the rapidly expanding world of the blogosphere, incessantly serving up "As We See It"s, as it were, only a few keystrokes away?

What is no longer within reach now is that distinctive community out of which the *Journal* came and which remained, however much the roster of editors and contributors grew, and however much the ongoing operation of the magazine became more centralized in the Eerdmans office, not only a continuing source of ideas and articles, but a wonderfully inspiring intellectual ethos sustained in part by shared — and, let it be acknowledged, sometimes self-important — stories that became mythologies. The founding editors never tired of regaling the younger guard with, for example, their account of Henry Zylstra's triumphantly naming the magazine at the outset "a periodical of Reformed comment and opinion," a remarkably unremarkable contribution, I always thought, from the great man. Then again, such is often the simplicity of genius. The founders certainly thought so here. The younger generation had its own stories to add — of, for example, the time Henry Stob was asked by one of the newer editors, in the service of a more enlightened etiquette, not to light up a cigarette after lunch, causing much silent consternation in a founder for whom the *Journal*, at least of cherished memory, practically *was* smoke. It was no less an authoritative figure than Henry Stob who, in another story, drew the delicate diplomatic assignment of telling Jim Daane that the magazine would not publish his series of articles criticizing Carl Henry, they having been judged as now anachronistic and unfair. Jim remained, I suspect, mildly peeved to the end of his life about this turndown, convinced that he, as Carl Henry's onetime associate, could see better than his *Journal* fellows the errors still latent in the Henry mind. The myth-making could extend in startling and eccentric ways even beyond any formal *Journal* business. "Nick," Harry Boer once announced to his editorial colleague Nick Wolterstorff, having appeared unannounced on the Wolterstorff doorstep proffering a package of Oreo cookies, "I'm here to discuss reprobation."

No *Journal* story was told — and retold — with more relish by the founding editors than of the moment when Wm. B. Eerdmans, Sr., enthusiastically began the magazine by laying down two dollars for its first subscription. Now, sixty years later, in a quieter gesture, the Eerdmans Publishing Company offers this volume of *Journal* pieces to those who will remember the magazine and to those who may wish to know it — as an anniversary gift in this centennial year, but even more as an expression of thanks for a gift with which it was entrusted for forty years by an unusually devoted group of editors, writers, and readers. Particular thanks are due on this occasion to the Calvin Center for Christian Scholarship for its financial and logistical support of this retrospective volume. *The Reformed Journal* is unthinkable without Calvin College and Calvin Theological Seminary, and it is gratifying that the Calvin community here recognizes the history of the magazine as, indeed, a part of its own. And our thanks, again, to Jim Bratt and Ron Wells for carrying off with such excellence a project that, like the magazine itself, was obviously a labor of love.

JON POTT

Acknowledgments

This book would not have come into being without the ready support of the Eerdmans Publishing Company. We thank William B. Eerdmans, Jr., and Jon Pott for adopting the project as part of the company's centennial anniversary celebration, and we appreciate Jenny Hoffman's efficient help in transforming the original hard copies into electronic files. We are also indebted to the Calvin Center for Christian Scholarship for its generous financial support of the project, especially to Susan Felch, CCCS director, for encouraging our proposal, and Dale Williams, CCCS program coordinator, for covering details as we moved forward. Finally, we are grateful to Lisa Eary of the Calvin College history department, who intervened in the production process at a crucial moment to help us along with her usual unflappable competence.

Introduction

The Reformed Journal was one of the outstanding magazines of religious reflection on the North American scene in the second half of the twentieth century. Over a forty-year span (1951-1990) it produced a body of original, well-informed, and self-critical commentary on the church and the world, in an era when both church and world were undergoing dramatic change. In the process the *Journal* made a notable contribution to the resurgence of evangelical Protestantism that reshaped the landscape of American religion and politics. If in the end — actually, all along — *Journal* writers disapproved of some of the fundamental tenets and conclusions of various parties in the evangelical house, that was an irony the *Journal's* better wits could ruefully accept. Its earnest spirit, however, never quit the contest.

Overall, the earnestness tended to prevail: these were, after all, Calvinists, in an era when the species was thought to be extinct; many of them descendants of Dutch Calvinist stock, for whom humor was traditionally more earthy than witty and thus inappropriate in discussions of godly things. Most of the *Journal's* writers regarded themselves also as progressives, if of a moderate sort — progressive in a very traditionalistic denomination; progressive among evangelicals, whose reputation during this era typically varied from Right to Hard Right; progressive because and not in spite of their religious orientation, in the face of a consensus among all right-minded people that God is not a forward thinker. The *Journal's* story, in short, is unusual enough to be interesting and substantive enough to merit the time to study it.

The volume before you collects some of the best writing of the *Journal*, first of all for your reading pleasure and for your intellectual

— indeed, we hope spiritual — edification. It provides a record of an intriguing interaction between Reformed thinkers and developments in American life from the start to the end of the Cold War, from the retreat of Modernism to an early peak of postmodernism, from the last phase of Christian America to the global explosion of non-Western Christianity. We think it important to make the *Journal*'s voice more accessible both for the record and as a resource that others might emulate in their own way in today's radically altered media environment. It is particularly useful, at a moment when Calvinists are said to be on the rise in American Protestantism, to show some broader dimensions of what that tradition can supply by way of theology, social and cultural commentary, and political reflection.[1] The eminent American religious historian Martin Marty once observed of the central evangelical fixation: "You're born again? Great! That took fifteen minutes. Now what?" This volume queries Calvinism's ardent believers, and equally ardent detractors, about its own mantra: "God predestined things? Great, that was an eternity ago. What now?" The *Reformed Journal* was a venture in answering that question.

*   *   *

The Reformed Journal was born in 1951 out of intramural quarrels in the Christian Reformed Church. The denomination itself had originated in 1857 when a sub-set of the newly arrived Dutch immigrants to the Midwest left the ecclesiastical shelter provided them by the venerable, east-coast Reformed Church in America in favor of greater autonomy and even stricter orthodoxy.[2] After some decades of bare survival the CRC bloomed with the high tide of Dutch migration to the United States in the 1880s and '90s and entered upon a period of vigorous theological discussion and institutional proliferation. Most important in the latter was the Theological School at Grand Rapids (founded 1876), which developed into Calvin College and Seminary.

---

1. See, for instance, Collin Hansen, *Young, Restless, Reformed: A Journalist's Journey with the New Calvinists* (Wheaton, Ill.: Crossway Books, 2008); and James K. A. Smith, *Letters to a Young Calvinist: An Invitation to the Reformed Tradition* (Grand Rapids: Brazos, 2010).

2. This historical review is explored in close detail in James D. Bratt, *Dutch Calvinism in Modern America: A History of a Conservative Subculture* (Grand Rapids: Eerdmans, 1984).

The schools, along with the denomination at large, felt the heavy hand of Americanization during World War I, and so spent the 1920s hashing out what sort and what degree of acculturation they should pursue. They vented the issue in theological arguments, specifically over the doctrine of common grace — the proposition that God shows real (though not saving) grace to all people, not just to the elect. The real-world stakes were clear: what did the people of God share with their non-believing neighbors? What were the possibilities and moral worth of American society? How separate should the church be from the world? The answer given by Synod, the CRC's highest assembly, was to affirm a minimal form of common grace as necessary for evangelization but then to magnify the antagonism between church and world by way of forthright condemnations of three forms of "worldliness": dancing, games of chance, and theater attendance — that is, the movies. The measures were as symbolically redolent as they were concretely binding upon everyday behavior, and they defined the ambience in which the *Journal*'s founders were reared.

It was not unreasonable to show a collective wariness during the decades of the Great Depression and World War II, but other strands of Christian Reformed culture generated countervailing attitudes. Yes, the church's children were educated in separate day schools, but there all subjects were to be taught from a Christian perspective, encouraging reflection on the whole world under the ultimate will of God. Yes, doctrine was to be strictly minded but behind that screen lay profound philosophical and theological questions as well as a long, robust tradition of Reformed thinking about them. The inquisitive young mind had license to go deep-sea diving. Yes, the reigning political culture in Dutch American enclaves was Republican, often of a pronounced isolationist and anti-New Deal tone; but only one generation back in the Dutch Reformed heritage lay the great work and witness of Abraham Kuyper, which could support other views. Kuyper (1837-1920) had formulated an ideology of and amassed an institutional apparatus to support an intentionally Calvinist project in politics and scholarship which tried to mount consistently biblical positions in defiance of the established secular spectrum of policy and opinion. On that Kuyperian basis some Christian Reformed leaders found reason to support the New Deal, to warrant involvement in international affairs, and to propose positive Christian interventions in the domains of scholarship and social action. The leading exponents of such approaches in the

CRC were Clarence Bouma, a professor at Calvin Seminary, and Henry J. Ryskamp, dean of Calvin College. Bouma was editor of and Ryskamp a frequent contributor to *The Calvin Forum*, a monthly journal of opinion founded in 1935 to give intellectual leadership to the CRC from the Calvin campus.

*   *   *

The end of World War II made such a venture seem more plausible. The war had swept hundreds of young people out of Christian Reformed enclaves into what was said to be a crusade to save civilization from totalitarian destruction. American victory in that cause made the world seem less hostile to efforts for righteousness, while the casualties suffered along the way made such efforts more urgent than ever. By contrast, the timid legalism, the petty customs, the reflex defensiveness of the old CRC seemed passé at best, irresponsible at worst. Such was the conviction, at any rate, of the young returning veterans who would be the *Journal*'s first editors: Henry Stob, who served on the staff of General Douglas MacArthur before returning to his position in the philosophy department at Calvin College; his cousin George Stob, erstwhile Army chaplain in Europe who was named professor of church history at Calvin Seminary in 1948; Henry Zylstra, an infantryman who received a battlefield commission in the Philippines before coming back to the English department at the college; Harry Boer, a Marine chaplain in the Pacific, who joined the seminary faculty in 1949 as professor of missions; and James Daane, a CRC minister and veteran not of the war but of doctoral training at Princeton Theological Seminary under the direction of Josef Hromadka, a reputed neoorthodox theologian from the newly Communist country of Czechoslovakia.[3]

Two items pertaining to the last three members on this list signaled a storm that blew up Calvin Seminary in the early 1950s and began to reconfigure the CRC in the process. By the late 1940s the seminary's long-time leader, the carefully orthodox Louis Berkhof, had retired, opening the way for assertive moves by Clarence Bouma. Boer and George Stob were his protégés and were appointed to the sem-

---

3. Personal details are given in George Stob, "The Years of the Journal," *Reformed Journal* 26 (March 1976): 12-13.

inary faculty in the face of strong conservative opposition. Their fresh and open attitude, in turn, brought them under suspicion of "Barthianism" — that is, of a view of scriptural authority different from the old scholastic propositional method taught by Berkhof. The matter was complicated by personality conflicts until the faculty could not even meet to conduct ordinary business. Bouma suffered a nervous breakdown that ended his career, and the Synod cashiered virtually the whole remainder of the faculty, including Stob and Boer. Rumors of doctrinal deviance went unsustained, despite assiduous investigation into those under suspicion. Stob moved on to the parish ministry; Boer took his professorial skills to northern Nigeria, where the CRC had long supported a mission. The *Reformed Journal,* founded as a progressive voice in the conflict, carried on the larger cause for the long run. A month later, as if to provide a foil, another magazine appeared on the opposite end of the CRC spectrum — *Torch and Trumpet,* known to its opponents as "Glow and Blow."

Yet, the broader scene of church and nation was also in the *Journal*'s sights from the start. The early 1950s was the heyday of McCarthyism and kindred hysterias about "un-American" opinion. At the same time a new generation of conservative Protestants was coming back from the sidelines where their parents had retreated as belittled "fundamentalists" following defeats in *their* theological battles in the 1920s. The younger set chose the label "evangelical" instead, mounted successful appeals through parachurch organizations such as Youth for Christ, and followed dynamic, positive leaders like Billy Graham, who refashioned revivalism for postwar venues, and Carl Henry, who called for a recovery of evangelical social concern.[4] In other words, the times required Christian Reformed attention to politics and to evangelicals, and that mandate too figured in the *Journal*'s inception.

The CRC had joined the National Association of Evangelicals (NAE) in 1943 to ease the process of placing chaplains in the armed services. Just as this was an unusual ecumenical move for so cautious a denomination, so, ironically, it was progressive voices in the church that in 1950 called for the decision to be reconsidered, lest the CRC lose its "Reformed distinctiveness" to fundamentalist "aberrations." The fi-

---

4. Joel Carpenter, *Revive Us Again: The Reawakening of American Fundamentalism* (New York: Oxford University Press, 1997).

nal straw was the NAE's official endorsement of John T. Flynn's *The Road Ahead,* a right-wing political screed befitting the McCarthyist times. When Lester DeKoster, a Calvin College professor of Speech (and a future *Journal* editor), protested against the volume's method and message, H. J. Kuiper, longtime editor of the CRC's official magazine and arguably the strongest voice in the denomination, twice called upon Synod to investigate whether DeKoster had been "infected with the Socialistic virus" and formally opposed his appointment as college librarian.[5] Against future complaints that their magazine was politicizing religion, the *Journal's* editors could reply that they were simply returning a favor.

The last and vital piece of the *Journal's* support structure was provided by the good offices of the William B. Eerdmans Publishing Company. The founder, "Bill, Sr." (1882-1966), had immigrated to the United States in 1902 with the intention of entering the ministry but took up the book business instead. He collaborated in the organizational process of the *Reformed Journal,* paid its first subscription, and provided all the logistical support from production to distribution to advertising and subscription management. His son and successor, "Bill, Jr.," maintained the same policy until the changing cost structure of the publishing industry required the company to give exclusive devotion to its book business. For the *Journal's* entire forty-year run, its managers and eventually editors-in-chief were Eerdmans people: Peter De Visser, David Wynbeek, Calvin Bulthuis, Marlin Van Elderen, and Jon Pott.

*   *   *

Once launched, the *Journal* steadily expanded its breadth of coverage, contributors, and readers until it was a noted presence on the evangelical Protestant scene. Simultaneously, the *Journal* provided a respected venue for the expression of confessional and biblical conviction among a (still) "mainline" Protestant readership. For most of its career the *Journal* was one of the few magazines — for a few years the only one — to belong to both the mainline Church Press Association and to the Evangelical Press Association. As one of the few organs read across

---

5. Stob, "Years of the Journal," p. 11 (source of quotations); Bratt, *Dutch Calvinism,* pp. 189-90.

that divide, the *Reformed Journal* served to make traditional Protestant conviction more reputable in mainline precincts while also setting a standard among evangelicals of top-notch, venturesome commentary on the whole range of concerns of modern public life.

Its mediating location perhaps helps account for the disproportionate number of annual awards that the two press associations bestowed upon the little magazine from Michigan. For their part the *Journal*'s editors located its strength in the Reformed tradition that was emblazoned on the magazine's masthead: a tradition that the *Journal* helped renew among its Christian Reformed base, that it helped encourage among readers in mainline churches which nominally stood in the Reformed heritage, and that it espoused over against the personalistic, individualistic, and culture-aversive habits inherited by many mid-twentieth century evangelicals. To many, the most striking aspect of the magazine was its combination of distinctive point of view and expansive range of commentary. Articles on theology and the deliberations of church assemblies spread out on the *Journal*'s pages, as befit a religious magazine, but so did reviews of literature and film, essays on higher education and aesthetic theory, and articles on philosophy and science — and sometimes the philosophy of science. The *Reformed Journal* gave persistent attention to important social trends like the civil rights movement and the rebirth of feminism, as it did to political controversies attending the Vietnam War and the rise of the Christian Right. It was also marked by ecumenical concern in giving space to the plight of Christians in Palestine and especially (sometimes almost uniquely) in publishing the leading Christian voices — black, white, and colored — in the resistance to South African apartheid. All this added up to a consistent body of reflection refracted through theological commitment, engaged with the state of the academic disciplines, and intent on articulating fresh positions above hardened, predictable habits of opinion.

*   *   *

The selections below aim to provide a representative cross-section of the *Journal*'s writing. We have included pieces from each decade of the magazine's career and across all domains of its concerns. We have tried to capture the *Journal*'s dynamic interaction with the context of the times, to show how it responded to — indeed, helped hone — the cutting edge of evangelical engagement with the culture. The major divisions of the book are chronological, each introduced by a few words setting the context and agenda of that period, along with a sketch of the principal ligaments tying each cluster of pieces together. A brief summary of the *Journal*'s course of development, therefore, will suffice here. For its first dozen years the magazine centered on in-house disputes in the Christian Reformed Church in opposition to the denomination's entrenched defenders of orthodoxy. The 1960s and '70s brought a quickening of socio-political concerns — issues of war and peace, race and civil rights, American foreign policy and Christian Zionism — along with responses to radical new proposals in theology and the erosion of the old "mainline" in American Protestantism. In the *Journal*'s last dozen years, the triumph of conservative politics in the presidency of Ronald Reagan prompted the magazine to offer a coherent, yet supplely expressed version of critical Reformed thinking in the Niebuhrian as well as Kuyperian tradition over against claims by such organizations as the Moral Majority and the Christian Coalition to speak for biblical Christianity.

In reviewing all these periods and topics we have put a priority on choosing good writing; happily, the *Journal* abounded in such. We are delighted to make some of it freshly accessible and to acquaint a new generation with (as we remind an older one of) definitive voices from an important venture in Christian thinking: philosophers like Henry Stob and his student, Nicholas Wolterstorff; theologians like Lewis Smedes and his colleague at Fuller Theological Seminary, James Daane; leading evangelical historians like George Marsden and Mark Noll; a pioneer of Christian feminism, Mary Stewart Van Leeuwen; and supreme prose stylists like Virginia Stem Owens, Lionel Basney, and Cornelius Plantinga. We have been able to include only three of the many poems the *Journal* published over the years, and only one of its many short stories — but one remarkable enough to deserve its place as the final word in the volume.

A Note on Style

As an anthology of historical materials, this book preserves the language and style in which the articles originally appeared. This will be especially noticeable with respect to gender usages, racial and ethnic terminology, and the capitalization of pronoun references to God. Most of the longer pieces in this collection were originally even longer — sometimes much longer! — and have been trimmed for inclusion here. Except at the start of essays we have marked deleted materials with ellipses. We have also from time to time altered paragraphing, punctuation, and italicization, since (especially in the early years) *Journal* writers preferred the first short, the last heavy, and strewed commas everywhere. Through all changes we have tried to preserve the author's particular voice and original argument. Readers who want to read the entirety of the original articles — and some others on the same or closely related topics — will be able to access these in due time at the Eerdmans website.

James Daane spoke for the founding editors when he declared that the postwar world required "a Reformed theology bristling with vitality and restless with creative energy." That tone and agenda are well captured in the opening essay in this section, Harry Boer's "The Cathedral," and the two selections that follow start to flesh out what such a project might produce. Lewis Smedes, who would become a *Journal* editor in 1964, appeared in its pages already in 1952 while a graduate student in theology at the Free University of Amsterdam. His piece issued a prescient call for sacramental renewal which would recur down through the years in the *Journal*'s columns, just as it would become a leading theme across American Protestantism later in the century.

The *Journal*'s serious but gentle critique of 1950s American culture is well put in John Timmerman's "The American Way of Life," the *Journal* debut of a longstanding member of the Calvin College English department and an eventual *Journal* editor. Timmerman's Christian-Idealist outlook came from Henry Zylstra, whose "Thoughts for Teachers" also demonstrates the literary method that a generation of Calvin students learned from this most influential of teachers. Zylstra's death in Amsterdam in December 1956 was a profound shock to the magazine and college alike; ironically, his classic Advent meditation, "Hospitality," ran that same month.

The magazine's more hopeful, if still measured, engagement with American society is evident in Sidney Rooy's reflections upon Billy Graham's 1957 New York City Crusade and Ernest Van Vugt's remarkably titled Calvin College chapel talk, "Pitch Your Tents Toward Sodom." Stronger assertions appear in Henry Stob's defense of academic freedom at a Christian college, written in light of both the recent imposition of "loyalty" oaths at American colleges and universities and recurrent suspicions in the CRC about various sorts of "unorthodoxy" at Calvin College. A frequent target of such, Lester DeKoster, never ducked a fight and invited controversy with his forthright assault on the prevailing assumption that being Reformed meant voting Republican. The truly egregious religio-political system of South African apartheid received the first of many *Journal* rebukes in the essay Harry Boer published at the dawn of the 1960s from his teaching post in Nigeria.

The inaugural period in the *Journal*'s history closed, as it opened, on a theological controversy, this one precipitated by Calvin Seminary professor Harold Dekker's revisiting the middle term of the old Calvinist acronym of TULIP: the doctrine of limited atonement. Dekker's article drew many critiques, one of the best being that of Peter De Jong, a future Calvin Seminary professor himself. The CRC Synod duly investigated the matter, only to decide in 1967 that, while Dekker had spoken a bit loosely, he was not guilty of doctrinal error. That decision marked the end of the reign of the conservative establishment against which the *Journal*'s founders had arisen, and arguably the beginning of their own ascendancy.

The Cathedral

HARRY R. BOER   *July 1953*

We who stand in the spiritual tradition of John Calvin think of him as a reformer and a theologian, as a writer of the *Institutes* and of the *Commentaries*. Only infrequently do we think of him as a preacher, and hardly at all as one who addressed the world of his day from the pulpit of a massive cathedral. That Calvin during the space of thirty years preached his eloquent sermons in the impressive setting of marble and stone structured in Gothic beauty is worthy of note. . . . His timeless witness was spoken in the symbolic setting of enduring stone hewn into the form of a heaven-pointing cross. When Calvin preached in St. Peter's it was already rich with three hundred fifty years of history. He who ascended the pulpit and they who worshipped in the pew were already then conscious of the weight of a tradition and of a cloud of witnesses who had gone on before. . . .

Dutch American Calvinists have quite left this tradition. We build houses of worship to last some generations and expect that then our great-grandchildren will erect new ones. But we will not be in those new buildings. Our spirits will be absent, lost in the ruins of the old. And because we will not be there, those who lived before us will not be there. Our posterity will stand alone, much as we now so largely stand alone. They will be conscious of a physical relationship to those who gave them birth but somehow strangely distant from their spirit and ideals, just as we now stand strangely distant from the spirit and ideals that lie at the fountainhead of our tradition.

Have we not become quite poor? Theology is the queen of the sciences in the Reformed tradition, but we have not produced a new thought, have not found a new vision in half a century. But there has been endless casuistry about the movies and divorce. Apparently isolated from all that went before or came after stands concern with the large problem of Common Grace in 1924. Why was no more heard about it for twenty-five years and more? Was it really theological and religious concern that lifted the problem to prominence a quarter-century ago?

I think that all this is the way it is because we have not the inner strength to build *cathedrals*. Like the rest of America, we have the *money* to build them, but not the inner strength. We have money to build a million-dollar science building. We have more millions for a commons building and dormitories and other such soulless structures. But there is on Calvin College's campus no cathedral, no small effort at one in the form of a solid, spacious, worship-inviting chapel. This the often emptily boastful descendants of the preacher of St. Peter's in Geneva do not have at the center of their denominational life.

Now I do not mean to say that we cannot build a cathedral-like chapel on our school grounds. Of course we can . . . for we are a determined people when we get going. But it would not, I fear, be a *cathedral*. A cathedral, to me, represents a profound human appreciation for history in its religious significance and development. It says that God is the Lord of History. Therefore it cuts the never-aging rock out of the eternal hills and fashions it into an enduring structure, a testimony to man's witnessing, consecrated, royal service to the God of time, past and present and future. That is a cathedral. That is a true cathedral. In such a cathedral one never stands alone. One stands in the consciousness of communion with and indebtedness to the past, and of a stewardship to discharge in the present and transmit to the future. It is this sense of history, the sense that builds cathedrals of stone or stately mansions of the soul, that we have lost in the Christian Reformed Communion. . . .

Can we again become [a cathedral-building people]? Assuredly we can. Did not Israel become a temple-building people after the long captivity? So we can again become a cathedral-building community. But first we will have to unlearn and leave our idolatries as Israel had to unlearn and leave its idolatries. The chilling and killing touch of a dead traditionalism, satisfaction with what great men said in living context to their day many years ago, living on them but not extending them, the substitution of legalism for the safeguards of the liberty wherewith Christ has made us free — these, all these, must go, and unfettered men must be free to preach the unfettered Word to a world that needs unfettering from a bondage that only free men can effect. This only people who live in the tradition of Calvin can do, people who live in the cathedral tradition.

The significance of Calvin is not so much that he said new things, but that he spoke old truths in a new way in living context with his day. He absorbed into himself all that was best in the long history out of which he had come and he knew how to use it in making the Scriptures speak their message for his generation. The Bible is timeless, theologies are its exposition in the concrete situation in which the Church finds itself. We must get away from the notion that has so long dominated our thinking that theology or dogmatics is simply a compendium of propositions. It must serve the Church in its existing need. Christ saves us not alone from the world but also in the world as sin expresses itself in any given era of the world's history. Kuyper spoke against the easy-going Christ-denying Modernism of his time. Calvin took issue with the traditionalism of Rome and with its denial of the liberty that Christ has given us. Against these evils he made the Bible speak. He passionately demanded the right to say what the Bible says and for more than thirty years he wrote its meaning in his study and preached its message in the cathedral, sending throughout Europe a wave of energy-unleashing life that has permanently affected Western civilization.

I knew it from reading the *Institutes* and now after visiting the cathedral I know more than ever that Calvin could not possibly have spent his days on the movie question; in defending the proposition that card-playing is sin but that the Church must not do anything about it because everybody is doing it; in holding that an illegally divorced person can never, never be a member of the Christian Church so long as the partner is living and then, after forty years, undertake to see if there is scriptural ground for such a position. We are called to more serious and responsible theological stewardship. Our preoccupation with trivialities and with improperly formulated problems has cost us the riches of our tradition and given nothing in its place. . . .

Can the Reformed tradition among us still be preserved, guarded and extended — above all extended — for only so can a tradition be preserved? Clearly the days of the Prophets are gone and we are fallen upon the evil days of Scribes and Lawyers with their precept upon precept, line upon line, here a little, there a little. Let us stand in the ways, and see, and ask for the old paths, where is the good way, and walk therein, that we may find rest for our souls. Let us remember the free spirit, the prophetic voice, the fearless witness of the man who preached in St. Peter's. Mayhap the Master Builder will yet make of our Communion a spacious Cathedral in which we may serve him. For His promise remains: I will raise up the Tabernacle of David that is fallen, and close up the breaches thereof, and I will raise up his ruins, and I will build it as in the days of old.

Common Grace Versus Individualism

JAMES DAANE   *April 1951*

The history of religious thought shows that the doctrine of common grace has arisen only in the area of Reformed Theology. It did not, and could not, arise in Liberal or Fundamentalistic Christianity, for the simple reason that neither Liberalism nor Fundamentalism believes in the Covenant. Both these versions of Christianity believe that God deals with men exclusively *as individuals*. Where God's dealing with men is regarded as a strictly individual affair, there is no question as to what the elect and the reprobate have in *common*. There is here no question of common grace.

Reformed theology, however, takes the idea of the Covenant seriously. It believes that God, as Triune, is covenantal in His very nature; that man, created in God's image, is also covenantal in his very nature; and that God, in harmony with His and man's nature, always deals with mankind in terms of a covenant. Thus, God deals with the whole mass of mankind through the Covenant of Works, and with a large group of people through the Covenant of Grace. From this it is plain that God deals with mankind not first of all as so many individuals, but as a group.

But Reformed theology believes also in election and reprobation. This means that within the large group there are both elect and reprobate — individuals whom God intends to save and individuals whom He does not intend to save. At this point the question of common grace arises. God deals with mankind in terms of a group and has a general attitude toward the whole group. Yet the group contains elect and reprobate, toward each of which He has a special attitude. What, then, do the elect and reprobate, *as members of a common group*, have in common? This is the question of common grace — a question that can arise only within a theology that takes seriously both the doctrine of the Covenant and the doctrine of election and reprobation.

Rev. Herman Hoeksema claims to believe in the Covenant of Grace. Nevertheless, in common with the Fundamentalist and the Liberal, he believes essentially that God deals with mankind as individuals. For, in Hoeksema's thought, God does not *first of all* deal with elect and reprobate together, *in their covenanted historical relatedness*. God has no *common* attitude toward *both* elect and reprobate. Consequently, Hoeksema denies both common grace and a common wrath. God *only loves* the elect, and He *only hates* the reprobate. . . .

Against this religious individualism — which Hoeksema shares with both Liberalism and Fundamentalism — Reformed theology maintains that God deals with mankind first as a group and only secondly with the individual *as an individual*. And even then He deals with the individual *as a member of the group*. This, Reformed theology maintains, is taking the covenant seriously. To think of the individual apart from the group, and to think of the elect and the reprobate out of the relationship to the covenant, spells an unbiblical individualism.

Man — Both One and Many

The mistake of defining the individual's situation apart from the group becomes clear from a consideration of man's nature. The nature of man is determined by his creation in the divine image. Man's nature is a reflection of God's nature. Now God is both One and Three; He is both One and Many. God's nature, therefore, cannot be defined in terms of One *or* Three, but only in terms of One *and* Three. Separation of the One from the Three is theological sacrilege. And since man is a reflection of God, man is also in his very nature *both one and many*. Hence, every definition of man which fails to keep the balance between the one and the many distorts human nature.

In the light of this Biblical definition of human nature, it seems plainly contrary to Biblical teaching to say that the individual is first, and that the community follows after and is founded upon the individual. To define human nature in terms of the number "one," and to get to the community by adding up the many "ones," is to go contrary to the Bible. Definitions of Church and of Society based on an alleged priority of the individual do not square with the Biblical view of the nature of both God and man.

The Fundamentalist subscribes to this priority of the individual. Consequently, for the Fundamentalist the Church is nothing more than the sum total of saved individuals. To regard the Church as no more than the sum of its parts gives a weak and inadequate conception of the Church. Political Liberalism also subscribes to the priority of the individual. For this reason its conception of democracy is not Christian.

The Bible shows man, by nature and in the covenant, to be both one and many. The "many" does not result from the totaling of "ones." Christian thinking begins with both — the many as well as the one. They are both given, by God, in the nature of man and in the fact of the covenant. For that reason the question whether the individual or the community is first is out of place in Reformed thinking. Priority belongs to both, because they are essentially simultaneous.

To avoid misunderstanding, it must be said that the individual is, indeed, superior to the State. The political state is an instrument of justice and order; it is a *thing*. A person is always superior to a thing. But to say that the individual is superior to the social community — which is not a thing, but a community of persons — is surely a mistake. To think that because the individual is superior to the State, he is therefore superior to the *social community*, is confused thinking. The Bible teaches that man is both one and many. And to claim that the one is superior to the many — the individual superior to the group — is as mistaken as to claim that in God the One is superior to the Three.

From "The Beginning"

The equal primacy of the many and the one in human nature is apparent, first, from Adam's sexuality. Because Adam is the many as well as the one, Eve is made from Adam's rib. Eve is an individual, yet she must proceed from Adam. Moreover, in the conjunction of their sexuality, children are born. Here too the "many" aspect of Adam's human nature finds expression. The whole human race, including Eve, proceeds from him. He is therefore the Head of the Family, and its Father. According to Biblical definition, the Father is the source or author, and the Head is that in which the many members find their unity — not vice versa.

James Daane

The equal primacy of the many with the one is apparent, secondly, from Adam's creation in the image of God. Regarded as a "single individual," Adam is not the image of God. The position that the individual aspect of the image of God is superior would demand the position that the "One" in God is superior to the Three — a thought which the Bible will not allow. Adam is the image of God precisely because he is also the many; because in his nature community is just as much first, and just as superior, as his individuality. Adam is the image of God because he is the many as well as the one. Because Eve can be taken from him, because together they can have children, because of this racial aspect of Adam's nature, he is the image of God. Hence, Reformed thinkers have pointed out that the image of God finds its full expression not in the single individual but in the race.

This same truth of equal primacy is apparent, thirdly, from Adam's function as representative of the race. This representative office is not worn by Adam as Saul's armor — as something that does not "fit" him. Adam can covenantally represent the race because he is the many as well as the one. God can deal with Adam and the whole human race as a group because Adam, in his nature, is the many, the race which proceeds from him. Just as God's nature and his covenantal method are in perfect harmony, so Adam's sociality and his representative office fit each other. If one asserts the priority of the one over the many in human nature, and the priority of the individual over the group in the social sphere, the very basis for the possibility of a divine covenantal method of dealing with mankind is lost. . . . [So too] the historical realm has been forsaken — the only realm in which common grace can exist.

The Sacrament of Community

Lewis B. Smedes   *October 1952*

There is perhaps no moment in the Christian life more intensely promising of spiritual reward than the celebration of communion. The Lord's Supper is a holy drama acted out in perpetual memorial to His passion. More than that, it is a sacred mystery through which God imparts to us the body and blood of His Incarnate Son. We probably never come more intimately close to the Divine-human Savior than when we receive bread and wine from His sacred table. Nor do we ever come closer to each other. It is the sacrament of communion in His death and is by that token the sacrament of Life, for, in His instance, death means Life. It is thus the sacrament of communion in His Life, or, we may say, it is the sacrament of Community Life — community in Him and in one another. My purpose now is to underscore one point about our sacrament, that it is a real and objective medium of grace of Community Life, and to make one application, that the Lord's sacrament may be the Divine response to one of our great needs.

The Lord's Supper is a memorial to the death of the Savior. The statement that the bread and wine are *signs* may be taken partly in this sense: "this do in remembrance of Me." The bread broken and the wine poured out are a kind of reminder that *as* the bread is broken so was His body, and *as* the wine is poured, so was His blood. They are, thus, a unique sort of Passion Play, a drama in symbolism, which we identify with the real drama of His suffering. It is this aspect of the sacrament which makes appropriate the singing of such hymns as "When I *Survey* the Wondrous Cross." As we participate in the celebration, we are reminded of Calvary, and are, or feel that we should be, stirred to pious sorrow and tearful gratitude for His incomparable sufferings for us. The sacrament is this, surely; but it is more too. It is indeed a memorial symbol of the Cross; but it is not enough that it be, to our minds, this alone. Apart from the fact of Christ's institution of bread and wine, the Oberammergau Passion Play or Rubens's painting "The Descent from the Cross" might conceivably accomplish this more adequately. If it were only a memorial, it would hardly be a sacrament in any real sense, nor a means of grace. The pious imagination stimulated by it might perhaps aid in our sanctification, but the sacrament itself would be an empty sign.

If the Lord's Supper were only a commemorative symbol, it would be ineffective to the extent that our imaginative and emotional response were inadequate to it. It is possible that many of us have known disappointment and even disillusionment in the sacrament because we have approached it with this incomplete notion. As a memorial symbol, it would be sensitive to a variety of very incidental and subjective factors. The explanatory sermon may be peculiarly inappropriate, the form inexpressively read, the celebrant's mind preoccupied with yesterday's misfortune or tomorrow's fears, or any of a host of other possible disturbances may be present. Whatever the immediate cause, a celebrant could reasonably feel that, somehow, the sacrament "did not take." And the implication is that to this person in this case the Supper was not a means of grace. But there is never an occasion for the believer to experience disappointment, for the sacrament does not wait upon experience. Nor can its gracious effects be measured by what we experience or feel we have experienced. The Lord Himself appointed it, and, with those who believe, He never fails to "keep His appointment."

The Communion, then, is not a mere symbol, but a genuine medium which the Lord has wisely chosen to feed us with His grace. The Catholics are wrong in saying that the Reformed sacrament is subjective and empty. The grace given in our sacrament is as real as the grace the Catholics contend is given in theirs. The presence of Christ in our sacrament is as real as the presence the Catholics contend for theirs. The reformers — at least those of Geneva — never conceded to the Catholic sacrament a more genuine efficacy, a more "real" grace than they believed to attend their own. The controversy was one of *kind* and of *mode*, but never of *reality*.

The reformers denied that the sacrament has an inherent capacity for infusing grace as a narcotic has capacity to stupefy or alcohol to inebriate. They disputed that the Lord was present in the sacrament only after a migration of the body and blood in its substance from its heavenly home. The sacrament is a medium of grace, they said, only because the Holy Spirit confers grace through it. Christ is very present, though His humanity is permanently stationed at the right hand of God, only through a miracle of the Holy Spirit. (Whence it is called a "Spiritual" presence.) The reformers rejected the Catholic notion that faith was *irrelevant* to the sacrament, but they denied just as insistently that the sacrament was *dependent* upon faith. Faith, said Calvin, was a vessel in which the participant carried away the grace given. But the presence or availability of the grace was independent of the receiving and carrying away. If I may be permitted a rough analogy, water is in the tap, dependent upon the spring or reservoir, and not upon the presence of a bucket, though the bucket must be there if water is to be carried away. It is this kind of correlation between faith and the grace of the sacrament which Calvin saw. The grace is objectively present, simply because the Lord promised it and gives it. And to all who believe in Him, quite apart from their emotion at the moment of celebration, He will give His sacramental grace. . . . As with all God's gifts, we do not reach out and grasp the grace of the sacrament. God stoops and gives. The point thus far is, I think, fairly clear. It is that the Lord's Supper is *His* supper. In it, He caters to our needs.

If this is so, there is strong reason for regular and frequent participation. The argument that celebration should occur comparatively seldom lest the sacrament become commonplace obviously falls. Such argument suggests a well-placed distrust in our sustained regard for the holiness of the sacrament. But it carries a suggestion of distrust in the sacrament as well. We may be thankful that the sacrament is not first of all a matter of our proper respect but of Christ's institution and promise. The Holy Spirit works with the sacrament, and His acts cannot become "common." There are, then, no principial grounds for limiting the celebrations to four a year. It may not be principially imperative that they be more, but the nature of the sacrament argues that greater frequency could be beneficial. Calvin thought it quite imperative that celebrations be very frequent, *at least once a week.*

Apart from the frequency of communion, the nature of the sacrament demands that it be given a place of pre-eminent honor in our liturgy. Need it be said that it must never be allowed to be a mere appendage, a kind of extra point for which we have no integral place in the body of the service, a dangling modifier in the liturgical sentence?

On Communion Sunday everything else is adjectival; the sacrament is the thing. . . .

There is one more note to be added. Christ has but one body to offer, and one Life. With that one body, and the one Life, He unites us all. . . . To all who believe in Him, Christ gives His whole self very really in the sacrament, that through participation in Him all are united to Him, and, hence, to each other. In the first paragraph, I called it the sacrament of Community Life. That is what the Lord makes it to be.

The application of this has already implicitly been made. It deserves, however, to be made more explicit. It is not uncommon to hear it said that we, the Reformed community in America, have two paramount needs. We need, it is said, a sense of community. We also need, it is perhaps more frequently said, leadership, a prophetic voice to show us the way out of our difficulties. The second "need" is perhaps considered the answer to the first: We could become united if there were a leader to unite us. Whatever the truth of this, it would be tragically ironic if we should neglect that means which God has supplied us of the deepest unity possible in life. The unity provided in the sacrament goes deeper than any sense or awareness. It is more real than any organization, and far more permanent than any unity inspired by such media as "mass meetings" and the like. We do, perhaps, need leadership. But we need each other more. And we need union with each other in the mysteriously deep sense that goes to the root of our being, that penetrates the heart of our life. It is, in fact, the community of Life that we need.

We may add that there is no community but that of Life, His Life become ours together. And it is so. . . . Participation in Christ — participation in each other: this is community, a community as real and more real than our own selves. It is the community of the sacrament, of the sacrament of communion.

Academic Freedom at Calvin

HENRY STOB   *August 1952*

There are at least two things that an academic institution is concerned to do. It is concerned to disclose truth, and it is concerned to publish truth. A college must be engaged in research, and it must teach. It must both investigate and disseminate.

These two functions are sometimes separated. The one is then assigned to the University and the other to the College. Expediency seems to require this. In reality, however, the two functions belong together, and they ought to be kept in the closest possible contact. A college such as our own, for example, even though it offers no advanced degrees and therefore cannot in strictness be called a university, must perform the university function of research as well as the college function of teaching. If Christian teaching is to be real there must be Christian scholarship beforehand. And if both are to be real there must be freedom — academic freedom: freedom of inquiry for the scholar and freedom of expression for the teacher.

But what are we to understand by *Freedom?*

There is in the notion of Freedom both a negative and a positive element. In current usage the negative element predominates and sometimes this negativity is erroneously regarded as exhausting the whole meaning of the term. This is a serious mistake. It remains true, however, that the term *freedom* does have an inalienable negative aspect. In this aspect freedom means *Freedom From.* It means Independence. It means immunity or exemption from something. It connotes absence of restraint, bondage, or subjection. It means to be loose from restrictions.

This negativity, far from being a negligible element in freedom, is the very essence of perfect or absolute freedom, such as is enjoyed by God. God is completely free. He is bound by nothing external to himself. He is in bondage to nothing. . . . Now man is created in the image of God, and because he bears the divine *image* he too has freedom, even freedom in the negative sense of Independence. But because he is *created* his freedom is a creaturely freedom, his independence is a creaturely independence. The adjective "creaturely" is important. It modifies man's freedom. It means that human freedom can never be described simply as exemption from "undue" restraint.

This implies, of course, that there are "due" restraints upon him. They are upon him precisely because he is a creature and thus subject to God, to God's laws, and to all the ordinances of God. But it also implies that he is entitled to throw off "undue" restraints. He is entitled to do this precisely because he bears the image of God. Being superior to nature and on a plane with his fellows, he may refuse to be victimized by the one or enslaved by the other.

It is this nice balance between liberty and restraint, freedom and subjection, that is the essence of the Christian conception of Liberty, and the very basis of genuine Democracy. Because there is a nice and delicate balance here, it has not always been preserved. To many, freedom under law, liberty under restraint, independence within the framework of an ultimate dependence, high dignity while in creaturely subjection, has seemed grossly contradictory and quite intolerable. . . .

*   *   *

It is this latter view that comes to expression in the liberal tradition of modernity, a tradition which has its roots in Renaissance humanism and its chief expression in secularistic scientism. It is this view that dominates contemporary discussions of academic freedom, and it is the bond of agreement even between disputants. What the so-called liberals are all agreed on is that academic freedom is freedom *from* — freedom from the apriori, freedom from assumptions, freedom from commitment, freedom from the dictation of religious faith, freedom from a sacred book, freedom from a dogmatic creed. . . . Were they to measure Calvin College against their definition they would be able to find on all the campus not a wisp of academic freedom. What they would find is scholars and teachers building on a Book, men and women pursuing their inquiries in complete reliance on an authoritative Word taken as the absolute rule of knowledge and practice, truth and life. And they would repudiate the whole thing.

Well then, that raises the whole question once more: Is there academic freedom at Calvin College? The answer to that question is twofold. At the level on which the so-called liberal asks it, the answer is, Yes. There is not at Calvin that spurious thing which he calls freedom, but there is genuine freedom, human freedom. The liberal notion of freedom is negative; it is freedom from. At Calvin it is positive; it is freedom for. For the secularist freedom is an end. For the Calvinist it is a means. The Calvinist wants freedom, but he wants it in order to attain a further goal. He wants it in order to attain his true place: under God who made him and above the nature he is called upon to rule.

It is clear to us at Calvin that we are creatures and therefore not wholly sovereign. We know that we do not and cannot exist in ultimate independence. We know that from the nature of the case we and all men have a master, and that by an inviolable law of our being we all serve one, the true one or a false one. We know, therefore, that the question of freedom is never rightly put until one asks: What Lord do you acknowledge? To what do you tie yourself? To whom or what are you basically and finally committed? And we know that there are only three possibilities here: Nature, Man, and God.

We at Calvin choose God, or are chosen by him, and we try to live and think by his Word. We bow at this one point and therefore are free at every other — free precisely there and completely there where a human being may and can be free — free of nature and on an equality with men. That is why we are deaf to communism; we have no ear for economic determinism. That is why we resist to the death all tyranny; having given our allegiance to the King of Kings we count no man our master — neither the man on horseback, nor the man in purple, nor the man in the mitred cap. We stand in awe neither of the man in the Cadillac nor of the man in overalls. We are not intimidated by academic nonsense, and we don't bow before the sacred cow of science. We are free men. And we are free men because we have our anchor in the bedrock of the universe.

The secularist, on the other hand, who prates of a human freedom proper only to God, is bound to lose both God and every freedom proper to a creature. On the level of nature he will become the victim of those mechanical monsters — bomb, plane, cannon — that he has the ingenuity to create but not the wit to control. And on the level of society he will fall before a succession of Mussolinis, Hitlers, and Stalins. Having no foot in heaven he has no power to resist the strong men of the earth.

The liberal doesn't want this slavery, of course. He hates communism, he hates tyranny, he hates the bondage of machines and gadgets. He hates them almost as much as he hates the sovereign God of Calvinism. He wants to be free of them all. But, of course, he cannot. He has to make a choice of masters. He has made his choice, and by it he shall be judged.

*　　*　　*

If the question be asked then: Is there academic freedom at Calvin?, the answer to the secularist in the liberal tradition is, Yes — freedom from the subjectivism, the relativism, the nihilism of the age; freedom from the frustrations, the anxieties, the pessimisms of the times; freedom from the brute uncontrolled "reality" that the unbelieving scholar has imaginatively projected and which, on his own showing, may turn at any moment and engulf him. There is freedom at Calvin: the freedom that comes from walking in The Way.

If, however, the question is asked on another level, by those who stand with us in the same commitment, the answer cannot be quite the same. If it be asked: Is there, within the framework of the Scripture and the creeds, freedom of inquiry and expression at Calvin?, the answer is, "Yes, but there could be more."

No doubt such an answer can always be given. There is no perfection in this world. There are and always will be accidental and arbitrary restrictions on liberty, even in the best societies. But this is no excuse for their presence. Despite all their actuality, arbitrary restrictions remain undesirable, and they are most undesirable in a Christian community. Here freedom is held as a sacred possession. Here liberty is strictly inviolable. This means that if anywhere, then at Calvin, there should be academic freedom, freedom from extraneous and non-academic restraints.

Let no one misunderstand. There must be restraint. There must be the quite academic restraint of the truth; not the restraint of some merely abstract, amorphous, undefined truth always in process, but the restraint of the truth authoritatively disclosed in Scripture and freely acknowledged in the creeds. By this the scholars and teachers at Calvin are bound. And they are bound by another thing. They are bound by the law of Love, by the obligation to walk humbly with their God and considerately and self-sacrificially with their fellows. But by nothing else are they bound, and with no other yoke should they be burdened.

They must not be compelled to establish anyone in his private conceits, nor to further the ambitions of any party. They must be free, within the framework of a shared commitment, to come to a conclusion that contravenes the majority opinion, or perchance the opinion of an articulate and militant minority. They must be at liberty to explore new areas of truth, and to do so in their own responsible way. And they must have the same liberty to hold at arm's length new ways of thought, however impatiently presented for adoption.

They should be given rein. If it turns out that any one of them has wandered off or become lost, let him be reoriented, or if he be perverse, cut loose. But they should not have men breathing on their necks and constantly peering over their shoulders. They can't work that way. What they need is trust. They must be free to attack knotty and complex problems in the knowledge that they have the confidence of the Church, and they must have the freedom to express and expose to public criticism tentative ideas that may require revision or abandonment.

They also need freedom from the weight of custom and from the tyranny of venerable names. What they need, too, is freedom from fear and reprisals. And what they need most of all is freedom from the sting of uninformed prejudice, freedom from name calling, and freedom from silent but enervating suspicion.

We have all together undertaken a great and delicate task. We have undertaken to construe the world in the categories of eternity. It is a terrifyingly responsible task. To discharge it we need the utmost degree of consecration and competence. Doubtless we need watchfulness too, but it must be the watchfulness of the friend who cares. We need the watchfulness of the brother that is quick to help. What we need is wisdom, loyalty, and charity. And this from all sides.

It will be agreed, I think, that of this we have not had enough. It is only, however, in the measure that we have it that the scholars and teachers at Calvin will be able to perform their demanding tasks. They need this climate, this room, this freedom. They need it in order to do their duty, to inquire into and articulate the whole body of Christian truth, to trace out according to their lights all its implications. They need this freedom for the truth's sake to which they are committed.

Thoughts for Teachers

HENRY ZYLSTRA   *September 1954*

In these days registration is due again. We shall have to be concerned once more, both on the school and college levels, to see that our students get a solid core of liberal studies. There will be that tremendous pull towards the practical. The Commercial Course will seem to make so much more sense than the Classical Course. Somehow, in practice, Carlyle's old definition of man as a tool-using animal appeals to us just as much as Calvin's idea of a God-knowing creature. It is an old tension, this one between the practical and the liberal arts. I quote from the younger Seneca as Macaulay quoted him in his essay on Bacon: "... philosophy lies deeper. It is not her office to teach men how to use their hands. The object of her lessons is to form the soul."

The object is to form the soul. That will be a good phrase to have in mind as we sit at the registration tables arranging the schedules of our pupils. Which shall it be now, Latin or Gregg[1]? The object is to form the soul. . . .

We have been using the word *integration* a lot in our discussions of education. It is a great word and no doubt we shall have to use it some more. Personally, I like the word *orientation*. It may be that we have spoiled it a little with our university Orientation Week and the like. Such a week is devoted primarily to helping the student find himself on the campus. But even the meaning of that is not bad for getting at what education is. For once I shall quote the dictionary to help establish a point. To orient, says Webster, means *to cause to face toward the east. It means to ascertain the bearings of a thing.* How much more impor-

---

1. A popular system of shorthand stenography taught in commercial courses in American high schools.

tant those bearings are for us teachers than the thing itself. We have to get squared around towards God if the universe is to make sense. Life is bewildering and meaningless without the fixed reference point. And how were one to find his way in a life of eternity with a map of time except he have a polar point, a Bethlehem, an Incarnation? Orientation: that is our work as teachers. We must give our pupils their bearings in life by causing them to face towards the east.

Arthur Koestler, in his novel *Arrival and Departure* (Macmillan, 1943), powerfully illustrates how a differing assumption or dogma changes the picture of reality. The facts we look at in our schools are very much the same as those that are studied in other schools. But the patterns we see — and life, like a painting, is a muddle until we discern the pattern — are different. Koestler says:

> As children we used to be given a curious kind of puzzle to play with. It was a paper with a tangle of very thin blue and red lines. If you just looked at it you couldn't make out anything. But if you covered it with a piece of transparent red tissue-paper, the red lines of the drawing disappeared and the blue lines formed a picture — it was a clown in a circus holding a hoop and a little dog jumping through it. And if you covered the same drawing with blue tissue-paper, a roaring lion appeared, chasing the clown across the ring. You can do the same thing with every mortal, living or dead. . . .

"If you just looked at it you couldn't make out anything." This, then, is the necessity of dogma in education, grounded in the religious nature of man. There is no possibility of finding oneself in the universe, of getting one's bearings, of being oriented, in neutral education. After that the question becomes, through the tissue paper of *which* dogma is one reading reality?

*　　　*　　　*

The point of departure for several of these ideas is my reading of Professor Frederick A. Pottle's book, *The Idiom of Poetry* (Cornell University Press, 1946). He has some good things to say also about a problem which is recurrent among us in our schools: namely, what may our students, our pupils, read? On this point of Christian liberty in the reading of books, Professor Pottle takes a strong stand. It might well serve, it seems to me, as a statement of our own ideal in this matter. He says:

We protect children from books that might cause trouble, as we keep certain kinds of food from them, but when they grow up they must decide by the testimony of their own lives and their own consciences. It was profoundly said by St. Augustine that all morality can be summed up in the injunction, "Love God and do what you will." The saying could as well take the form, "Love God and read what you will."

Dr. Pottle understands the considerable threat to the morality of the young in some contemporary literature, but he thinks that the best way to deal with it is to build up positive resources of strength: "The church would do well to worry less about the demoralizing effect of contemporary literature and more about the sincerity, persistence, and competence of its training of the young."

Dr. Pottle is one of those modern minds who have the honesty to admit that "Every man, without exception, has his orthodoxies. . . ." There is always an area of dogma, an area of things which we take for granted. For most people of our time this uncritically accepted area is the scientific one. "Without being taught to do so," he says, "we assign all 'truth' to the province of science. Whatever science cannot manipulate we feel to be unreal or untrue." But other basic assumptions lead to a different kind of quest from the modern, and to the acknowledgment of a different kind of evidence. "How could men," asks Professor Pottle, thinking of the Middle Ages, "be content to remain so ignorant of ascertainable facts?" The answer is clear: "Because they were 'making sense' of nature in a framework (the theological) which interested them more than the scientific. . . ."

The same was true of the Greeks, though their dogma differed from that of the Middle Ages as well as from that of the Modern Age: "Is it not clear that the ancient Greeks could have made every discovery in science on which we pride ourselves if they had thought it worthwhile?" This is perhaps our hardest work as Christian teachers and the most inescapably obligatory: namely, to discriminate dogma, to discern within which framework a particular book, or period, or author is "making sense" of reality. . . .

*   *   *

Koestler thought that the scientific framework by which in the modern time men have chosen to make sense of life and reality would give way again to one of "intuition and ethical belief." We teachers should be alert, I think, to this change which has been heralded by many prophets of our time, particularly by men of letters, and which does indeed seem to be already well under way. A new and different dogma, in the sense of these notes, is shaping up in the middle decades of this century. The change seems to be a change from Liberal Man and Natural Man to Religious Man. Some think of it as likely to be a bigger change than that which happened at the French Revolution, and as big a change as that which took place at the Renaissance. We seem to be moving from an age of science into an age of faith.

Perhaps, though, I should not call it an age of faith that we are entering upon. I remember being admonished against it by Wystan H. Auden, a writer who has been especially sensitive to just this shift of dogmatic climate here under discussion. . . . [He characterizes it] in an off-hand clause which seems to me very happily struck off, and one of the most important sentences recorded in our decade. It comes at the end of his book, *The Enchafed Flood* (Faber and Faber, London, 1951): "We live in a new age in which . . . the necessity of dogma is once more recognized, not as the contradiction of reason and feeling, but as their ground and foundation."

It may be that before century's end — and, after all, dates do not govern spiritual epochs — this of Auden, and its equivalent in, as I say, many other writers, will be the text to exegete in characterization of our time. Those of us, if any, who have practically as well as theoretically escaped the liberal and positivist dogma of a scientific framework of interpretation, will presumably welcome the return of an acknowledged religious dimension. For it is dogma that determines what we mean to recognize as evidence.

The return to the religious way of making sense of reality will not, of course, solve all of our problems. Being religious is not synonymous with being Christian. A whole new set of advantages and disadvantages may be ahead of us. There will be disadvantages, too: irrationalism and resurgent naturalism can come back in the guise of religious affirmation. But when the issue no longer is whether or not there is to be a faith, but rather one of which faith it is to be, we shall be more honest and direct with each other all around. Meanwhile we teachers must be alert to the changing soul of the times.

Pitch Your Tents Toward Sodom

Ernest Van Vugt   *December 1961*

The life story of Lot is a disappointing one. It showed such promise at its beginning, but ended in such utter failure. While he was closely associated with Abraham, things went well, but from the time that he separated from his uncle and "pitched his tent toward Sodom" one disaster seems to have followed another. With the defeat of the kings of Sodom and Gomorrah he is taken captive, but when rescued by Abraham he returns to Sodom and his former life. When next we hear of him, certain destruction is imminent. There follow in rapid succession these events: Lot's escape from Sodom, the destruction of the cities, the miraculous metamorphosis of his wife, the flight of Lot and his two daughters to the mountains, and the machinations of these two daughters whereby Lot unwittingly became the progenitor of the children of Ammon and Moab. On this ominous note his story ends. He seems to have lost everything — excepting his own soul, for the Apostle Peter in his second epistle refers to him as "that righteous man."

This story may on the surface seem to have a very simple moral lesson to teach, namely, that the Christian cannot associate with unbelievers with impunity; that whenever he does go out into the world his own moral stability is bound to be shaken and the salvation of his family gravely imperiled. Thus it was with Lot.

But surely it is not true that righteousness must always give ground in the face of unrighteousness, that truth must forever be on the defensive, and fight a losing battle at that. St. Paul was often most successful as a missionary in the cities where wickedness of every kind, including that sin to which Sodom has given its name, seemed to control the minds of men.

Can it be then that the missionary is alone responsible for extending the frontiers of Christ's kingdom, and that the mission station is to be the sole outpost of his army? Although there may not be many who would say so, there are many who by their actions give assent to that position. But certainly that is not the only kind of action by which Christianity in the early centuries of our era transformed the world. In addition to the missionaries there were the many in the professions, in industry, and in politics who brought their Christianity to bear upon the culture in which they found themselves and so helped to transform it.

Was it not then a mistake for Lot to "pitch his tent toward Sodom"? In the light of the outcome it would be difficult to deny that it was. But it was so not merely because he was righteous, and "the men of the city wicked exceedingly before the Lord." At any rate, Abraham did not try to dissuade Lot from going. And what arguments could he have used? He himself was living among the heathen.

There is an essential difference between these two men, and in this difference there lies in part the reason why Lot should not have moved to Sodom. Abraham was very much aware of his calling. It is said of him that he "looked for a city which hath foundations, whose builder and maker is God," and that he "desired a better country, that is, an heavenly." But "Lot lifted up his eyes, and beheld all the plain of Jordan, that it was well watered everywhere," and he seemed to forget that he was but a "stranger and a pilgrim on the earth." Motivated by the desire for riches, he cut himself and his family off from the people of God, that is, from Abraham and his house, and enticed by the allurements of the cities of the plain, he soon left off living in tents, the symbol of the pilgrim, and moved into Sodom. Lot erred then in forgetting that the believer has here "no abiding city," and that though riches increase we are not to set our heart upon them. . . .

Although it is Lot's wife that scripture admonished us to remember, we ought not ignore Lot himself. But I do not think that his biography gives us an excuse to isolate ourselves in fear as though what God has given us is merely to be preserved by us and not shared with others. It does, however, serve to point out the dangers involved in our encounters with wickedness, and illustrates the high price that one who leaves the safety of the Christian community can pay for his failure to be adequately prepared and wholly committed to advance the cause of truth.

No man who lacks the courage of his convictions (or worse yet, lacks convictions) and no man who does not understand the issues involved should in his naïveté venture into the contemporary Sodoms as a quixotic champion of the truth and thus perhaps do more harm than good for the cause of truth. For truth is often an object of contempt to the wicked because it lacks suitable defenders. But was there ever a time when the world was in greater need of such to witness for the truth? . . .

No one has a greater responsibility to provide that kind of witness than does the graduate of a Christian liberal arts college, and no one has a better opportunity to prepare for that kind of service than does the student at such a college. Here through the various disciplines you can be led not only to a clearer understanding of the truth in its various manifestations, you can also be taught not to be content to condemn your culture, but to assess it, to evaluate it, and to correct and reform it in the light of Truth as personified in Christ. . . .

Many of you will upon leaving here pitch your tents near to Jerusalem. That is as it should be, and you will find enough of the spirit of Sodom there to demand the best that you have. I urge others of you to prepare to pitch your tents toward Sodom — some of you toward the Sodom of politics, others toward the Sodom of science, of the arts, of industry, and wherever such as you are needed. But do not ask what Sodom can do for you, but rather what you can do for Sodom and, being warned by the mistakes of Lot, act in the awareness of the high stakes involved. Sodom and Gomorrah were destroyed for want of ten righteous. How many righteous may yet be needed to avert the threatened destruction of our civilization?

No one will deny that there are dangers in meeting the world on its own ground, but they are not as great as the dangers in living in the world on its own terms. And you need not go it alone! St. Peter ends his reference to Lot with these words, "The Lord knoweth how to deliver the godly out of temptations."

The American Way of Life

JOHN J. TIMMERMAN   *September 1953*

The American has always been something of a paradox; he has from
the beginning worshipped God with a glance to Mammon, or worshipped Mammon with a regretful awareness of God. In recent years,
however, the traditional idealisms have become dimmer, and the pride
and satisfaction in things more intense, so much dimmer that the Vice-
President of General Motors could in a speech at the industrial cavalcade "The Parade of Progress" identify the American way with the
booster's paradise, an endless profusion of things.[1] Mammon towered
above the rows of gleaming cars.

The cavalcade was interesting. The film showed arrestingly beautiful industrial designs. The cars and planes had the hard glamor of superb craftsmanship in steel and color. Here was creative industry, a
fruitful wedding of natural form and the dream of man, no mere imita-
tion of nature but rather a fusion of the geometrical lines and balance
of the bird with beaten metal. Ask the fact for the form, said Emerson;
here it was bird become jet plane. But most interesting of all was the
keynoter's speech in which he undertook to define the American way
of life. And that way consisted of a geometrical ratio in the increase of
things: more and better cars, more and better planes, more machines in
a paradise of instruments. The hope of the exhibition, said the speaker,
was to set a boy dreaming — of things. . . .

Was the speaker right in identifying the American way of life with
the abundance of things? Then the "past is a bucket of ashes," and then
the great voices of the American past are no longer even echoes. For

1. The "Parade of Progress" was an annual promotion tour sponsored by General
Moters, resumed in 1953 after a twelve-year hiatus.

the Puritan put the city of God before the city of man. . . . Despite the sordid branches, the main road of the American Revolution was called *Freedom*. Emerson and the Romantics said things must not be allowed to vault into the saddle and control mankind. Whitman's hope of democracy rested upon ideal values — brotherhood not social security. The great reformers from Garrison to Bryan, the countless ordinary Americans who have been Christian, the late humanists have all recognized a law above the law of the thing.

If the speaker was right, these voices have had their day. But it seems to me that he was misreading both our past and our present. Nobody would deny that the pioneer gouging out the continent, that Franklin, predatory capitalism, manifest destiny, pragmatism, and instrumentalism are American. They are peculiarly American, but they are part, not the whole or central trait, of our paradoxical American character and way of life. The speaker was then both right and wrong. My fret was that he never mentioned the end for which the means exist, and my worry is that he may be more right than I think.

I did not expect the speaker to quote Emerson on the danger of too many possessions; I have no quarrel with technology as such. I am no agrarian, and I don't care to move to Walden Pond to study the emerald pickerel. I would like to drive any new General Motors car. I am fully aware of the crucial importance of automobiles in the American economy. What distresses me is the careless confusion of ends and means, the resting in the materials of civilization, the sacrifice of ends to means. What is the paradise of machines for? Of that there was not a word, and I believe, without being naive, that there should have been such a comment. If we rest in the machines, we will eventually become machines. We will resemble the traveller who runs his car six hundred miles a day. Instead of landscape he has seen green lights, filling stations, and license plates. He has become a living joint between wheel and pedal. He is part of the Ford he drives. My point is that the real American sees beyond the means to the goals which they should serve. He has the "vision of latitudes unknown," and the vision goes beyond the dizzy thrust of the jet plane. It penetrates to the pattern of the ideal man, and at its best finds the ideal man in the Word of the Lord.

Since America has always had plenty, and since Americans have always had craft and energy, she has always been threatened by things. Mammon has always stood by with his hands full of gold. The astute Puritan traders, the canny Dutch, the solid Jersey farmers, the prosperous Quakers, the lavish Virginian planters merely begin a list of the exploiters of the fathomless resources of America. And only too often the Puritan found his heart in the counting houses of Boston. The pressure of things reached its unsavory peaks in the Gilded Age of Grant and the scandals of the Harding Administration. And the circle came full in the twenties when a descendant of the Puritans occupied the White House in Washington and said that the business of America was business. . . .

Even though materialism may be the dominant trend in American life, it cannot yet, I believe, be called the American way of life. The essential American tradition is still alive in many places. Dissent is still with us. The Puritan and Christian speaks in the noble verse and prose of Eliot, the humanist is alive in Frost, and even the American satirists like Wolfe and Lewis, whom we so often belabor, score heavily. There is alive yet the residual Puritanism in the social reformers and humanitarians. There are many believers who hold to a Christian ideal that always determines the use of things, that regards them as valuable only in relation to men, and man as valuable only in relation to God.

But the candle may be guttering at times, even among us. We need to be on guard; we need to check the use of our energies. Do we preserve for spiritual activity a wide margin of the leisure which machines provide? Is our leisure creative as well as recreative? Do we value freedom as we ought? Most men, said Thoreau, lead lives of quiet desperation. They will always do that if they live in things. Absorption in things can only satisfy a society of adolescents. Americans need a pep-talk like *Life Begins at Forty* because they have by that time neither mastered things nor acquired enough of them. If one does not master things one can never acquire enough of them. Success is measured by the bank account, and that is never big enough, for the person caught by the lure of material success would rather drive a Cadillac on time than a Ford paid up. Life begins when one becomes aware of the central meaning of spiritual values, when it is God-centered. If the American way of life is to be in things, most adult Americans will lead lives of quiet desperation.

The Graham Crusades — Shall We Participate?

SIDNEY ROOY   *June 1958*

The big question facing every church in the area to which the Billy Graham Evangelistic Team comes is, "Shall we be a participating church or not?" It was this question that recently faced the Christian Reformed churches in the Eastern area. The question occasioned much discussion and debate, much soul-searching and prayer. How that question affected me, how it was answered by one of our Eastern churches and by its pastor, I should like to share with you.

The story begins some two years ago. A group of Christian laymen and ministers had invited the Crusade team to metropolitan New York. Mass media took up the Graham Crusade plans and began to follow their progress. The team refused to come, however, except by invitation of the Protestant Council of Churches in New York City. This it subsequently received.

. . . [The author follows with close and lengthy reflection upon "dangers" that accepting Graham's invitation possibly entailed: first of all, compromise with theological liberalism; next, the practices of a faulty ecclesiology. Those addressed, he turned to considering the Crusade's methods and then to measuring its results.]

Churches, some 1500 strong, joined in the execution of the Crusade. Some months have now passed. And the all-important question comes, Has it been worthwhile? Have the long-term results been good, or bad?

The answer is, They have been partly good and partly bad. Possibly much of what we call bad has been the result of bringing to light what was already weakness Perhaps the bad effects can best be summed up by the word *superficial,* and that especially in two respects. First, there are those people whose commitment to the Lord Jesus Christ now seems to have been superficial. Their zeal has been short-

40

lived. Perhaps at first they attended church irregularly and continued to do so. Perhaps they attended Sunday school before the Crusade and afterward still did not attend worship services. Perhaps they were really only children, and their childish enthusiasm has waned. Perhaps only curiosity brought them to the front, and profession of commitment became their excuse for being there. Whatever the practice or reason may have been, the superficial character of their "conversion" has become evident.

Second, there are those members of every church who have been adversely affected by the Crusade, or at least so it seems. Some of these people thought Graham sermons were good ordinary diet for the church, which Graham himself disavows. Some were zealous "missionaries" when Graham was in town but now have settled back into that old, but comfortable, niche of inactivity. Others have become more critical than helpful in the mission program of their church.

Now the question at this point is whether the Crusade is responsible for this superficiality. That it became the occasioning factor, no one would deny. It seems more realistic, however, to assume that there was something wrong before the Crusade began which it brought to light and accentuated. In regard to the temporary conversions, it must be remarked that a wholly unwarranted and unwholesome division between evangelism and doctrinal preaching has often been made in the churches. Responsibility for this rests with technical sermonizing and indiscriminate pew-sitting alike. In regard to the second kind of superficiality which the Crusade has brought to light — temporary mission zeal and the spirit of criticism on the part of church members — it should be said that these shortcomings are more the reflections of basic character defects than the results of a relatively brief series of evangelistic meetings.

But there have been many long-term effects of the Crusade as well. First, new converts have been added to the churches. This was the first intent of the Crusade and this has been accomplished. It is true that many of our churches have not shared in this harvest, but this has been due more to half-hearted or non-participation than anything else. A lady who came to faith on June 5 in [Madison Square] Garden last year recently made public profession of faith in one of our churches. A former Roman Catholic was led to a full commitment to the Lord through a lady connected with the Crusade, and he is now a very active member of one of our churches.

Second, trained and experienced counselors are now providing assistance in the work of personal calling in the community and are continuing worthwhile Crusade contacts by letter. The value of the experience gained in learning to lead a seeking soul to the Lord cannot be overestimated. Most of us are able to teach, or to talk in general about our faith, but we are dumb when it comes to getting on our knees with an inquirer and persuading him to accept the Lord. Nor can the value of continued Crusade contacts be questioned. One of our counselors wrote for many months to eight of the "spiritual children" directed to him, and he still continues correspondence with some.

Third, some churches which had been dying through disinterest or through perversion of the truth have secured a new lease on spiritual life. The result of new babes asking for the milk of the Word from those who had been content to feed husks has been wholesomely disquieting, and those who serve difficult mixed pastorates are gaining support from new believers.

Fourth, the preaching of evangelical ministers has taken on more personal and Scriptural directness. We are tempted to exhort our people to the gates of glory, and this may be well. The lack of emphasis, however, on the Scriptural teaching of conversion is only one indication of our preoccupation with the sheep within the fold and our lack of contact with the lost sheep of our community. When we stand face to face with these lost sheep, our preaching takes on more of the freshness, liveliness, and relevance of the Gospel.

Fifth, a new awareness of the universal character of the Lord's Church has been made real to all of us. It is impossible to attend meetings and work shoulder to shoulder with consecrated Christians of other denominations and not become increasingly aware that much is to be gained through closer contact with each other. There are many who seek what the Lord has entrusted to us, and there is much we can learn and have learned from others. Our reluctance in seeking closer contact has shut us off from some of the treasures God has for us.

Reformed Does Not Mean Apartheid

HARRY R. BOER   *May 1960*

When in January, 1958, I attended the meeting of the International Missionary Council in Accra, I sensed for the first time, in conversations with African representatives, an ominous fact that has in the past year proven all too true: in their sponsorship of Apartheid, the whites in South Africa have to reckon with the open hostility not only of their black compatriots but with the direct opposition of all of Africa south of the Sahara. This opposition is to be distinguished from the criticism and opposition of the rest of the world — it is and will be more intense, more threatening, and is based not only on a conception of human rights, but on a racial identification with oppressed brethren on a continental scale.

This fact has been brought home sharply during the past few weeks as a result of the recent tragic developments in the Union of South Africa [the mass shooting of black Africans at Sharpeville, the subsequent successful sympathy strike, and the attempted assassination of Prime Minister Henrik Verwoerd]. . . . Can the catastrophe of civil war in South Africa and possibly war on a larger scale still be avoided? Alan Paton, the well-known South African author of *Cry, the Beloved Country,* wrote in a recent issue of the *New York Times,*

> The Nationalist comforts himself that the Afrikaner has always had to struggle, that the new crisis is nothing new. But in his heart he knows that this crisis is the last crisis of all. . . . Events like the recent tragedies help to open his eyes, but what he needs to bring him out of the pipedream is a decisive order from the outside world.
>
> It must be an order to bring to an end the second greatest Christian apostasy of the twentieth century, or to take the consequences. Many of us pray that such an order will soon be heard.

The order, I am convinced, cannot be given by "the outside world." The [South] African Nationalist is blinded. Elsewhere in his article Paton compares him to the blinded Samson who brought destruction to his enemies and himself together. His concern for his way of life in the present seems to cancel out the possibility of concern for an inevitably tragic future. No pleas, no warnings, have induced such concern in the past. It is not likely that any moral "orders" will induce it in the future.

There must indeed be an order. But it must come from *outside the world*. It must come from God who created all men in his image, and from the Christ who died and rose for all men regardless of their color, creed, or culture. It is God in Christ who must speak, and only his decisive speaking can halt the march to the abyss.

How does God speak? He speaks in many ways and various. But one way in which he enlists men to speak with him and for him is to speak through the Church. We, the body of Christ, are his chosen instrument to declare not only his salvation to the nations, but also his righteousness, his holiness, his justice.

The non-Dutch churches of European background in South Africa have expressed their deep concern over the developing situation. How widely official pronouncements of these bodies reflect the average layman's point of view is anyone's guess. Fact is that the whites of both British and Dutch extraction stand behind the government or, if not wholly that, behind some sort of a program that will ensure the retention of white superiority. The opposition United Party may *speak* more moderately than the Government; whether it will *be* more moderate in a showdown remains to be seen.

*   *   *

As it is the universal embarrassment of whites to be of the same skin color as the proponents of Apartheid, so it is the universal embarrassment of Reformed people and churches to be of the same ecclesiastical and religious family as the South African Dutch. Should we, the Christian Reformed Church in America, not speak to the Reformed churches in South Africa? We are of Dutch extraction; we are Reformed; like them we are a Reformed planting on another continent; in Northern Nigeria the Dutch Reformed Church of South Africa honors us by entrusting us with the continuation of mission work which for more than thirty-five years they have carried on with self-sacrifice and devotion. Have we not a special responsibility here? Are we not in particular charged with laying upon the Reformed churches in South Africa the prior claims of God's love and justice? Can we not do so in the humility of the realization that we ourselves are not without guilt in the scandal of American segregational practices?

Should not healing for the South African nation arise first from the Church in its midst? Is not the Christ in her midst the power of God unto salvation? Must not the Church speak to the conscience of the nation? Should she not, in fact, be what Archbishop Temple once called the Church everywhere, namely, "the conscience of the nation"?

But how can the Reformed churches in South Africa be the prophetic voice of God to the nation when they are bound by the same prudential concerns that govern her worldly national community and government? The Reformed churches in South Africa cannot speak the healing word until they rise above the prudence of their own fears and live in the wisdom of God which is foolishness to men. Is it not at this point that the Christian Reformed Church should speak to her fellow Reformed churches in South Africa? Could not a strong voice speaking in love *within* the family possibly be more effective than the pleadings, warnings, and criticisms of churches outside the theological and ecclesiastical family?

It may be said that we really do not know the South African race problem, and that the better one gets to know it the more he is inclined to speak with restraint. This is doubtless true. But what is even more true is that no race may permanently lord it over another race, that a policeman's gun is a poor substitute for freedom under law, and that disenfranchisement and second-class citizenship for two-thirds to three-fourths of a nation's population cannot possibly be squared with Christian conceptions. . . .

Is Christianity, as the Moslems maintain, the white man's religion? And is the Reformed segment of it a particularly hateful expression of the white man's superiority complex on the religious front? Does Calvinism call for Apartheid? These are questions that the intelligent African is or will soon be pondering. If we are concerned to gain standing and acceptance for the Reformed faith in Africa, then now is the time to disown, clearly and unambiguously, any sympathy with the attitude that our Reformed brethren in South Africa take to Apartheid and all its attendant evils. Such action may not greatly affect life in the

United States, but it would show that we are our sister's keeper; it might awaken some in the Reformed churches in South Africa to the lateness of the hour of the day in which there is time to act; and it would help the Reformed mission in Nigeria to say and to show that Reformed does not mean Apartheid.

Calvinists and Democrats

Lester DeKoster *October 1958*

He who enters upon the discussion of politics is commonly fore-
warned that such discussion often generates more heat than light. The
precept of caution is to leave the subject strictly alone. But we all know
that the duty of making political choice confronts each citizen who
contemplates seriously the responsibilities of citizenship. For most
Americans, in this year 1958, the range of effective political choice lies
between the two major political parties, Republicans and Democrats. It
is to this situation that the following discussion is oriented, laying
aside for the time the possibility of other alternatives.

No party, major or minor, has a monopoly on the virtues, nor on
the vices, of political program and conduct. It is this fact which freights
political decision heavily with problems, and requires of the citizen
thoughtful and persistent pursuit of the issues as change and circumstance shift focus and perspective. But one is surprised, if not dis-
mayed, to discover that amid conditions so complex as those of the
twentieth century, there are Christians who quite sincerely assume
that a Christian commitment does not stimulate discussion of the issues which divide the two major parties but, on the contrary, settles it.
This assumption comes to expression in such a question, asked rhetor-
ically as if the answer were foregone, as "*How* can *you*, as a Christian,
be a Democrat?"

A number of replies rise in one's mind in response to this query;
and one of these is the subject of the article which follows. Orthodox
Christianity, as coming to expression in Calvinism, does not, I believe,
prohibit support of the general aims and achievements of the Democrats, nor does it necessarily settle one in Republicanism. Rather, I
shall suggest that there is, in fact, much in the political history and

practice of Calvinism which exhibits remarkable affinity to the history
and practice of the Democratic Party, particularly in that area where
the state and economic life interact. . . .

[My thesis] can be made in two points: (1) Admitting at once that
history wears many faces and allows of many interpretations, I nevertheless think to discern that Calvin and Calvinism have stood, in the
large, for the positive intervention of the state in the social and economic life of the people for the promotion of the general welfare. And I
think it true that this state intervention did not destroy capitalistic enterprise, but rather has tended to curb its abuses and to unfold its
potentialities; for the development of capitalism and the spread of Calvinism went hand in hand. (2) This selective and controlled intervention of the state in the social and economic life of the nation, not to
transform nor to destroy capitalism but rather to discipline and to develop it, has been, as I understand and endorse it, the overall program
of the Democratic Party, and both the intent and result of much legislation devised, sponsored, and in large measure enacted by Democrats.
Nay more, hardly an original legislative enactment designed *to promote
positively the spread* of prosperity *under capitalism* has been devised,
sponsored, and enacted by any other political party, on the national
level, since the days of Theodore Roosevelt.

Placing these two historical phenomena side by side — Calvinism
in politics, and the achievements of the Democratic administrations of
our generation — does *not* lead me to conclude that non-Democrats are
non-Calvinists, *nor* does it imply that Republicans are fuzzy on their
Calvinism or disloyal to their faith. But I am led to contend that support
of the main outlines of the Democratic program has been, and is, by no
means out of line with historic Calvinism; but, rather, is quite clearly in
the spirit of Calvin's Geneva, in the tradition of the Puritan-Calvinists
of Scotland, England and New England, and in harmony with the program of our Calvinistic brethren in Holland across the sea. . . .

In Geneva

[T]he Geneva of the sixteenth century breathed, economically, modern
air. Capitalism and private enterprise were well known there, and
business was not the puzzle to Calvin which it is said always to have
remained to Luther. The "bourgeois revolution" was, by the calcula-

tion of some scholars, no less than two hundred years on its way by Calvin's time; and he was himself schooled in the legal bases of property, trade, and contract. Which, then, of the three alternatives — that of umpire, regulator, or participant — represents the relation of state and economic life in Calvin's Geneva?

That the state was umpire there is no doubt. . . . No one, it is likely, who is seeking illustration for the thesis that they govern best who govern least will turn to Calvin's Geneva. Nor is that school of economic theory which proclaims each one's inviolable right to do as he likes with his own apt to find any more support in the practices of Geneva than it can discover in the teaching of Calvin.

But did this city also go beyond the second alternative, strict *regulation* of economic life? It did! Writes Dr. H. H. Meeter, "Calvin advocated public loans for the poor and refugee, measures relating to public health, statistical inquiries into the income of districts, the fixing of the price of corn and wine and other commodities, the determination of a proper rate of interest, and even the ownership and operation by the State of a silk industry for the twofold purpose of increasing the revenue of the State and giving added employment to the citizens. In fact, so much social legislation was enacted by the Genevan government at the time and through the influence of Calvin that his government has been termed Christian socialism. While the government of Geneva was anticommunistic — and thus cannot be called socialism as we know it today — it, nevertheless, stressed emphatically the duty of the government to provide for the public welfare in material, cultural, and philanthropic matters."

Were it useful, this quotation might be complemented by others in similar vein from Choisy, Troeltsch, Weber, and more. For the purposes in hand, however, it may be maintained that Calvin's Geneva *regulated* economic life with grim enthusiasm, and crossed the line into *active economic participation* with some abandon. . . . Knox, and the Puritans in Scotland and England, hewed much to the same line, though he without real political power and they able to exercise what they preached. In New England, writes Tawney, "naturally the authorities regulated prices, limited the rate of interest, fixed a maximum wage, and whipped incorrigible idlers." They sought also to control profits, and one of the ministers of Boston, sermonizing on nine principles governing trade, gave as the first that it was unlawful to suppose "that a man might sell as dear as he can, and buy as cheap as he can."

Lester DeKoster

The Netherlands

In sum, Calvinism in England, Scotland, and New England did but
echo Geneva. All this, however, was long ago and came to pass when
church and state had hardly been clearly separated. What of the modern world? When we turn to the Netherlands we find that once more
the story is much the same, in an industrial nation in many ways parallel to our own. Whether we select from Professor Diepenhorst's practical exposition of the program of the Calvinistic Antirevolutionaire
Partij a list of social legislation endorsed by that party and largely enacted into law through its influence, a list which reads like a precursor
to the Rooseveltian New Deal; or whether we quote from Dr. Meeter's
summary of the work of Kuyper and Colijn; or whether we extract
from Kuyper or Colijn or Talma themselves; or whether we work back
from the volume, *The Responsible Society* (in Dutch), published this
very year, we cannot escape the conclusion that Calvinism in the Netherlands has by no means restricted itself to viewing the state as only an
umpire over the economic life of the people, but has gone on to the second and third of our alternatives. . . .

The broad outline is clear: Calvin and Calvinism have seen state
and economic life not as enemies, nor as strangers, but as associates in
achieving the total welfare of the nation. And in this partnership, the
task of the state has been understood to be *umpire, regulator, and participant*, all three, as a need for each became clear.

Calvinism and Capitalism

But perhaps by now the reader who has himself done a little grubbing
about in these matters is puzzled. He well remembers reading that it
has been the work of men like Weber, Troeltsch, and Tawney — though
not entirely in unison — to show that Calvinism and capitalism flourished together not only, but as cause (Calvinism) and effect (capitalism). This conclusion is endorsed by Miss [Georgia] Harkness, though
with reservations, after her own survey of the evidence. How is it,
then, the question arises, that Calvinism encouraged capitalism, if it
stood in fact for state regulation and also for state participation?

The answer is puzzling only to those who mistake economic Liberalism of the *laissez-faire* school for Calvinism. To Calvin it was quite

clear, one may conclude, that regulation and intervention by the state, if *controlled* by the concepts of freedom and general welfare, are not harmful but medicinal to capitalist development. Calvin was no enemy to private enterprise. On the contrary, as Troeltsch puts it, "Calvinism . . . is the only form of Christian social doctrine which accepts the basis of the modern economic situation without reserve." . . .

What Calvin embodied in thought and practice was the persuasion that Undisciplined Activity, whether in economic practice or in society at large, led to disaster. To curb excesses by law was clearly the duty of the state, and to extend this discipline to careful state regulation of enterprise was also the practice of Calvin's Geneva. Moreover, the state, in Calvin's time and under the guidance of Calvinists since his time, has moved into economic participation in the national life, where private enterprise has left gaps to be filled or where spirit-maiming burdens might be lifted from the shoulders of the poor and oppressed.

And as a result of reaching and crossing what Tawney calls this "watershed" in the history of religio-politico-economic relationships, wherever Calvinism took root there capitalism flourished. And it flourished, not in spite of Geneva, but in the tradition of Calvin; and, *what is more,* when capitalism over-stepped the bounds set by Geneva and went madly off on its own, it in due season spewed forth Karl Marx!

Our problem, as Christians in politico-economic relationships, is not to escape Calvin, nor to take pains to explain him away under new slogans, but rather it is to take him seriously. So doing is not to abjure all state regulation of, and participation in, economic life, but so to control these activities by religious principle that the general welfare may be promoted, not by hobbling but by developing the creative powers inherent in capitalism itself.

The Democratic Program

This attitude toward state regulation and participation in economic life is, as I view it, implicit in much that the Democratic Party has accomplished since the day of Woodrow Wilson, and more emphatically, since the time of Franklin Roosevelt. Whatever may have been the variety of motives present to the minds of those who shaped the New

Deal, there is, I think, clear evidence also of the same apprehension of the relation of state to nation which has characterized Calvinism since the days of Geneva.

And the result has been much the same as those results which attended the progress of Calvinism across Europe and America. The New Deal and Fair Deal did not stifle private enterprise, nor choke the national economy. On the contrary, despite the tremendous energies absorbed by purely military production, the nation has in twenty-five years made strides so gigantic in economic progress that it is not only our grandfather's standards of living which have been revolutionized since 1929, but our own. If the New Deal and the Fair Deal have really been poisonous to free enterprise, then "on what meat," indeed, "doth this colossus feed?"

. . . The work of Roosevelt is now commonly understood to have been directed to rehabilitating and redeveloping the American free enterprise system, bitterly as that work was assailed at the time. And I think it may be truly said that what Roosevelt, from his own point of view, like Karl Marx from a quite different point of view, and, again, like John Calvin from his own vantage point — I say, what all of these men clearly understood was that the laws of economics, if left uncontrolled by the laws of morality, lead to tensions, to chaos, and to the oppression of the poor. And the insight which Roosevelt sought to turn to constructive ends, as Marx sought to turn the same insight to destructive ends, Calvinism had long insisted upon using for the development of private enterprise, namely this insight, that the state is not the enemy of the people but their servant, not their tyrant but their aide, *if properly employed.* . . .

For the solution to modern problems is never simple. Economic life might be left to its own, and then Karl Marx would someday meet it on the downhill road. But this *laissez faire* has never been Calvinism's way. Calvinism has stood for active participation by state in national life, with an eye to national welfare. In such participation there are, as I say, risks of over-stepping the bounds. But every virtue has within it the occasion to defects; and *for gain in politics, as in business,* one must run risks. Indeed, living is itself the running of risks. Our task is to seek the gain, and to guard against the risk; and with an eye alert to this dual responsibility, and acting in the ways opened to us by the blessing of political freedom, we as Calvinists can find a place for service in the Democratic Party, 1958.

And when I think on these things, if you will allow me one half-facetious remark, kind reader, then let me say that when someone asks, "How can you, as a Christian, be a Democrat?" I am tempted to reply, with what I hope is a twinkle in the eye, "How can you, as a Calvinist, be anything else?"

God So Loved — ALL Men!

HAROLD DEKKER   *December 1962*

The most basic and comprehensive of all missionary principles is the love of God. In divine love missions finds both its conception and its initiation. "God so loved . . . that he gave . . ." From God's love missions draws its motivation and its methodology. As Paul put it, "The love of Christ constraineth us." Moreover, the message of missions is a message of the love of God. It proclaims that God is love, that He has acted in love for man's salvation and that this love demands decisive response. How much did God love? So much that He gave His only begotten Son. So much that He emptied Himself; He gave Himself. The amount of the love is indicated by the amount of the gift. That means no less than an infinite love.

Love without limit! Can an unlimited love be limited in its scope? Can an unrestricted love be restricted in those whom it loves? Can the infinite love of the incarnation have as its object only a part of mankind? Hardly. Neither does the Bible teach this. Rather we are told, "God so loved *the world* that he gave." Whether taken as the cosmos or as the human race, "world" in this passage clearly covers all men. By no strain of exegesis can God's redemptive love be confined to any special group. Neither the language of this verse nor the broadest context of Scripture will allow any other interpretation but that God loves all men. . . . [There follows commentary on various biblical passages.]

The universal love of God stands out in Scripture in bold beauty and unimpaired power. It is regrettable that some theologians, for the sake of a limited election, place limitation on the love of God. The most extreme and destructive form that this takes is the arbitrary interpretation of words such as "world" as "elect world," and "all men" as "all elect men." This kind of limitation has neither hermeneutic nor dog-

54   *1951-1962*

matic justification. However, a basically similar compromise of the Biblical paradox is made by those who distinguish between two kinds of love in God, positing a *qualitative* difference between God's love for all men and His love for the elect. Their view is not altogether unlike the view of those who say that God loves elect men and hates all other men. Essentially these two views are different forms of a double-track theology which drives a wedge into the very nature of God and which sacrifices Biblical realism to logical structure. God's love is love. It cannot be something else. Where in Biblical language or concept is there a qualitative difference within love as *agape?* Where in man's experience with God is there something which is at one and the same time both love and other-than-love? A *qualitative* disjunction between different kinds of divine love is a sheer contradiction in terms. It safeguards neither the love of God nor the decree of election.

*   *   *

This leads us to a consideration of the relationship between universal divine love and the atonement of Christ. If God's love in giving Christ is universal, is the atonement universal? Or is it limited? Before answering this question we must carefully understand the terms which it uses and the alternative which it poses.

Just what is the Reformed doctrine of limited atonement? As far as the average reader of this journal is concerned, the definition of Louis Berkhof may be considered representative. We quote from his *Systematic Theology:* "The question with which we are concerned at this point . . . relate[s] to the design of the atonement. Did the Father in sending Christ, and did Christ in coming into the world to make atonement for sin, do this with the design or for the purpose of saving only the elect or all men? That is the question, and that only is the question." (pp. 393-395) · · ·

[After criticizing Berkhof's use of biblical evidence, the author takes up] what the Canons of Dort have to say. The question for Berkhof is the design of the atonement as such. To this detached question the Canons do not speak. They speak of the design of the atonement as far as its "saving efficacy" is concerned. The relevant statement (from II-8) is as follows: "For this was the sovereign counsel and most gracious will and purpose of God the Father, that the quickening saving efficacy of the most precious death of His Son should extend to all the elect, for bestowing upon them alone the gift of justifying faith, thereby to bring them infallibly to salvation; that is, it was the will of God that Christ by the blood of the cross . . . should effectually redeem out of every people, tribe, nation, and language, all those, and those only, who were from eternity chosen to salvation and given to Him by the Father; that He should confer upon them faith, which, together with all the other saving gifts of the Holy Spirit, He purchased for them by His death."

"Limited atonement" as taught by the Canons is not precisely the same, it seems, as that taught by Berkhof. Dort did not deal with the design of the atonement in general, as Berkhof does. It dealt rather with the design of the atonement in specific connection with efficacious application of saving grace. Contrary to the Arminians who taught the atonement was intended to apply enabling grace to all men, Dort insisted that the atonement in no sense was intended to effectuate saving grace for all men. The key phrases in the above excerpt from the Canons are "saving efficacy," "justifying faith," and "effectually redeem." But Berkhof deals with the design of the atonement in a broader sense and it seems clear that the Canons of Dort do not demand adherence to the doctrine of limited atonement in exactly the way he sets it forth.

Limited atonement as construed by Berkhof is apparently more a logical inference from the doctrine of election than a Biblically demonstrable doctrine. If any doctrine of limited atonement is allowed to stand as mere logical inference, without compelling Biblical evidence, it must be recognized that by equally logical inference from the doctrine of election one may hold that God loves not all men but only some, and that God's sincere offer of the gospel is not for all but for a limited number. We must accept the paradoxes of Scripture wherever we find them, not merely where they suit our dogmatical predilections.

*   *   *

Now let us return to our original question. Is the atonement limited or universal in its design? The answer depends on what we mean by design. As far as the atonement is concerned, four factors may be distinguished when we speak of design: *sufficiency, availability, desire,* and *efficacy.*

First, can those who recognize the *sufficiency* of the atonement for all men, as Berkhof certainly does, deny that this was part of its *design?* If universal sufficiency is not part of the divine design of the atonement, it is an accident, an unintended byproduct. Any such conception is of course theologically impossible and amply discredited by the Bible.

Second, is the salvation which the atonement provides *available* to all men? Indeed it is. Otherwise the well-meant offer of the gospel is a farce, for it then offers sincerely to all men what cannot be sincerely said to be available to all. Moreover, Scripture such as Titus 2:11 is very precise at this point: "For the grace of God hath appeared, bringing salvation to all men."

Third, does God *desire* the salvation of all? This we have already shown. Can God's desire for the salvation of all men be dissociated from His design in the atonement? Not according to logic or, more decisively, Biblical teaching. I Timothy 2:4-6 says about the design of God's desire: "Who would have all men be saved, and come to the knowledge of the truth. For there is one God, one mediator also between God and men, himself man, Christ Jesus, who gave himself a ransom for all."

There are, therefore, three senses in which we may legitimately speak of the atonement as being universal in design, i.e., the *sufficiency* and *availability* of salvation for all men and the divine *desire* that all will receive it. The only point at which Scripture and the Reformed confessions point to a limited design in the atonement is at the point of *efficacy.* Only there can a doctrine of limited atonement be formulated which does not do clear violence to Biblical teaching concerning the universal love of God.

Seemingly, Berkhof did not recognize adequately the complexities of the concept of design with respect to the atonement. But he has faithfully and cogently set forth the essence of the historic Calvinistic view that as far as the actual salvation of men is concerned there is a limitation of numbers which is embraced in the eternal purpose of God and in the design of the atonement. When it comes to the efficacy of the atonement there can be no doubt that its existential limitation is to be explained ultimately in terms of the sovereign disposition of divine grace. On this score the Scriptures, explicated by the Canons of Dort, are decisive and convincing.

The doctrine of limited atonement as taught by Berkhof and others has commonly been used to place a taboo on the proposition that Christ died for all men and on any statement by a missionary to unbelievers such as, "Christ died for you." Supposedly such language is Arminian. Actually it is not necessarily so. There is no warrant in Scripture or the Reformed confessions for disallowing such expressions when they are used in any one of the first three meanings explained above. If the Church is unwilling to say in any sense that Christ died for all men and refuses to say to unbelievers, in addition to "God loves you," "Christ died for you," it places the infinite love of God under an illegitimate restriction.

The doctrine of limited atonement as commonly understood and observed in the Christian Reformed Church impairs the principle of the universal love of God and tends to inhibit missionary spirit and activity. God so loved *all men* that He gave His only begotten Son! May this great truth permeate the life and witness of the Church in full power.

Does God Love All Men Alike?

Peter De Jong   *March 1963*

I have often felt that there has been a tendency among us to do less than justice to some of the texts of the Scriptures that stress the general invitation and call of the gospel. In calling attention to that in his *Reformed Journal* article, Rev. Harold Dekker does the church a service. However, his article goes much further than that and in its effort to make his point makes claims that, it seems to me, are thoroughly unbiblical and that if accepted must prove destructive to the very gospel Professor Dekker is concerned about promoting. . . .

We notice that the article at the outset defines the love of God in speculative rather than in Biblical terms. "Love without limit! Can an unlimited love be limited in its scope? Can an unrestricted love be restricted in those whom it loves? Can the infinite love of the incarnation have as its object only a part of mankind? Hardly." It ought to be observed that this kind of argument must lead not only to universal atonement but to universal salvation, and that, of course, none of us is ready to accept. The only guide to what our doctrinal position is to be must be the plain teaching of God's Word. What we might imagine to be worthy of the expression of infinite love carries no real weight at all unless we are ready with equally consistent logic to go along with Modernists, Neo-Orthodox, Seventh-Day Adventists and Jehovah's Witnesses to argue that the love of God makes such a thing as eternal punishment inconceivable.

If we are to take our position on the basis of the Bible, we shall have to observe that the assumption that there is no qualitative difference between God's love for all men and His love for the elect seems to rob the Biblical word and concept of election of all real meaning. Doesn't the term "elect," in whatever way it is used, always mean that those so distinguished are "called out," "separated," brought into a special relation of friendship with God different from that of the rest? Countless examples may be cited. . . . [The author follows with several.]

The article attempts to maintain that there is no "qualitative difference between God's love for all men and his love for the elect" by evading or ignoring the thrust of such passages and appealing to a few other places where the death of Christ is spoken of in a more general way. Admittedly, we face problems in this matter we cannot fully solve. As Rev. Dekker says, "We must accept the paradoxes of Scripture wherever we find them, not merely where they suit our dogmatic predilections." It is better to leave unsolved problems than to resort to forced exegesis, as has sometimes been done. But this good advice of the writer is precisely what in this article he does not do. He makes sweeping generalizations that contradict, as far as I can see, a large body of Scripture teaching. Where in the Bible can one find one example of gospel preaching in which the individual unbeliever is told, "God loves you and Christ died for you"? If God's Word nowhere teaches us to address the world in this way, what right does anyone have to demand that we do so, or to condemn the churches' refusal to do so?

The Arminian, Modernist, and, more recently, the Neo-Orthodox influences have all been toward wiping out the Biblical distinctions between church and world. Karl Barth in particular has repeatedly tried to deny this distinction and again and again in his writing tends toward universalism. It is significant that one of the common charges made against the Neo-Orthodox movement has been that it has proved to be singularly impotent in generating missionary enthusiasm. Professor Dekker is concerned about promoting mission enthusiasm, and we appreciate that — but we can hardly promote a good mission program with an unbiblical interpretation of the love of God that obscures the Biblical distinctions between church and world.

The love of God, however important, is not the only truth or consideration with which we need to be concerned in our missionary effort. Other teachings are also important — that of the judgment and wrath of God among them. In the same passage in which Paul says, "The love of Christ constraineth us," he also says, "For we must all be made manifest before the judgment seat of Christ — knowing therefore the fear of the Lord, we persuade men" (2 Cor. 5:10, 11). This aspect of the gospel is becoming far too generally ignored in our time, and may have something to do with the weakness of the churches' life and missionary efforts. Let us not forget that "the great awakening," which in the early history of our country went far toward Christianizing a largely non-Christian population, did not arise out of the proclamation of an indiscriminate love of God to believer and unbeliever alike, but from a presentation of the gospel of God's love against the background of a warning of the wrath to come.

We need to stress the truth that "God so loved the world," but let us not try to improve upon it by reading it "all men" or "each individual man," and let us not forget the rest of it, "that he gave his only begotten Son, that whosoever believeth on him should not perish, but have eternal life." And let us not neglect the context and corollary, "He that obeyeth not the Son shall not see life, but the wrath of God abideth on him."

He Bore Our Griefs

Jacobus Revius   *March 1963*
translated by Henrietta Ten Harmsel

No, it was not the Jews who crucified,
Nor who, Lord Jesus, spit into your face,
Nor who betrayed you in the judgment place,
Nor who with buffets struck you as you died.

No, it was not the soldiers fisted bold
Who lifted up the hammer and the nail,
Or raised the cross on Calvary's cursed hill,
Or cast the dice to win your seamless robe.

I am the one, O Lord, who brought you there.
I am the heavy cross you had to bear,
I am the rope that bound you to the tree,

The whip, the nail, the hammer, and the spear,
The bloody, thorny crown you had to wear:
It was my sin, O Lord, it was for me.

This poem is taken from the Over-Ysselsche Sangen en Dichten, the collected poems of
the Protestant Baroque poet of the Netherlands — Jacobus Revius (1586-1658). He presented the two volumes of poetry as a kind of epic of the Christian Church, beginning
with creation and the fall and continuing in his time in the bitter struggle between the
Reformed Dutch and the invading Spanish. The sonnet printed here is taken from that
part of the "epic" which mourns the suffering and death of Christ.

Hospitality

HENRY ZYLSTRA   *December 1956*

Among the older American Christmas classics, none is more charming than Irving's inimitable *Sketch Book*. I was reading those five Christmas chapters in that book again a while ago, and I found myself longing for the ingratiating warmth and liberality in the manor houses of yesteryear. The thing that comes to grand expression in Irving's sketches is the old time Christmas virtue of *hospitality*. Said the old Squire of Bracebridge Hall: "I love to see this day well kept by rich and poor; it is a great thing to have one day in the year, at least, when you are sure of being welcome wherever you go, and of having, as it were, the world all thrown open to you."

It is quite right that this virtue or grace of hospitality should be so firmly associated for us with Christmas. The association is a natural one. Two of the things, certainly, that make for hospitality are the *guest* and the *gift*. Both of these were uniquely present at Christmas. St. Benedict set it down as a rule of his order: "Every guest who comes to the monastery shall be received as if he were Christ Himself." Such, surely, is the basis of the generosity and love we show *our* guests at Christmas, and such, rightly taken, is the foundation of all Christmas hospitality whatever.

Time was when the very word *guest* quickened the pulses and set up a high expectancy. One sees eager children, wistful at the window pane, awaiting the cutter's arrival. It may be that we have lost something of the keen edge of this expectation in the humdrum of our secularized lives. But time was when distances were long, travel was hard, and visits were a privilege. It was then that the host appreciated the guest, and the guest the host. And if we have lost the fine edge of expectation in our regimented holiday procedures, this may also be because not everything is in order with our charity. One of our American poets, Mr. Auden, at least, writes of clearing up the debris after a trying holiday:

> *. . . Now we must dismantle the tree*
> *Putting the decorations back into their cardboard boxes —*
> *Some have got broken — and carrying them back to the attic.*

> *. . . There are enough*
> *Left-overs to do, warmed-up, for the rest of the week —*
> *Not that we have much appetite, having drunk such a lot,*
> *Stayed up so late, attempted — quite unsuccessfully —*
> *To love all our relatives, and in general*
> *Grossly overestimated our powers.*

We ought all, of course, in this Christmas season to be those children at the window impatiently asking again and again, "Is He coming?" And if ever there ought to have been an excitement of expectation it was when, in the fullness of time, prophecy yearned for fulfillment in the coming of the Divine guest. This was He who was announced in Eden as the One that should bruise the serpent's heel. The procession of the prophets marched towards Bethlehem from Balaam to Malachi with a mounting crescendo of urgency. The whole past was converging upon this present. This was the Branch, the Root, the Stem. Micah had been very specific: "Thou, Bethlehem Ephrata, though thou be little among the thousands of Judah, yet out of thee shall he come forth that is to be ruler of Israel." But there is no need here for calling upon the prophets for further witness: the words of Handel's *Messiah* are ringing in our ears. The point is clear: Our Lord ought to have been an *expected* guest.

But what now of the hospitality, the welcome, the entertainment He received? Think again of Washington Irving's words: Christmas the one day on which we can be sure of being welcome anywhere, and of having, as it were, the world all thrown open to us. The world, all the world, was most certainly our Lord's due. "All things are delivered to me," He said. "God," wrote the author of the Book of Hebrews, "hath in these last days spoken unto us by his Son whom he hath appointed heir of all things." Long ago, in the Book of Genesis, the father Jacob had sent his son Joseph to his own, and they had said, "This is the heir: Let us kill him." Our Lord explained it in a parable: "Surely they will reverence the Son." But they did not accord Him this welcome. They put Him to death.

Joseph and Mary came to the inn, and they were waved away. Such was the Christmas Eve hospitality accorded the Heir of all things, Him to whom the world should have been all thrown open. Later He would give some hint of His natural right to the things that were refused Him, as when He sent His disciples for the colt on which to ride triumphantly into Jerusalem. If they were prevented from loosing the animal, those disciples were simply to say: "The Lord hath need of him." But this hour was not now come. There was no room at the inn.

We need not, at this late date, be berating the desk clerk in that old Palestinian hotel for his lack of respect. The natural man, of whom there is much in us all, does not easily recognize spiritual things. The poor man did not guess that eternity might have impinged upon time in the guestbook of his establishment. He did not know, as a poet would put it later, that twenty centuries of stony sleep were about to be vexed to nightmare by a rocking cradle. He may have come with our best world's wisdom, and mumbled something about "first come, first served."

First come, first served indeed. This was the Alpha, and He should have been served first. But there was no room. So it was that our earth received its honored guest. Afterwards, on occasion, it is true, He found hospitality in that friendly cottage in Bethany. But that was an oasis in the desert of general neglect. "Foxes," He said, "have holes, and the birds of the air have nests, but the Son of man hath not where to lay his head." The expected guest was a *rejected* guest. He came to His own and His own received Him not.

Obviously, our own Christmas hospitality will be merely sentimental unless we begin by opening the homes of our hearts to this royal guest ourselves. . . . Joyce Kilmer put it this way:

> Unlock your door this evening,
> And let your gate swing wide;
> Let him who asks for shelter,
> Come speedily inside.
> What if your yard be narrow,
> What if your house be small:
> There is a guest is coming
> Will glorify it all.

Consider, finally, the words of our Lord: *Behold, I stand at the door and knock. If any man hear my voice, and open the door, I will come in to him and sup with him, and he with me.* That is the penultimate word on hospitality. May we pray for the grace to receive Him into the homes of our hearts. May we praise Him for the great grace of condescending to us, entering into us, and lodging with us. May we unbar the gates of our pride, and kindle within the hearths of our souls a love that can respond to His own. May He himself prepare within us a table of offerings acceptable to Him. And may He dine with us now and evermore.

Two dramatic events in the year 1963 signaled a new outward turn in the *Reformed Journal*'s attention: the August "March on Washington" which occasioned Martin Luther King, Jr.'s most famous speech, and the assassination of President John F. Kennedy at Dallas that November. The second phase of the *Journal*'s career is most distinguished by the increasing space it devoted to the social and political aspects of American life. Much of that attention fell into the categories laid out below: race and civil rights, politics in general and the Vietnam War in particular, and later in the era, the rebirth of feminism and the issue of abortion rights.

This commentary defied some lines of association that hardened later on. Henry Stob, through the early '60s a self-professed Republican, mounted a case against the alliance of "Fundamentalism and Political Rightism" that still holds true today. Lewis Smedes argued against both the Vietnam War *and* the Supreme Court's expansion of abortion rights in *Roe v. Wade*. James Daane took a similar position out of his civil rights advocacy earlier in the decade. On the other hand, Lester DeKoster kept true to the Cold War side of his traditional Democratic convictions and defended the Vietnam War all along. By opportunity and estrangement he left the *Journal* in 1970 to become editor of the CRC's official periodical, *The Banner*, and thus a successor to his old prosecutor H. J. Kuiper.

The magazine never lost its religious focus, however. One of its landmark contributions to the developing evangelical movement was Lewis Smedes's interrogation of Carl Henry's program for evangelical social ethics. Smedes concluded that Henry did not have one — rather, an individualistic ethic writ large. Richard Mouw, a Calvin College philosophy instructor who would later join Smedes as professor at (later president of) Fuller Theological Seminary as well as a *Journal* editor, made his *Journal* debut by drawing out the activist ecclesiology implicit in Smedes's position. Simultaneously, the magazine was engaging the varieties of "secular theology" that made such dramatic news in the day, culminating in the proposition that God was dead. Tellingly, it was a poet and literary scholar, Roderick Jellema, who made the most trenchant response in the *Journal*'s pages. The times' growing sense of extremity registered as well in a twenty-year retrospective on Hiroshima and in the *Journal*'s choice of film for its first movie review: Ingmar Bergman's *Winter Light*. The CRC Synod had lifted its proscription of theater attendance just the year before.

Significant editorial changes were behind the magazine's more lively and supple ways. In 1960 it began the "As We See It" feature in the first pages of each issue — briefer, punchy statements of opinion and reflection than were permitted by traditional full-length articles. The column became the *Journal*'s distinguishing mark thereafter. With the appointment of Calvin Bulthuis as its first editor-in-chief, the magazine achieved a new level of consistency and professionalism. Bulthuis's untimely death on Christmas Eve 1971 elicited a poignant reflection from his longtime friend Lewis Smedes, one of several pieces that echoed the yearning for community so typical of the American 1970s, and of the *Journal* along with it.

In Memoriam [On JFK]

LESTER DEKOSTER   *December 1963*

Where were you, when the shock wave set off by the President's assassination engulfed you in its passing?

The moment remains starkly fixed in one's memory, indelibly impressed by a rending of that veil of custom and indifference that commonly shields us from the fearful alternatives of life and death. Wherever we were, whatever we were doing . . . we shall not forget.

Where have we come, now? Past the point of hatred, which is murder? Past the point of bitterness, which nourishes hatred? Past the point of suspicion, which nourishes bitterness? To deeper sympathy, richer understanding, more disciplined thought, word, and deed? To rededication to that subtle nobility, basic sanity, profound humanity which is fundamentally American, and for which the President lived and died? If so, this martyred man shall not have died in vain.

Where were you? We shall not forget! Where have we come? Can we remember?

The Evangelicals and the Social Question

LEWIS B. SMEDES   *February 1966*

No single person has done more to awaken the fundamentalist conscience on the score of social ethics than has Carl Henry. Thanks in
large measure to his educated conscience-pricking, evangelicals today are struggling toward a conscious viewpoint on social questions.
Others before him — notably neo-orthodox people like the Niebuhrs
— had chided fundamentalists for their apocalyptic neglect of social
questions. Others — notably Calvinists like us — looked down their
noses at fundamentalism for its myopic view of the gospel and its
bearing on life. But Carl Henry spoke to fundamentalism from
within.

He spoke with considerable historical learning and theological
awareness. And he hit fundamentalism where it hurt — its stubborn
insensitivity to the social struggle. He knew that fundamentalism was
contributing to the social question if only by way of its quietism and ir-
responsibility. What he achieved is a *conscious* commitment to the social revelance of the gospel. This newfound commitment — or re-
commitment — is one of the earmarks of the evangelicalism for which
Dr. Henry is a leading spokesman.

Lately, Dr. Henry has felt pressed to defend the record and argue
the genuineness of evangelical concern. The civil rights struggle has
forced everyone, including the evangelicals, to examine their position
and sometimes to defend it. . . . Dr. Henry [has done so in] an impressive statement on social ethics in *Christianity Today*. He called it "Evangelicals in the Social Struggle." Coming when it did, it bore the marks
of an evangelical manifesto. Dr. Henry's piece deserves study and
comment. We offer ours with the understanding that, in many respects, we are in the same boat with him. We do not have all the an-

swers either. Like Dr. Henry, we are only working towards a viable and meaningful social ethic for today's world. . . .

The Strategy

The evangelical strategy for improving society is based upon the cleavage between regenerate and unregenerate men in society, and upon the moral influence of the regenerate segment on the unregenerate. . . . Social ethics is very simple, then. The gospel makes men good. Good men make good societies. The one element still needed is the will of good men to get into society and do something. Dr. Henry urges them into the struggle to use their supernatural potential for good. The fields of opportunity are wide open. The evangelical, he writes, "can and ought to use every platform of social involvement to promulgate the revealed moral principles that sustain a healthy society and that indict an unhealthy one." . . . This is not a strategy for a direct approach to a change in environment. It is not a strategy for an immediate change in social structures by law. It is one that calls for evangelical preaching — from the pulpit and by individuals across the bench from one another, preaching with conversion as its goal and, that failing, with an appeal to "enduring values."

There is much to be said for this approach. A society of immoral men living under an ideal legal structure is hardly by that token a good society. The leaven of good men of good will is, without any question, an inexpendable ingredient of a good society. But does this help us along toward a *social* ethic? Dr. Henry knows as well as anyone does that Christian history is shamefacedly strewn with sad stories of regenerate men pressing with ugly manners toward absolutely wrong-headed goals. He knows that regenerate men have done and are doing some stupid and harmful things with full assurance that they have "revealed moral principles" behind them. There has got to be some hint as to where the regenerate of society ought to lead the rest of society. As a moralist Dr. Henry knows this, and he has some answers. So, until we hear him tell the evangelical what he ought to be for and what he ought to be against, and how he ought to work for the right goals, we have not gotten to the gist of his social ethics.

But, even on this point we have some questions.

(1) Dr. Henry pins his hopes on the ability of regenerated men to

"influence humanity to aspire to enduring values." How earnest are his hopes . . . [and] how much hope does Dr. Henry have? This is not a cute trick to catch someone in a contradiction. If you are skeptical about laws and changes in environment, if you rely instead on the personal influence of good men to get others to elevate their own values, you have got to assume considerable moral readiness in the unregenerate, or you had better forget about social ethics and stick to evangelism in the narrowest sense.

(2) Dr. Henry says there is little point in changing environment. For when a man emerges transformed from a bad environment, he will not be long in setting out to change the environment. But why should he? Why should not he, too, stick to evangelism? Why should Dr. Henry encourage the second generation of regenerate men to alter environment when by the terms of his own ethics changing the environment is of dubious worth?

(3) Does Dr. Henry take into full awareness the fact that a bad social situation often prevents even the best willed Christian person from fulfilling his Christian obligation? . . . While we all know that a change in environment does not automatically turn bad men into good men, we know that a bad environment can keep a good man from doing the good as he ought. And by the same token, a good environment can inhibit a bad man from *doing* evil. And isn't this what *social* ethics is all about?

(4) Where does Dr. Henry get his confidence that regenerate men can be depended upon to overcome their own prejudices, shortsightedness, pride, and inertia? Dr. Henry will probably answer that he gets his confidence from faith in the Holy Spirit. But is this something you can presume upon? . . . To base a social ethic on the personal powers of the regenerate to spread the overflow of his own values into society is to make of social ethics a risky adventure.

(5) Finally, just what is the regenerate man — informed by "revealed principles" — to do about large hard-core areas of social deprivation? What does he do about the dislocations and hardships brought on people by shifts in the national economic and social patterns? Is he to "promulgate revealed principles" there, in the hopes that people victimized by these things will "aspire to enduring values"? . . .

The Tactics

This is the question of who does what when. And the rub here comes when we ask what government ought to do and what the church may do. Dr. Henry is eager to keep the areas of responsibility very clear. The role of the government is to maintain justice. The role of the church is to practice love. Law is the province of government. Compassion or benevolence is the province of the church. These are the ground rules for evangelical consideration of tactics in social action.

The reasons for keeping compassion out of government are curious. One of them is that benevolence is bound to be partial, discriminatory. Compassion is a form of love, and "love is preferential and shows favor or partiality." Government, in justice, must be impartial. I am at a loss to know where Dr. Henry comes by the notion that love is always partial. Our Father, we are told, sets the pattern for human benevolence precisely in His compassionate impartiality. He lets the sun shine and the rain fall on the just and unjust alike. Is it not the *essence* of compassion to show no favor and to be impartial?

The other reason for keeping compassion out of government is that compassion tends to push the government toward the welfare state. The welfare state is Dr. Henry's bête noir. He does not tell us why it is evil; he assumes, perhaps, that every literate evangelical will know why. What is the alternative to the welfare state? Why, the just state, of course. The "best alternative to the welfare state is the just state." Now, Dr. Henry must know that this gets us nowhere. If, when ill, I am told that the only alternative I have to surgery is sound health, I know my doctor is kidding. When Dr. Henry tells us that the best alternative to a welfare state is a just state, I am sure that he is not kidding; I am equally sure that he has not shed any light. What *is* the role of government in Dr. Henry's social ethics? . . . [It seems] that the government's function is to see to justice in the land. But it tells us little unless we begin defining some of these rights that must be assured and protected.

Dr. Henry does mention something about property rights being fundamental. I suppose he would add the right to vote, the right to travel, and the "right to work." (The latter meaning, not the right of every man to a job, but the wrong of any *union* to keep him away from his job.) But does every man have the right to provide decently for his family? Does every man have the right to live where he can afford a house? Does every man have the right of access to public accommodation? Does every aged and poor man have the right to adequate medical care? Are these rights — or are they matters of benevolence? If they are rights, then, by Dr. Henry's own definition, the government has an obligation to at least try to assure every man of them. And this would not be an exercise in compassion, but in law and justice. . . .

The net impression of Dr. Henry's essay is that evangelicals do not yet have a social ethic. They have a personal ethic for regenerate individuals. They do not have an ethic that prescribes a way of action and form for human society. We do not blame evangelicals for this. As we said earlier, we are in much the same boat. But with a difference. We insist that there has to be a social ethic derived from Christian principles, an ethic which prescribes a manner of life for *society* — the organic form of corporate human existence. We insist that environmental forms are terribly important to any social ethics. And we insist that government has a positive calling to see that the various segments of the organic society share properly in the social and economic privileges and responsibilities of the common wealth. The call of the gospel to conversion and regeneration is not compromised, we believe, by saying that evangelism is not a substitute for social ethics. For, apart from the salvation of individuals, there is a God-willed structure for society which we must seek to know and apply. And only as we look to this will we be involved in Christian social ethics. As I said, we do not blame evangelicals for not having achieved a social ethic. What we are eager to know is whether they really want one. . . .

What Social Structures? Some Remarks on Professor Smedes's Alternative

CARL F. H. HENRY   *May-June 1966*

To me it seems ironic that the Church, precisely at the time when she is lusting for novel forms and structures of her own, and is becoming increasingly unsure of what elements of fixity characterize her own community, should suddenly have become endowed with a divine afflatus for revising the social structures of the world. I do not imply that the Christian Reformed Church is re-examining its own structures (self-examination in view of biblical imperatives would be wholesome in all denominations), but there is little doubt that we now find an energetic espousal of new patterns of social involvement on the American scene. If changing social structures is the decisive test of the Church's real engagement in social ethics, it is remarkable that the Christian Reformed Church . . . has so recently gained this insight, and that we seem here to have an instance of the Church learning from the world (if not from the post-Marxist world) what her main social duty is.

While I insist that individual Christians ought to be politically active to the limit of their *competence,* and that they are obliged to join in the struggle for the just state and to seek the improvement of civil law, I would hold that whatever pertains to the world is provisional except as it has a basis in the revealed will of God for the social orders. As I see it, the purpose of civil government is preservative, not regenerative; that is, it is to protect human rights and sustain peace by the promotion of justice and order. It is ridiculous, therefore, to imply that although I am for civil rights I am not necessarily for civil rights *legislation.* Law and liberty, insofar as we deal with legitimate rights, belong together (I wish that Professor Smedes would himself not so swiftly exempt the right-to-work debate from this context). I thought President Johnson's civil rights message to Congress was his high hour, and wrote him so — although I thought it was no business of the institutional Church to endorse any specific legislative proposal in the name of the Church, and still have personal reservations about some aspects of civil rights legislation. . . .

Professor Smedes does not like my emphasis that except in dire emergency the responsibility of the state is in the realm of rights (which are non-preferential) and not of compassion or benevolence (which is preferential). He thinks that benevolence should not be left to benevolent individuals but is a proper role of government, not simply on an emergency basis but ideally and normatively. He thinks, it appears, that "the essence of compassion" is "to show no favor and to be impartial." Hence we are left with the overall impression that, as Professor Smedes sees it, the welfare state is neither evil nor partial, but preferential and ideal. He insists that "there has to be a social ethic derived from Christian principles, an ethic which prescribes the manner of life for *society* — the organic form of corporate human existence."

It is this "God-willed structure for society," as Professor Smedes calls it, that I now call on him to formulate precisely, and hopefully in the context of the teaching and example of Jesus and the apostles. I am myself convinced that the Church has much to say and do in the world. But I am not inclined to applaud either the direction that Dr. Smedes seems to be pointing, or his identification of the main concern.

The Church has the social task first of ordering its own life as a community of the faithful in distinction from the world of unbelief, and this it does under God for the sake of all mankind. In this ordering of the life of the redemptive community it ought to mirror what is implied in a good society — not simply as stipulated by law and grudgingly appropriated, but as impressively achieved on the basis of *agape.* Not that ecclesiastical norms ought in turn to be implemented by governments in the world. The state has its own specific mission and limits and, while the good state will require nothing contrary to the social commandments of the Decalogue (Rom. 13), its province is not the compulsion of benevolence but the preservation of justice and order. Only as the Church powerfully reflects the direct authority of Jesus Christ can she effectively witness to the world of the perils of ignoring the lordship of the invisible King whose claims the world spurns.

Where Do We Differ?

Lewis B. Smedes   *May-June 1966*

Dr. Henry reiterates that "law cannot transform people while the Gospel can." This is the limit of the usefulness of laws in our striving toward a just society. . . . Now, I do not know of any Christian moralist who supposes that laws can transform people. I certainly do not. But I do think that reliance on the Gospel of personal regeneration as the evangelical strategy in social ethics is inadequate. It is for this reason, undoubtedly, that I set greater store by law in achieving a good society than does Dr. Henry. I gather that he thinks of the usefulness of law primarily — though probably not exclusively — as deterrent, inhibitive, protective, and not as potentially creative of a better social structure. Still, his endorsement of the civil rights act keeps the door open for a more positive view.

To Dr. Henry the purpose of government lies in the realm of preservation. . . . [But] what is the government supposed to preserve? The answer: human rights and peace. The means: "by the promotion of justice and order." To this, I say Amen! And when I note Dr. Henry's insistence on his approval of civil rights legislation (does this include the Civil Rights Act of 1964?), I get the feeling that we are not far apart. But was this a merely preservative act? It certainly was also a creative act. It was a decision by government to provide (by law and enforcement) a new social status for one group within the population, a status that had been denied them by a social structure imposed and sustained by another group. If Dr. Henry espouses this kind of governmental "preservation," I am happy to settle for the term — as long as it can be given this sort of content.

But Dr. Henry is wary of my readiness to carry this kind of governmental involvement over into the economic sphere of life. Why? Do people have no economic rights besides the right to keep what they already have? . . . [People] have a right to keep what they have earned, Dr. Henry says (property rights). But do they have no *right* to a share in the common goods? Do children have no right to be part of a family living in an environment where family life is truly possible? Do the elderly poor have no right to adequate medical care? Do fathers of families have no right to provide for their families? And does government not have a summons from justice to see that these rights, too, are honored as far as possible? That Dr. Henry did not wish to go into such questions is his privilege. But unless we evangelicals do come to terms with these and similar questions about the nature of men's rights, we are not going to advance into a relevant social ethic for our time. . . .

It is my hope that the evangelical of today, awakened as he is to a revitalized social concern, will give new thought to the question of the nature of man. And if this discussion, modestly begun on these pages, could ripen to a full-scale discussion on another level, the question of individualism will have to be prominent on the agenda. The net impression left on me still is that expressed in my other essay: Evangelicals have a personal ethic for regenerate individuals. They do not have an ethic that prescribes a way of action and form for human society. I think the Calvinist tradition provides the most promising base on which to develop one.

The Church and Social Specifics

Richard J. Mouw   *July-August 1969*

Faithful readers of this journal will be well aware that there is a difference of opinion among evangelical Christians as to how specific the Church's pronouncements are to be vis-a-vis social matters. Those of us who think it obvious that the Church should often be *very* specific in this area are apt to be puzzled by, and perhaps suspicious of, the attitudes of Christians who are, by their own confession, concerned with the "social implications of the Gospel" and who are yet anxious to place definite restrictions on the political-economic aspects of the Church's proclamation. . . .

With this justification I desire to do a little prodding. My text is the following comment, authored, I presume, by Dr. Carl Henry:

> When evangelical Protestants deplore the Church's meddling in politics, they surely do not disown its proper role in enunciating theological and moral principles that bear upon public life. And now they are called to make a bold new inquiry into questions that concern the social and political ethos. Although the Church has no mandate, authority, or competence to say *yes* or *no* to political and economic specifics — except perhaps in some emergency that may require a *no* to preserve the Christian faith, witness, and life — it must set the principles of revealed morality in dialogic relation to modern alternatives.

I find these remarks both perplexing and encouraging. First, my perplexity. In one very brief phrase the writer manages to raise at least two distinct, and debatable, issues. He states that "the Church has no mandate, authority, or competence" to pronounce on social specifics.

On the Church in Society   79

Richard J. Mouw

Granting, for the present, that having a *mandate* to do something and having the *authority* to do it amount to nearly the same thing, to claim that the Church has neither the mandate nor the authority to speak on social specifics clearly differs from the claim that the Church has no *competence* to do so. Bodies often have the competence to decide matters over which they have no authority; and it also happens that a body will have the authority to decide issues while lacking the competence to do so.

Now the Lord of the Church, presumably, would not give the Church the authority to do that for which it has no competence; or, better, if He gave the authority to the Church He would also *give* it the competence. So the important issue is whether the Church has the authority to speak on social specifics; independent of *that* question the issue of whether it has the competence is irrelevant.

The editorial writer, however, chooses to pronounce on this latter issue, and I can see no reason for thinking that his pronouncement is correct. The Church's competence, he holds, does not extend beyond the ability to enunciate general "theological and moral principles that bear upon public life." What is curious is that while the writer holds that the *Church* is incompetent for the task of getting beyond these general principles to social specifics, the *laity* does not completely share this incompetence; for he goes on to ask: "Are evangelical churches really encouraging laymen to wrestle earnestly with such issues, not on the assumption that the Church has revelational solutions to secular specifics, but rather on the assumption that devout men motivated by biblical standards can contribute significantly to public dialogue, to public policy, and to public leadership?"

One wonders: if the layman, by hearing these general principles enunciated from the pulpit, can with some degree of effectiveness "wrestle earnestly" with specific issues, why cannot the *enunciator* of those principles, by the hearing of his *own* enunciations, *also* do some effective wrestling? Must we assume the intellectual inferiority of the official church proclaimer in comparison with the "devout men" who hear him? Is it not conceivable that the abilities of both parties to bring the principles to bear on specific matters might be, in general, equal? Surely the writer does not mean to claim that the Church's official spokesmen are peculiarly inept at wrestling with specific issues, but, rather, that they have no authority to do so in their official capacities.

But the competence which is apparently being ascribed to the layman here is itself of a vague sort. For the writer clearly denies that *any-one* can, in any straight-forward sense, derive specific social solutions from the data of revelation. There are, he tells us, no "revelational solutions to secular specifics." But is this true? Consider the following pattern of reasoning. The Scriptures clearly teach that strong family bonds should be preserved; now suppose that a particular piece of "secular" legislation were proposed which would have as an obvious result of its enactment the widespread deterioration of family bonds. An intelligent Christian, then, would know the following claims to be true: (1) God disapproves of the widespread deterioration of family bonds, and (2) this piece of legislation, if adopted, would promote the widespread deterioration of family bonds. Would he not also, then, know the following claim to be true? (3) God disapproves of this piece of legislation (all else being equal). Of course, (2) is not a "revealed" claim, but it is not a claim whose truth it is impossible to discover. And if (2) could be known to be true I do not see how any person with a grasp of the fundamental laws of reasoning could fail to derive (3) from it and (1).

Is there any reason to think that official Church spokesmen cannot arrive at *many* specific claims in the manner just described? The issues that our writer seems to be confusing are these: whether, on the one hand, a Church spokesman can *arrive* at specific judgments, and whether, on the other hand, having arrived at them he has the authority to *reveal* his conclusions. That the Church can do the former, I suggest, is obvious. The question cannot be, then, whether the Church *can* decide on specifics but whether it has the mandate to *announce* its decisions. I am tempted to argue that the Church does indeed have the authority to make claims like (3) above. . . .

[In Dr. Henry's] comment that is our present concern there is a remark, added almost as an afterthought, that makes a concession on this point. And this is where I find my encouragement. The writer qualifies his sweeping denial of the Church's authority (and competence) to speak on social specifics, for he allows that there might be "emergency" situations wherein the Church may be required to pronounce a specific *no*. Although the authority and competence of the Church in these special circumstances are limited by him to the making of negative judgments, it would seem that a recognition that the Church *can* say *no* when the matter is serious enough gives us a basis for gauging what the Church's attitudes are toward run-of-the-mill policies and proposals. For when it chooses *not* to speak we can infer that its position is one of approval or neutrality, or that it does not consider the matter crucial enough to merit a pronouncement. If *exceptions* to the Church's lack of authority and competence to speak on specifics are permitted, then the Church's *silence* becomes a kind of pronouncement.

Even here questions arise. If the Church has, on occasion, both the authority and the competence to decide that a specific proposal or policy is to be *rejected*, why, by the *same* criteria it uses in deciding to disapprove, could it not also on occasion decide to *approve?* Surely the competence for disapproving implies the competence for approving; so it must be, once again, that the issue is the Church's authority and not its competence.

How, on this view, is the Church to know when it has the rare authority to pronounce a specific *no?* The answer given is that it is obliged to speak only when its pronouncement is necessary "to preserve the Christian faith, witness, and life." In this I find comfort. For this is surely a criterion which parties on both sides of the dispute can accept. I, for one, would accept this as a hard and fast rule: *the Church must only pronounce on specifics when there is a threat to the Christian faith, witness, and life.* We cannot approve the Church's promiscuous "meddling" in politics; rather, the Church's proclamations in the social arena must be motivated solely by its firm commitment to the preservation of the Christian way.

But I would add that threats to the Christian way are not rare; the Church constantly faces one continuing "emergency" situation. For *sin* has permeated the hearts of men, radically affecting their lives, both personal and social, in all aspects — including the political and the economic. And the Church is obliged, even given a mandate, to bring to all sinful situations both the judgment and the Gospel of God.

What is encouraging about the view we have been discussing is that it so often seems that our disagreement with many of our evangelical brothers is rooted in what are apparently very different views of the nature and mission of the Church; one often understands them to be denying that the Church should *ever* make the kinds of pronouncements which many of us want the Church to make. But with the author of these remarks there is, it would seem, no such *basic* disagreement. We are agreed that, on occasion, the Church is obligated to speak a specific word in the social arena. We are even in apparent agreement as to what criterion should decide just when that word should be spoken. Where we disagree, it seems, is over *how often* the obligation for the Church to speak specifically arises. And on *this* issue I am inclined now to accuse our writer of not taking very seriously the thought that human society is in a general state of "emergency." But this is such a hard saying that I wonder whether I have yet understood him.

Mississippi Versus . . . Meredith?

Lester DeKoster   *January 1963*

For some months now the world has watched what Governor Barnett calls the "great commonwealth" of Mississippi and its tax-supported University engage in well-nigh mortal combat with Mr. James Meredith, citizen — and, also in the Providence of God, Negro.

Mr. Meredith was born a citizen. He was also born a Negro. He had nothing to do with either. James Meredith did not choose to be a Negro. But if he did not, and if a choice was nonetheless involved, who made that choice for him? The answer to the question is not obscure. Mr. Meredith is clothed in color by his Creator.

And yet the question at Oxford, Mississippi, is precisely this: *color.* Nothing else is so centrally at issue, even now that competence to continue is being edged into the contest. Were it in fact a matter of entrance requirements, or of qualifications, or of citizenship, or of ability to pay, or of aptitudes or attitudes on Mr. Meredith's part, then no doubt the question of the extent of his personal responsibility would be involved; but the State's case rests on one issue only: *color.*

If, then, the State of Mississippi and its school are engaged in a contest over color, they are only accidentally fighting with Mr. Meredith. Their real quarrel, though they seem unaware of it, is with Him who draped Mr. Meredith in black; and it is His judgment in such matters that is on trial at Oxford, Mississippi, and elsewhere these days. Perhaps no one has said loudly enough, or perhaps few people care, that it is an awful thing to fall into combat with the living God — even when He is hidden in blackness.

If God, not Meredith, is the giver of color, then to draw the battle line on color is to confront, in Meredith, God. Then to hoot at Meredith is to hoot at God; to scorn, in Meredith, God; to threaten, in Meredith,

God; to ostracize, in Meredith, *the living God!* Does someone suppose that Ford stands behind its cars, and General Motors its trucks, and your shopkeeper his wares, while God plays deadbeat to the works of His hands?

The Abolitionist, John Brown, reminded the Court which condemned him to death that the Judge to whom they were despatching him would in due season meet them all — and, time having gone by, so it has happened. Brown's judges have, one by one — no mob to whip up courage there — made their way to *The* Judge, to give account of their treatment of John Brown. So might those, like Mr. Meredith, fighting still in the cause for which John Brown gave his life, remind not only the Governor of Mississippi and his hirelings, but us all: it is with God that we contend when we discriminate, according to color, and when we deny human rights that we can in final truth neither institute nor alienate. And, they might remind us too, if we do not find this out now, we are certain to discover it later, when we pass from grace to judgment.

The Answer Is Blowing in the Wind

JAMES DAANE   *September 1963*

The marchers came to Washington. They marched the short distance from the Washington Monument to the Lincoln Memorial, on a street called Constitution Avenue. They sang and waved banners, they prayed and made speeches, under the brooding figure of Abraham Lincoln.

The District of Columbia was afraid. Its people stayed home. Downtown offices were half-staffed. Instead of snarled traffic, the streets were quiet — as on an early Sunday morning. Business was off 80 to 90 percent. But there was no violence. The 200,000 marchers were orderly, polite, apologizing for the slightest inadvertent social infraction of good manners.

The moral dimension of this historic sign of social revolution was as big as the Washington Monument. The whole protest was a glowing tribute to the character of the marchers and their Negro leadership. The march was short, but the sound of moving feet and the echo of the pain and hurt of the Negro soul sobbed out in Negro spirituals and folksongs, will linger long in the historical memory of the American people. There was something Christlike in the patient restraint of long endured pain and injustice. There was something of the cry, Father, forgive them, in this people who though long reviled, reviled not again. Although they and their children had suffered from the law's long delay, they were not calling fire from heaven. They did not seek to eliminate the white man, but to join him and his way of life.

There were no threats. But there was quiet intent, and unconcealed determination. They want their legal, democratic, American rights, and they want them now. Their patience revealed a controlled impatience, and there were clear suggestions of its limits. Their protest was public, morally controlled; they sought by nonviolence and due processes of law the rights that men cannot honestly deny are their rights. Their behavior stole the consciences of their oppressors. Convinced that no man has a right to set the timetable for another man's freedom, they want their freedom now. All of it. They will not be satisfied by a gradual reception of the rights they should have had long ago. They do not intend to wait another hundred years. And what American who glories in the spirit of 1776 can blame them?

What does it all mean? As the song goes, "The answer, my friend, is blowing in the wind." If the American people are unwilling to live by their own political beliefs and traditions, if Congress does but little, and if the South is unable to read the social signs of our times, what is now public, peaceful, non-violent, may well become sullen, bitter, non-public, and violent. Wild revenge and bitter frustrated acts of reprisal could easily replace the mood of a Mrs. Medgar Evers, who publicly asked that there be no hatred for the shotgun destruction of her husband one night.

There are 20,000,000 Negroes in America; they are caught up in the winds of social change that blow across the earth, winds that will not be stayed because their time is come. No responsible Negro leader wants to say what will happen, if nothing happens. They continue like Martin Luther King to say, "I have a dream," or like James Baldwin, to quote spirituals, "God gave Noah the rainbow sign; no more water, the fire next time." Freedom moves through the land. The God of justice moves in the earth. We can ignore the answer that blows in the wind only to our hurt and shame.

We Went to Alabama

EDSON LEWIS, JR. *April 1965*

It was early in the morning (6:30 a.m.) when we entered Montgomery, "The Cradle of the Confederacy." Following the now famous (or is it in-famous?) highway 80, we soon found ourselves driving down a street alongside the state capitol building. State troopers were everywhere: at the intersections, in large clusters around the capitol building, by their patrol cars. I don't think we were impressed by the large number of troopers as we were by the muted threat of their presence. We knew that these troopers could not be relied on to defend us later in the day if we needed defense. The possibility that we might be running away from their club-swinging fury before the day was over could not be erased from our minds. We felt somewhat lonely and exposed as we drove be-tween the rows of patrol cars that symbolized an authority whose record had been sullied by unwarranted brutality and violence. Our New Jer-sey license plates told everyone why we were there and what we in-tended to do. We were almost aliens in a foreign country, though we had come nearly 1,100 miles to affirm that an American is never an "out-sider" when he is in any one of the fifty states. We felt in some small measure the ominous threat and unnerving presence of what others have referred to as the "police state." The traditional symbols of author-ity and safety had become our actual or potential enemies. We sensed that the troopers and even the guardsmen, some of whom wore the Con-federate emblem on their helmets or jackets, and one of whom spit on a clergyman in our Tuesday group, could really not be trusted. The sense of this veiled threat remained with us the whole day, and to some extent all the time we were below the Mason-Dixon line. . . .

One of the most rewarding things about our journey was the op-portunity to become acquainted with the Negro citizens of Selma in whose immediate company we were privileged to march. Some of them were old and bent. Others were young and eager to present their petition for freedom. Many (even some of the young girls) had been beaten and jailed because they dared to protest against the iniquity of the "system." We were impressed by the teenagers, finding in them a strength of personality and integrity of purpose not often found in teenagers elsewhere. They had achieved a level of commitment and human dignity that made them rich indeed.

*   *   *

The line of march took us first through the Negro section of Montgomery. There the atmosphere was festive and hopeful. People on porches or sidewalks waved and shouted their encouragement. My wife and I were particularly touched by the small Negro children who were lined up at intervals along the way to wave at us, sometimes under the supervision of their old grandmother, who no doubt was telling them to stand straight and tall, and to wave, and to have hope in their future. She was there to keep the tragedy of her own years from infecting the lives of these little ones.

What a contrast this was to what we felt and saw in the white section of Montgomery! There the atmosphere was heavy with hostility. There we saw four small white boys on top of a sedan, not one of them old enough to be in school, but old enough to know that they didn't like the marchers. One of them was "mowing down" the marchers with his toy gun. His elders on the porch of the nearby house seemed to give their approval to this imaginary slaughter. We could feel sorry for the Negro children who had so hopefully waved, for the suffering is not yet over; but we could have wept for the white children with the toy gun who were innocently assimilating the fear and blindness of parents more concerned about states' rights, property rights, legal rights, etc., than about truth and justice; parents who did not hesitate in the dark of the coming night to use gunpowder in the sick attempt to overcome their fear and blindness. . . . There could be little doubt that in the downtown streets of Montgomery that day it was the glowering, smoldering, immobile whites who were in slavery. They were the ones who were afraid. They were the ones who desperately needed freedom from the bigotry that was burning out compassion, self-understanding, and even self-respect from their lives.

We had read of this sort of hostility before, but now it was directed toward *us,* and this was new. For a day we stood in the shoes the Negro had been standing in for decades. And we marveled that the marching, singing, smiling Negroes around us did not seem to be afraid or bitter. We marveled at the purposeful good humor of our Negro companions who have been tried in the fires of abuse so long, and have taken it with so much more grace than we would expect ourselves to exhibit under similar circumstances. In the glare of the sunlit streets of Montgomery the myth of white superiority (in morals, intelligence, etc.) shriveled up into a lie as the singing Negroes and the sullen whites looked into each other's faces. For a while, at least, the downtown streets of Montgomery were saying that the issue is rather clearly *not* that of "getting the Negro up to the level of the rest of us," but that of getting the rest of us up to his level. And in the measure that this is true, the real problem is *not* whether the white man can accept the Negro, but whether the Negro will be able to accept the white.

*   *   *

It was heartening to see the number of clergymen in the march (both Negro and white), and to know that the Christian Church, to some extent, was coming out from behind its stained-glass windows to identify with the suffering and the oppressed. It is just possible that God will use the Church's involvement in this struggle to bring the long-needed renewal that His people await. But I found myself haunted by those angry white faces, contorted as though by some demonic spirit. What is the Church going to do about them? Having identified with the Negro, the Church has not thereby completed its ministry. What about those on the downtown sidewalks of Montgomery who swelter in the oppressive heat of ignorance and blind bigotry? What about those who are in mortal terror because their false god of white supremacy is crumbling? . . . Perhaps a more basic question is, Is the Church ready to be uncompromisingly true to the Gospel so that it can be a help to these people? The question is not so much one of tactics, but of faithfulness to Jesus Christ. The question is, Will the Church *be* the Church? Are the churches ready to call men to the things that matter, and to say that what is happening to the oppressors and the unconcerned is much more dangerous than what is happening to the Negro, notwithstanding the shots in the dark, the concealed bombs, the cattle prods, the club-swinging troopers? These are the painful and as yet unanswered questions that we brought back from Alabama.

*   *   *

Whatever thought we may have had that we were going south to help the Negro was pretty effectively erased by those Negroes with whom we marched. They ended up helping us. We needed them more than they needed us. We saw and heard them blessing those who have persecuted them, praying for those who have despitefully used them, and forgiving their enemies. They were ready to march for justice and their country whether we had come or not. Is there any doubt that the future strength of the Christian Church and the health of our democracy lies with those who can do more than talk about these things? Can there be any question that it lies with those who are willing to lay down their lives for righteousness' sake? It is just possible that on that memorable Tuesday and Thursday we marched with those who shall be the custodians of the future of democracy.

I am well aware that all Negroes are not like those with whom we marched. There are those Negroes who are apathetic, dejected, and broken in spirit. There are those whose egos have crumbled, and whose initiative has been forever crushed. There are Negroes who wander in the wilderness, who no longer even care to recover the dignity and humanity they lost long ago. There are Negroes who have no desire to join the marches because even the desire for freedom is gone. These are Negroes, may God help us, *who have believed and still believe what the white man has been saying about them.*

The Negroes with whom we marched are those who are standing up to say that what the white man has been saying is a lie. The marching Negroes are those who believe *what God says about them,* and this has made all the difference in the world. When God's word is accepted, and the contradictory word of the white man rejected, then freedom is found. And I for one am ready to share my future and my children's future with people like these. For a nation to be destroyed, it is not necessary that its citizens be wicked, but only blind and spineless. Well, the people with whom we marched seemed to have the vision and commitment required by our times, and it was a privilege to be allowed to walk by their side.

Humanitarian Snobs?

GEORGE STOB   *January 1967*

The thing seems self-contradicting. The humanitarian is the man with the big heart, whose interest in people is governed simply by his respect for their humanness. The humanitarian loves men because they are men — not because they're polished, poised, rich, accomplished, or even good. They all rate with him in his concern for basic human rights and needs. He's not choosy. It's the human that counts for the humanitarian.

But it sometimes appears that in the endeavor to promote their humanitarianism some humanitarians turn to unhumanitarianism. They play the part of humanitarian snobs. So do Christians, who are supposed to be the best of all humanitarians. And so we get Christian snobs. Or Christians who are un-Christian.

It is not surprising that Christians should be un-Christian in many things. We do confess to having "only a small beginning of this obedience." But there should be a bit of shock to find we are un-Christian in the very exercise of being Christian, or disobedient in our very obedience.

This happens, it seems to me, in some of our noble efforts for the achievement of racial integration. We have no objections, we assure ourselves and others, to having Negroes for our next-door neighbors. After all, there are some "good, clean Negroes," and these are presumably the kind that our non-objection covers. And so we become discriminating non-discriminators.

The exploitation of this spirit has become part of the tactic in promotion of racial integration by Human Relations groups. Fearful residents are being assured that new housing is being sought by "well-educated" as well as financially qualified Negroes. And part of the program of some Human Relations Commissions is the distribution of a "fact-sheet" on the minority family moving in, providing "personal background on the family, including age, occupation, education, religion, and the number of children." We are asked to accept regardless of the color of the skin, and then invited to accept on evidence of social or cultural acceptability. We are asked to be non-prejudiced on the basis of prejudicial considerations.

There is, of course, no such thing as neighborliness with reservations. The Good Samaritan story is full proof of that. So is the whole Gospel of Him who there taught us what neighborliness means. And in these days following our celebration of His coming all the way from His sinless glory to be neighbor and brother to us, we may be thankful He didn't come looking for "good" sinners, and that He didn't come with a "fact-sheet" to help Him find a good place for His move-in.

Good Friday 1968

HUGH KOOPS *May-June 1968*

On a cool, damp evening in early 1961 I went to the ballroom of a large south Chicago hotel to hear Martin Luther King. The sidewalk outside the hotel and the lobby inside were teeming with people pushing to enter the room where King was to appear. I looked around to find some friend who might stand with me as we pushed forward. Only a scattered white face here and there might possibly be familiar. The majority of those who came to hear King were black, and I felt fearfully alone.

We waited in the ballroom uneasily. Finally someone made the announcement that King was detained in Atlanta. In his place was his assistant from the Southern Christian Leadership Conference, Ralph Abernathy. There was some mumbling among the crowd, but all were quiet when Abernathy finally began to speak.

I do not remember what Abernathy said. I was too involved with my own feelings to listen carefully or to remember well. I know he began to speak about the sufferings of the Negro and the injustices of American society. My short stay in Hyde Park, and my study of the Woodlawn community in south Chicago, had made this suffering and injustice apparent to me. I do not recall that he said anything I did not already know.

But what did I know? What I knew about suffering and injustice I knew from the safe distance that separates white and black, the comfortable middle-class and the impoverished lower-class, an educated graduate student and the poorly trained dropout from an inadequate inner-city high school. As I listened to Abernathy I felt the response of the audience to his words. They knew, not from study or observation, but from experience and anguish what he described.

As the audience responded I felt myself responding with those who surrounded me. I began to feel a disgust toward white America, a loathing of the comforts of the middle-class, an aversion to everything an education seemed to represent. As the listeners began to say "Amen," I whispered softly with them.

But the words stuck in my throat! Was it the movement of the young Negro at my side, or the fixed stare of another across the hall? No matter. Somehow I sensed that I could not be at one with this crowd. I was white, and middle-class. They were black, and poor. Every "Amen" I said to Abernathy was a "No" to myself. And every "Amen" said by every Negro there was a "No" to me. To affirm what was said was to condemn what I represented. Suddenly I became very afraid, of myself, and of the crowd. For if I had come to loathe white America, how much more had those who surrounded me come to hate what I seemed to be. The speaker had barely begun, but the room seemed intolerably warm, and the door so far away.

But slowly the mood changed. From his portrayal of the present, Abernathy moved to a vision of the future. King's colleague led us to King's vision from the mountain. And the way into that future was the way of nonviolence. It was a way counter to every emotion that had arisen within my own heart, and contrary to anything I could expect from those around me. But Abernathy was insistent. I listened, my ears trying to keep up with the speaker, but my every sense tuned to the response of the crowd. I felt a struggle before me, a battle waging in the ballroom between the righteous indignation of an aggrieved minority and the pleading of an impassioned Christian trying to turn the corner from wrath to forgiveness, from violence to nonviolence. And the struggle taking place *before* me took place *for* me. I felt like the strength could deliver me, and white America, from the "justified" hostility toward myself which I had seen not only in those who surrounded me, but in myself as well. Were the case against me built on justice alone, I knew I was condemned, by the "Amen" from my own throat. The case *must* rest on charity!

Abernathy won! My champion, my advocate, my mediator was victorious.

We joyously sang, "We Shall Overcome," my arms locked hand-in-hand with Negroes on either side as we swayed to the rhythm of our victory over hatred. I walked from the hotel smiling with new-found friends. Only later, after I had locked the door to our apartment for the night, did the terror of those moments return, only for an instant.

Ever since, I felt that Martin Luther King was for American society what Ralph Abernathy was for me that night. He, like Carmichael and Brown, was keenly aware of suffering and injustice, but he also had a vision of a Promised Land, entered by grace. It took all the energy and charisma he possessed to hold back the Negro sensitivity to human justice which invites violence. King often stood alone as an advocate of divine justice, a righteousness surpassing that of retribution for prejudice and discrimination.

On April 4 I stood again in a crowded room. The whisper spread from ear to ear, and finally the message was out. Martin Luther King was dead. The terror returned. Was I without a champion? Has American society no mediator? Is there no one left to turn back the crowd?

Is this how the disciples felt when Christ was crucified? How long must we wait through these hours of darkness? When will we enter the Promised Land? How can we recognize the risen Lord when he appears?

Who Is Twentieth-Century Man?

RODERICK JELLEMA   *December 1966*

We talk a great deal these days, rightly, about keeping the Church "relevant." But relevant to what image of man-in-our-times? Who is twentieth-century man? What is his mood and outlook? To what is he receptive? Is he most accurately personified by John F. Kennedy, the Beatles, Saul Bellow, Stokeley Carmichael, W. H. Auden, Ronald Reagan? Or none of these? . . .

Like all big and exciting questions, this one has no simple, pat answer. The significant and astounding thing about this one is that it is answered with such sharp variance by the literature of our times and by the theological writings of our times. The condition of man's soul as it is reflected in modern literature is not at all the condition that is being spoken to by the new theologians. The drifts of theological discussion since World War II seem to me most vulnerable just here, where they hope to be strongest. The mind and temperament of modern man which the new theologians wish to accommodate does not really seem to exist. The new theologians may be attempting to be relevant to a man who is largely an outmoded fiction. . . .

Much of what has gone on in the theological discussions and movements of the past twenty years centers around Rudolf Bultmann's "demythologizing," the very latest forms of this being Bishop Robinson's *Honest to God* and the vaguely defined death-of-God or "Christian atheism" movement. . . . The assumptions that underlie the new theology and its quest for meaningfulness — including assumptions about twentieth-century man and his outlook — are analyzed in two recent books by the Canadian theologian Kenneth Hamilton. *Revolt Against Heaven: An Enquiry into Anti-Supernaturalism* (1965), and *God is Dead: The Anatomy of a Slogan* (1966). Hamilton does a critical survey, not a hatchet-job; he gives explications of some of the varieties of the new theology (and wins Altizer's praise for the fairness and lucidity of his treatment); he offers illuminating critical approaches to these theologies; but mainly he probes and traces and explores the roots of this anti-supernaturalist theology as they push their way back to the pre-Barthian theological past.

Already that metaphor of roots in the past sets one to thinking. Kenneth Hamilton traces them back in a straight line to Schleiermacher — and then, of course, to a secondary root-system still further back, all the way back to the Enlightenment. What we are getting in the new theology, Hamilton demonstrates, is an extension of the nineteenth-century liberal tradition: the supernatural is denied as untenable, God's immanence is stressed to the point of making Him earthbound, and religious beliefs are achieved not in response to divine revelation but as "the product of our own perspective on the universe." Those three points are a fairly good summary of post-Enlightenment religious accommodation to the vagaries of intellectual history. It is understandable that such thinking would be attractive to modern theologians who recoil from Karl Barth's insistence that man be confronted with the Word which enters history bearing its own authority — understandable especially if they lock themselves up with theological journals and ignore the possibility that man's outlook has changed since the days of Schleiermacher. But on what authority do these theologians, with their tap root trailing back 150 years to Schleiermacher, presume to speak so urgently for and to and in terms of *contemporary* outlook and *contemporary* sensibility? Can we imagine a school of "radical" poets fomenting a "revolution" of "acceptable" poetic theory which is geared to Wordsworth's generation? It begins to appear as though all this urgency to make theology meaningful to contemporary man reveals more about the public relations of the new theology than about its germination.

And indeed, Kenneth Hamilton's two books are quick to point out the chaotic lack of agreement among these theologians when they try to delineate the modern outlook with which theology "must" harmonize. They seem to agree, in Hamilton's phrase, "that the Christian Church is compelled to run before the wind and not to set its course into it." (This new movement seems strangely passive and fatigued.) But which wind is the surest wind of the times? The scientific revolution, surely; they are all sailing before that wind, assuming that scientific thought has banished the supernatural and the miraculous from man's credibility. I shall want to say something about that hypothesis later. But from that elementary (and nineteenth-century) response onwards, they cannot agree about what the incontrovertible contemporary world-view is. For Bultmann, it is the (non-Christian) world-view of Martin Heidegger. Hamilton wryly concludes that for Bultmann "Heidegger has to speak first, so that God may be heard subsequently." Paul van Buren, hesitant to commit himself to any very specific world-view, seems to insist only that it be current and "secular" and "empirical." Ogden wants to go further than Bultmann in demythologizing the Gospel, translating it for "cultured men," translating it "into a language that enlightened men today can understand" — but the culture and enlightenment turn out to be existentialist. Van Buren tells us that he "wonders where the left-wing existentialist theologians have found their 'modern man.'" Well, I wonder too. But I wonder just as much where van Buren has found his. William Hamilton, the third name (with Altizer and van Buren) most associated with the death-of-God theology, quite frankly admits that he finds his notion of the spirit of the age in the surface fads and tides and fashions of our secular culture. If that sounds like a shaky source for the unshakable world-view to which theology is supposed to conform, at least it is contemporary. Altizer, the only figure in the movement who is oriented toward mysticism, seems to think that contemporary man is receptive to a rediscovery of the sacred; but this proposition he has arrived at not by taking the pulse of contemporary man, but by building a theory out of oriental gnosticism, Hegel, William Blake, and Nietzsche.

At times the new theologians seem almost deliberately and cynically ignorant of the soul of their own times. William Hamilton seems to be looking for it where one could never find it articulated: in the polls and the newspapers. Although Harvey Cox, author of *The Secular City*, lives in an age in which artists and philosophers are almost obsessed with their painful assaults on "the question of meaning," to a point of irritation, he announces that "modern man" no longer asks the question of meaning. In an age when literature is almost choking itself on a heavy diet of "myth" and "the rediscovery of myth," Bultmann is busy "demythologizing" the Bible to make it more palatable to "contemporary man." Even Altizer, who seems closer to the soul of the times than these others, is finally open to suspicion as a faulty diagnostician. While the scholars and critics try to account for

the phenomenal resurgence of historic Christianity in modern literature (Gerard Manley Hopkins, T. S. Eliot's *Four Quartets*, C. S. Lewis,
Edwin Muir's *One Foot in Eden*, W. H. Auden, Christopher Fry), Altizer
tells us that there has not been a Christian poet in the last 150 years. . . .

If literature is an accurate reflection of the soul of the times, the
new theology is on the wrong track in its attempt to address that soul.
For the literature of our century — which is "radical" in the true sense
of the word — suggests a very different picture of man's condition. If I
read that literature rightly, there are strong indications that modern
man is rejecting the limits of mere "understanding"; that he is receptive to myth and mystery and miracle; that the intellectual heritage of
the last two centuries is drying up; that his loss of belief in man is con-
ditioning him to seek redemption from outside himself and history;
that image and symbol are vehicles of truth; that his growing sense of
the absurdity of life pushes him perilously near to the absurdity of the
cross. But that is matter for other articles. I only want to focus now on
the proposition that the new theologians are not speaking very often to
or in the name of twentieth-century man. They are not radical — not
nearly radical enough.

Barth and the Abiding Question

Lewis B. Smedes   *February 1969*

I wondered, when I read of Barth's death, whether he had gotten around to doing what he once said he was going to do, first thing, when he got to heaven. He said he was going to ask St. Paul what he meant by his talk in Romans 1 about God's visibility in nature. This, he said, was going to be his first order of business in glory. I wonder what Paul told him.

"Calvin," Barth is reported as saying, "is in heaven and has had time to ponder where he went wrong. Doubtless he is pleased that I am setting him right." I cannot be absolutely sure, but I have a hunch that Barth is pleased right now to have had Paul set him right so soon.

That Barth should have been so eager to get Paul's word on Romans 1 is really not surprising. I think Barth's entire enterprise is all about that question. What is God's relationship to history? Barth's work was born in a volcanic protest against an easy identification of the Almighty with the upward climb of man and his society in history. The Christ who was heralded in the Gospel as the Redeemer, Judge but also Savior, of culture, too innocently (except in God's eyes) had been turned into an example of culture's own redemptive powers. And Barth thrust the world apart from God, thrust culture apart from Christ, divided them by an incredibly powerful theological foray against those cultured appreciators of the acculturated Christ.

But Barth's divorce of culture from Christ, of nature from God, became, I think, his own albatross. I suspect that his own enormous labor in theology was made harder for him because of his initial exaggerated demand for a word of grace and judgment, of revelation and redemption that was unaffected by human history. My own greatest feeling of

Theology   101

uneasiness in the house Barth built comes precisely at this point: the bearing of Christ on culture.

Revelation, for Barth, seemed to linger just above history — breaking in close enough to show through, but never involved enough to be part of it. The divine word of grace, too, rolls majestically out over all of history, comes as the over-arching affirmation of the whole world. All shades of grey are wondrously proclaimed as white in God's gracious affirmation of it all. God's terrible No, His awful reprobation of the world, was exhausted at the cross, and only His joy-inspiring, unambiguously good Yes was left to be spoken and repeated over and over again. But that surprising Yes *to* the world sounded out *over* it. And it sounded without equivocation. It was like a gigantic tidal wave of grace that always stayed out at sea. It was always a promise. But did it ever get inside the world, cut through it, changing it, dividing it, and transforming it here and now? Is there a powerful point of contact between Christ and culture? Gratifying as is Barth's magnificent stand against liberalism's willingness to let culture swallow Christ, I am inclined to regret Barth's unwillingness to let Christ get involved with culture. I may be wrong, and others will insist I am, but I find the point of contact between Christ and culture hard to find in Barth's grand theological castle.

Christ and culture! This is still the abiding question. Call it by other names, if you will. Call it revelation and history, redemption and history, God and the world. It is the same question. Barth's enormous answer, developed in profundity and learning within every volume he wrote, is obviously to be reckoned with. But theologians will have more to do than write commentaries on Barth; and they are doing more than that now, considerably more. Evangelical theologians in particular have their own work cut out for them here. For a place to begin, however, with all of Barth's epoch-making greatness duly praised, I think one does better with Calvin.

Barth's joyful voice is silenced — on earth. He now has better theologians to talk to than any he met here. And, as he put it, he will be singing Bach joyfully before the throne of God and, maybe more to his liking, he will be joining the angels at home on Saturday night to sing Mozart. (He even understands Mozart better now.) One day he will be singing the new song, neither Bach nor Mozart, in the Christ-transformed culture of the new earth. And then we will all know a lot more, about Barth too, but especially about God and His way with our world.

Complaint of a Conservative

Howard G. Hageman   *July-August 1972*

Someday someone with greater skill than I should do an extended study of what I consider the greatest swindle of the twentieth century, in the United States at least. I refer to the way in which a bunch of radicals have taken over the conservative cause and labeled it as their own.

It would be easy to find illustrations in the political field. To take an obvious example, a true conservative who repeats the pledge of allegiance to the flag is simple enough to assume that it means what it says, "with liberty and justice for all." Therefore, when he discovers that there are places in America where liberty is not enjoyed by everyone or where justice is meted out on disturbingly different scales, he sets out to do something about it. What happens? He is met with all kinds of hoots and catcalls from the *soi-disant* conservatives of the radical right who tell him that he is disturbing the peace, upsetting the status quo, or even betraying the best American tradition. But what is the best American tradition? Is it trying to make the country mean what it says or is it seeking to find all kinds of meretricious reasons to explain why we never really meant it in the first place? And who is the real conservative?

Or take the religious scene. In denominations of the Reformed tradition in the US, it is not uncommon to find the classic Lutheran stance — that church and state each has its own sphere of activity and neither interferes with the other — palmed off as the true evangelical position. But is it Reformed? Shades of John Calvin or John Knox! Yet when a conservative Reformed churchman claims that it is high time that the church stood up to the state in the best prophetic tradition to say, "Thou art the man!", watch all the phony conservatives claim that he is a dangerous liberal.

Let's be more theological for a moment. In vast areas in Reformed Christendom, the mishmash called 19th-century evangelicalism is widely accepted as the faith of the fathers. To put it bluntly, Billy Graham is regarded by many Reformed church people as the Elisha to John Calvin's Elijah. Let it be said that from a Reformed point of view, all this is theologically defective if not disastrous, and the cries can be heard from Grand Rapids to Boston and back again. But what are Reformed churchmen to do with the sacramental and catechetical inheritance of their faith? All they have to do is insist upon it in the face of popular evangelicalism and they may well find themselves cast out as heathen men and publicans.

I do not exaggerate. We are face to face with an American orthodoxy which is a dangerous counterfeit of the historic Reformed faith. We are continually being caught up in a political radicalism which in the name of status quoism is gradually but surely eroding our constitutional heritage. And saddest of all, many folk who consider themselves true conservatives sit by and applaud.

I do have a suggestion. Make the Declaration of Independence and the United States Constitution required reading. Make the three forms of Unity[1] priority information for all who claim to accept them. Then perhaps we can ask with some intelligence, "Who is the real conservative?"

---

1. The confessional standards in the Dutch Reformed tradition: the Belgic Confession, the Heidelberg Catechism, and the Canons of Dort.

Misplaced Battle Lines

BERNARD RAMM   *July-August 1976*

Harold Lindsell, the editor of *Christianity Today,* defends the following theses in this book [*The Battle for the Bible*]:

(1) Belief in biblical inerrancy is an absolute part of the definition of an evangelical, and if an evangelical denies this doctrine he is not technically an evangelical (pp. 139, 210);

(2) from that it follows that the watershed among evangelicals is the doctrine of biblical inerrancy;

(3) its importance to theology can be shown by the dreadful consequences in groups who deny the doctrine as shown in the history of the Lutheran Church, Missouri Synod, the Southern Baptist Convention, Fuller Theological Seminary, etc., etc.;

(4) all evangelicals who believe the doctrine should unite in a campaign to propagate and defend the doctrine.

Lindsell makes it difficult to criticize his book for several reasons. For one thing, he claims to be writing for popular consumption (p. 13), yet the book bristles with theological issues requiring scholarly discussion. On his view, one of the things to be revealed at the second coming of Christ is the inerrancy of Scripture (p. 211), so to disagree with Lindsell is to be found in the goat's corner at the Second Coming. The devil is busy testing all, but those who believe in inerrancy are best protected. Hence to disagree with Lindsell is to be caught in the devil's corner already (p. 183).

The Battle for the Bible bristles with problems of many kinds, but we shall concentrate our remarks on the author's thesis of the central role of biblical inerrancy in present day evangelicalism.

(1) *The concept of inerrancy.* Both "inerrancy" and "infallibility" refer to the absence of any contradiction in a work. They are not concepts

Bernard Ramm

which mandatorily or by necessity invoke the divine. A text on mathematics may be inerrant. At best, inerrancy might be a *sufficient* reason for holding to the inspiration of Scripture, but something else is needed for a *necessary* reason. Lindsell's entire book lacks a *necessary* reason . . . for accepting Scripture as the Word of God. Historically, that necessary reason has been either the *autopistia* of Scripture or its christological content. Just as serious is the total absence in Lindsell's presentation of the Reformation doctrine of Word and Spirit. Even the witness of the Spirit is downgraded (p. 183). Nor is the hat tipped to Calvin's majesty of Scripture.

Further, we are not home free if we claim there are no errors in Scripture. Anybody who has lived with biblical criticism through the years knows the clusters of problems we face on every page of Scripture. If we told a logician that there are no errors in Scripture but thousands of problems (not an exaggeration in view of the huge books on Old and New Testament introduction), he would die laughing. We must not have a view of Holy Scripture which — to use a current philosophical phrase — dies the death of a thousand qualifications.

(2) *The only hole in the dike?* Lindsell's argument is that inerrancy is such a crown doctrine that to surrender it is to surrender all. The little hole in the dike enlarges until the great heresies of liberalism and Bultmannianism enter the church without any possibility of being evicted. But is this really the case in the whole range of church history? Is not Arianism in Christology the heresy of heresies? It seems to me that Lindsell is claiming too much for a view of Scripture. We can have some first-rate heresies by surrendering other doctrines, too, such as the Trinity, the Incarnation, the atonement.

(3) *Ought we divide here?* Lindsell's book suffers from oversimplification. Christians come in all sorts of shapes, lumps, contours! Theologians and their theologies are also uneven, irregular, obviously creatures of history or culture or victims of genes. To reduce the issue of the faith down to Lindsell's view of inerrancy (there are others!), and with that divide sheep and goats, saints and heretics, and predict the course of denominations and schools and theologians, is all too neat, all too simple, all too precise. The Christian world comes too sloppy, too expansive, too irregular to be so neatly analyzed.

Further, it leads to oddities. By having a *sufficient* reason for the inspiration of Scripture but not a *necessary* reason Lindsell makes all sectarians and cultists into evangelicals in that they too believe in the inerrancy of Scripture. And that isn't all! Such stalwarts as Kornelis H. Miskotte, Helmut Thielicke, Otto Weber, and Helmut Gollwitzer, who have fought liberalism, existentialism, and Bultmannianism on the continent, are suspect because they do not believe in inerrancy, but some eschatological fanatic who believes in inerrancy is theologically safe!

I think Thielicke tells us where the dividing point is in his work *The Evangelical Faith.* In his language Cartesian theology is the theology of liberalism (Schleiermacher) and of existentialism (Tillich, Bultmann). To them the root of theology is man's religious potential. Non-Cartesian theology is evangelical theology, which affirms the incarnation of God in Christ, the cross, the resurrection, and the new birth by the power of the Spirit.

(4) *Misplaced battle line?* One could fondly wish the only difficulty with Scripture were the need to iron out a few contradictions here and there. But certainly the battle for the Bible in modern times is much larger than reconciling contradictions. The contemporary battle for the Bible asks whether most of biblical history is credible, or whether all we have of the true words and deeds of Jesus is a demitasse full of shreds, or whether the Prison Epistles and the Pastoral Epistles are Pauline, or whether Revelation is anything more than a weird book of Christian apocalypticism.

(5) *Whom will it convert?* I presume Lindsell wishes to (i) confirm the faithful in inerrancy; (ii) stabilize the uncertain; and (iii) woo back those who have given up inerrancy. I expect he will be successful with the first group, bat .500 with the second, and lose the third. To prepare for this review I reread a famous article by A. A. Hodge and B. B. Warfield — "Inspiration," in *The Presbyterian Review* for April 1881. There is no essential difference between the theses of this article and Lindsell's book. The old debates about original manuscripts are passé; the argument that we can have many problems but are safe if we have no errors is threadbare. For the alert, highly trained evangelical Lindsell's entire book has a *déjà vu* cast to it. I don't think Lindsell has any idea how thoroughly he will turn off those evangelical scholars who know that the battle and the issues are elsewhere and must be elsewhere.

(6) *A neglected tradition?* To argue as if one were inerrantly sure of inerrancy is to write — in Luther's terms — a theology of glory. Luther was impressed with the contradiction between the cross of Christ and

ordinary human ways of thinking. It has been said that the most marked character of his theology is that it is a theology of the cross, of the crucified God. Hence we must also have a doctrine of the Scriptures which is of the same heartbeat as the theology of the cross.

In the words of the British theologian Thornton, God's written Word is in the form of humiliation just as the Son of God in his incarnation. It too shares the brokenness, the servanthood, the masking of the divine glory as the incarnate Son. Or in the thought of the Dutch Old Testament scholar K. H. Miskotte *(When the Gods Are Silent),* Yahweh of the Old Testament leads a hidden, mysterious existence, for he alone will be worshiped and adored. And we dare not have a version of Scripture that betrays the nature in which Yahweh encounters man.

(7) *The issue is important.* I do not wish to leave the impression that Lindsell has not raised an important issue. He certainly has. The integrity of Scripture is extremely important for theology. We can never surrender *sola Scriptura.* In evangelical theology the Holy Scripture is the supreme and final authority in matters of faith and conduct. Further, the concept of evangelical is not indefinitely extensible. There is a line in the critical assessment of Holy Scripture which when crossed separates one from the Word of God. I agree to all this. But for my own tastes I find much more satisfaction in G. C. Berkouwer's book *Holy Scripture,* if for no other reason than that it is more in the great tradition than Lindsell's.

Accommodation

NICHOLAS WOLTERSTORFF   *October 1963*

In a Christian college, can there be any attempt to *accommodate* the gospel of Christ to the "wisdom" of the pagans? Can there be any attempt to *synthesize* the proclamation of the Word of God with the best that has been said and thought by the world? Of course not. Impossible. How could any Christian, let alone any Reformed Christian, think so?

Why do I even raise the issue? For this reason: In our Reformed community today there are a number of institutions of higher learning that have either recently been formed or will apparently soon be formed — institutions, that is, in addition to Calvin College and Seminary. Now and then the supporters of such institutions and of movements behind them — especially those supporters who are also adherents of the philosophy of Dooyeweerd and Vollenhoven — try to advance their cause by intimating that at Calvin College and Seminary there are a number of people who try to accommodate Christ to the world. They write as if there is a division of mind among us as to whether or not the Word of God should be synthesized with the thought of the world. They seem to think that in asserting the wrongness of such accommodation and synthesis they are either preaching a very new truth that some of us have not yet heard, or an old truth that some of us have not yet accepted.

The answer to such accusations had better be blunt. They are false, plain false. There is nothing to them; and to talk as if there were is to be either grossly misinformed or willfully misleading. Whether or not we should accommodate ourselves to the world is not at all an issue in our community. No mature person in our community, or at least none of whom I have ever heard, holds that we should synthesize the message of the Scriptures with the thought of the world. And the fact that this conviction is universally shared among us is, so far as I can tell, nothing new. Our Reformed community in America has always shared it. It is the cornerstone of our whole educational system.

On what do we disagree then? Why all the smoke? The differences among us arise over specific issues. Is *this* a case of accommodation? Is *that* a case of synthesis? I myself believe that Dooyeweerd and his followers have seriously accommodated themselves to the non-Christian philosophy of Immanuel Kant. But I certainly do not believe that they *intend* to do this, nor do I believe that they themselves *think* they have done so.

So there's very little point in saying to each other, with a large overflow of rhetoric, that we Calvinists must be opposed to accommodation. Of course we must be. All of us have for a long time now been convinced of it. What would be of use is that each of us try to show where and how one of our brothers has, so far as we can see, accommodated the gospel of Christ to what is antithetically opposed to it. Unless we can talk seriously and carefully on specific issues there is no use in talking; wild, unsubstantiated accusations are evil.

Further, if we are seriously interested in the truth and not just in propagating some partisan view, we will want to see to it that the person who holds views differing from our own gets an equal opportunity to express and defend himself. For the person who makes the charge of accommodation may be the one who is in error; he may be the one who, on the issue discussed, has accommodated Christ. All of us do in fact accommodate Christ to the world, for none of us is perfect, but none of us holds this for an ideal. He who casts stones to break glass, himself lives behind glass. So these discussions on specific issues that I have urged must not only be firm, but also conspicuous for their charity.

It will not serve the cause of Christ, though it may serve other causes, to accuse each other of intending to synthesize the *kerygma* of the Scriptures with the thought of the world; nor will it serve His cause pridefully to accuse others of in fact synthesizing without ever being willing *seriously* to consider the possibility that we ourselves have done so. What would serve His cause is firm and charitable discussions aimed at learning from each other.

In Memoriam: T. S. Eliot

GEORGE H. HARPER   *January 1965*

The death of T. S. Eliot in London on the fourth of January will no
doubt be followed by many articles in the literary press and in a renewed interest in his life and writings. Readers of the *Reformed Journal*
will recall that he was the subject of more than one article or review in
these pages, especially during the time that Henry Zylstra was one of
its editors. It seems appropriate, for several reasons, that the *Journal*
take notice of Eliot's death and provide its readers with a brief account
of his life and a short view of his work and the influence he had on
some of his readers. . . .

His influence as a poetic revolutionist began in 1917 with the publication of "The Love Song of J. Alfred Prufrock," still a puzzling poem
despite the seas of critical exegesis that have washed over it. His longer early poem, "The Waste Land" (1922), which incorporated apparently unconnected echoes of many other poetries in several languages
and several ages in an attempt to objectify the decay of the spirit in
post-world war Europe, established his position as the leader of the
new poetry of the century, a position he has not relinquished. . . . His
place in modern art and thought is secure, and he should be seen for
long to rank with, and perhaps before, Joyce, Picasso, Webern and
Schoenberg, Gropius, and, in slightly different spheres, Wittgenstein
and Barth.

But it is as a Christian man working calmly at his calling that *Reformed Journal* readers may choose to remember him. He will doubtless
be in their minds in a section reserved for C. S. Lewis and other vocal
intellectual and artistic Christians of the century. His Christian commitment was made known early and unobtrusively, and could be seen
in all that he did — it pervaded his poetry, his criticism, and his stance

as an intellectual and artist. It was these qualities of the man, as well as the sheer *fun* of the poetry, that Henry Zylstra urged as Eliot's claim on the attention of students in the 1940's at Calvin College, and it was not long before many in the college were sending off to the booksellers for Eliot's poetry and criticism. The poetry caught, through its wryness and oddity (which was yet somehow *right* for the times), the attention of students; and the criticism, which sometimes seemed to help to explain the poetry, provided a kind of intellectual discipline and stiffening needed in the world of un- and even anti-Christian art and poetry and thought. Students of Henry Zylstra, and of his colleagues, could see for themselves that the highest intellectual life was livable for the Christian too, despite all the evidence that the "world" so easily seemed to provide; and it was bracing to know that this kind of heroism was not merely parochial — the heroism that Grand Rapids gave some scope to, they saw, was possible in London and Paris, in Cambridge (both), and by a kind of adjustment also in smaller towns and cities closer to Grand Rapids.

The *Times Literary Supplement* (London), for which Eliot often wrote, in a memorial editorial expresses a thought that is as applicable to Christian students of poetry and criticism in Midwestern USA as it is to English students: to have read Eliot young, especially after the experiences of World War II, was to have found a new world; with his death, that somehow dies too. . . .

Twenty Years After the Bomb

Steve J. Van Der Weele   *September 1965*

The dropping of the first atom bomb, as everyone knows, brought the Second World War to an abrupt end. There was a consensus of approval for this strategy, and for those who did raise dissenting voices — and there were some — Winston Churchill had an answer difficult to refute at the time: So far as he knew, he observed drily, none of the protesters had sons on the ships already dispatched to engage the Japanese. But somehow, nothing has been quite the same since. The physicists, as Robert Oppenheimer noted, have known sin; and man, despite the nuclear test ban, has been compelled to take seriously the possibility of death by nuclear annihilation.

Thoughtful citizens, especially Christian citizens, will respond thoughtfully and prayerfully to the memory of the events of August 6, 1945. As in other instances, poets can be helpful in this. Although in general poets have found the specter of the bomb too horrendous to cope with in poetry, several prominent ones have done so forcefully and relevantly. Perhaps readers of the *Journal* will find helpful a brief resumé of the contents of three of these poems.

The first of these is an eight-line poem by Chad Walsh, "The Tragical History of Dr. Faustus." Mr. Walsh updates the story of the necromancer who was not satisfied with knowledge appropriate for human beings. Through a bargain with the devil, he hoped to attain knowledge considered illicit for mankind. For this, of course, he mortgaged his soul, and the devil presided over the bankruptcy. Faustus goes to hell. Now, says Mr. Walsh, we are compelled to bury Dr. Faustus and his knowledge under a ten-foot protective barrier of concrete. He succeeded in disturbing the spirits he sought to command; they have mushroomed upwards miles above his grave. Unfortunately, the doc-

Steve J. Van Der Weele

tor has neglected to master that part of the formula which will recall these spirits and sing them back to their state of rest.

John Wain's poem on this subject, entitled "A Song About Major Eatherly" (from the collection *Weep Before God*), concerns itself with the psychological and moral toll that the dropping of the bomb exacted from Major Claude R. Eatherly, pilot of the plane that dropped the second bomb, the bomb that fell on Nagasaki. A quotation taken from *The Observer* of August, 1958, and placed by the author of the poem as an introduction to it, supplies the important facts. In the wake of his mission, Major Eatherly began to have disturbing nightmares. According to his wife, he would scream out in a sickening cry, "Release it, release it!" He next incurred brief periods of insanity, which the doctors described as "extreme nervous depression." Major Eatherly was discharged and awarded a pension of $237 per month. However, he refused to accept the money, interpreting it as a reward for the murder that had been inflicted on the Japanese cities. He then resorted to petty thievery, for which he was committed to Fort Worth prison.

Wain's poem begins with the words: "Good news. It seems he loved them after all. / His orders were to fry their bones to ash. / He carried up the bomb and let it fall. / And then his orders were to take the cash, / A hero's pension. . . ." Wain then proceeds to reflect on the major's desperate attempt to retrieve his manhood, his humanity, his capacity to love. The major did once hate the Japanese — he hated them because, as is true for all of us, he hated those who compelled him to kill them. The trapper hates the fox because the fox will gnaw its own leg to free itself. Those who must seek a murderer resent having to kill him. And this is the reason Major Eatherly became involved in hating the Japanese.

The incendiary terror released by Major Eatherly, states the poet, was actually a reversion to an earlier phase in the thought of the Western world: the assumption that the proper punishment and purification for sin is heat, flame, the hot fires of purgation and of hell. However, we became too sophisticated to take this seriously: "Those emblematic flames sank down to rest. . . ." Nevertheless, even though men's hearts grew increasingly cold and insensitive, the fires of hate and passion continued to consume men's spirits, and consequently they were never permitted to forget the terrifying potentiality of the elemental force of fire. And so men conjured a second hell, "And Major Eatherly took off at dawn." . . .

The poem ends with a tender and wistful hope for the major, and suggestions for us, his fellow citizens, on how to deal with him. Do not judge him by the ordinary laws applicable to property. Let his petty thievery go unpunished. He is living in another moral dimension. Let us hope that his nightmares may subside, and do not force him to accept his pension. Above all, let us somehow make him understand that his mental and moral disarray have not been lost upon us. Let us leave him a note as he sleeps: "Say nothing of love, or thanks, or penitence: / Say only 'Eatherly, we have your message.'"

Edith Sitwell's work, *Three Poems of the Atomic Age* (from her *Collected Poems*, pp. 364-374), is written in three parts, to which she has given the following titles: "Dirge for the New Sunrise," "The Shadow of Cain," and "The Canticle of the Rose." Although each section is relatively independent, the reading of the whole poem produces a magnificence and epic power not fully realized in the individual sections. Still, all the themes are contained in each section, though the organization varies in terms of the emphasis the poet wishes to achieve.

The poem is a lament about the atomic atrocities of Hiroshima and Nagasaki. It is also a prayer. It is contemplative, not melodramatic. It is an anguished cry, but not merely a display of futile hand-wringing. Sometimes the poet indicates directly her emotional involvement, then again she is more objective and assumes a prophetic stance. The force of the poem is to summon man back to God, to persuade him to accept the divine offer of spiritual renewal, to prompt him to embrace the healing force of the crucifixion of Christ. Nothing less than this stupendous act of divine grace is an adequate response to the fiendish act which man, after having discovered knowledge with which he could not cope, poured out his hate in diabolical irreverence over two Japanese cities in August, 1945. . . .

What happened physically to the Japanese cities is only what had happened prior spiritually to the heart of man. Whereas God is sacramentally present everywhere (". . . the Son of God is sowed in every furrow . . ."), the great fission that the bomb made in the earth represents the cleavage that man had already established between his fellow man and towards God during his centuries of migrations and flight. The chaos that ensued, the disruption of the normal cycle of life's processes, revealed in a terrifying way the extent to which man had opposed God's laws. The sun and the earth seemed as if they would change places. The entire solar system was metaphorically wrenched from its orbit. The contrivance that dealt this violence was the complete antithesis of the creative intent of God's universe. The growing blade of wheat was blasted. The springs of life and fertility shriveled up in the withering heat of this holocaust.

What occurred at Hiroshima and Nagasaki was a cosmic blasphemy. The effect was to pulverize all distinctions. The categories of victim and murderer, just and unjust, Lazarus and Dives, have vanished: "Mother or Murderer, you have given or taken life — Now all is one!" Those who survived physically, though blinded, as well as those who saw into reality in that blinding flash of light before they were annihilated are also equals: "There was no more hating then, / And no more love: Gone is the heart of man."

But even this atrocity will not bring wisdom to men. Not all will seek for spiritual wholeness, or seek to allay the hunger of their souls by seeking for the true sources of light and life and joy. Avarice and greed, "the leprosy of gold," will still compete for man's loyalty and allegiance. Stupidly and perversely men will still ignore the summons of Christ, who alone can come "to the inner leaf of the forsaken heart." But only through His passion can new life and growth proceed from suffering and death. Although the ashes of those who were killed will rise up in judgment, Christ is the "ultimate Fire / Who will burn away the cold in the heart of Man." He provides resources to restore true light, humanity, fellowship and communion.

I recommend these poems as aids to reflection twenty years after the first victims of atomic warfare lay dead in the streets and suffering in the hospitals.

The Piety of Despair:
Ingmar Bergman's *Winter Light*

BERNARD VAN'T HUL   *September 1967*

Film critic Dwight Macdonald is presumably right when he says that the popular indifference to Ingmar Bergman in this country may be attributed to the "gloom" which pervades most of his works. And Macdonald himself thinks of such Bergman films as *Winter Light* that in them Bergman is "too much fascinated by the questions of God, man, the meaning of life, and the problem of evil." One hears similarly patronizing objections to Bergman from acquaintances who find him "too grim, too stark, too medieval, too Calvinistic." I think that Bergman's fascination with "questions of God, man, the meaning of life, and the problem of evil" is redeemed from morbidity by an arrestingly powerful imagination which, though not finally Calvinistic, sees much of life steadily and finds it grim. . . .

Taking place during one day in rural contemporary Sweden, the events of *Winter Light*'s episodic-seeming plot are easily accounted for. The sickly, severe, middle-aged preacher (Thomas) of a small state Lutheran church serves the Mass to a handful of rural stereotypes in an opening scene which firmly establishes the oppressive tone of gloom which will not be once mitigated throughout the picture. Among the communicants are a somber-faced and obviously distraught fisherman, Jonas Petersen, and his impassive pregnant wife who, in the vestry after the service, detains Preacher Thomas and leaves Jonas behind for a talk with the dominie. She hopes that a counseling session will ease her husband's anxiety. In this session the preacher's stock irrelevant questions betray a compassionless insensitivity to the problems of such as Jonas; the preacher becomes impatient with Jonas' timid reticence; and instead of comforting his parishioner, the preacher assails him with an agonized and self-deprecating confession of his own doubt and distress with what he calls the distance, then the silence, of God.

Confused and embarrassed by these strange pastoral confidences, Jonas flees to shoot himself dead, as Thomas learns before getting home from the church. On his way to inform and console the now-widowed wife of Jonas, Preacher Thomas superintends the removal of Jonas' body from the river bank where he died, then spends a painful half hour or so with Marta the village schoolteacher, a nervous, plain-faced spinster who, though among the communicants in church, frankly disavows belief in Thomas' God, yet loves Thomas with an almost maternally solicitous and utterly self-surrendering love. During this half hour in Marta's schoolhouse, Thomas frets himself into a merciless renunciation of Marta's love; he is *"sick* of her" and specifies, as though in support of his contempt, her nervous mannerisms, her myopia, her eczema-inflamed hands — among other frailties that the flesh of preachers' mortal parishioners is heir to. From flesh and its frailties this fastidious preacher would keep his distance. ("Leave me alone. . . . I must get out of the maze of idiotic trivialities.") Though wounded in the heart's core, Marta will stay devoted, attending doggedly and despised to sickly Thomas.

. . . Having stupidly counseled Jonas to his suicide and having brutally trampled out the flickering pride of loving Marta, Thomas leaves Jonas' widow all uncomforted, with her children and the funeral arrangements to care for. He makes his sick and tired way to the vesper services which, as his living requires, he must conduct. But before the service Thomas must endure, as though his private pain were not enough, the lay-theological discourse of the arthritic sexton. Wondering why vespers should be conducted at all (since no one attends), the sexton presses Thomas for some light on the meaning of the Passion. Doubting Thomas has little light to share. He has only curt answers for the sexton, whose talk touches the quick of his own problems. And Thomas broods until time for the bells over his decision to go on with the vespers. He achieves the pulpit, looks out over the empty rows, and intones (for only despised Marta, the cynical organist, and the confused sexton to hear) the beginning of the service with which the movie ends: "Holy, holy, holy . . . the whole earth is full of his glory. . . ."

Thus Thomas, who has struggled to be "free" of parishioners' problems and of the thralldom of his very faith, ends this day by persisting in the formal gestures of his office. Few who watch this preacher's struggle with doubt in performance of duties will find him an admirable character. The confident saint, for whom faith implies unwavering certitude, will judge Thomas a blasphemer. The liturgical words of his mouth clearly belie the meditations of his heart. The unbeliever, for whom common sense precludes both faith and blasphemy, will think Thomas a somewhat neurotic and altogether inept establishmentarian fraud. . . . If in the vesper service with which the movie ends there is not one sure believer on either side of the pulpit, either the confident saint or the cocksure cynic must be right: Bergman's preacher is blasphemer or fraud.

Unless, whatever the movie maker's intentions, still another judgment be allowed for — that Thomas' ineptitude may be, for struggling sinners such as Thomas, the only alternative to rank hypocrisy that life in the empirical church affords. When God is silent; when one's frantic hypotheses in favor of the impeachment of God culminate in a coughing spell at the altar rail; when one has driven the fatherless and widows outside of the affliction that is his own feelingless ministry — then, if just as vespers are about to begin, one comes to a first awareness of misery and a glimpse of deliverance, the alternative to blasphemy or hypocrisy may be the absurd alternative to pray, specifically for help in one's unbelief, and to sustain out of unclean but momentarily unfeigned lips, "Holy, holy, holy . . . full of his glory."

Call Thomas' piety the piety of despair. Such piety is surely at the edge of blasphemy when, as the better and enduring substance of the saint's heavenly certitude gives way to silence and cold winter light, one merely speaks the words. Unless the merely spoken words become, as Thomas speaks them, more than mere. Unless, as in winter light there is only somewhat of a darkness, there be something, in the words of contrite impotence, of substance.

Whatever Bergman's intentions, his movie dramatizes vividly a problem that is no less the concern of contemporary Christians than it was of the wavering disciples themselves. The problem relates doubt to belief; and the behavior of Bergman's preacher raises, in the believer's mind, the question of ritual as a means of grace to those who pray for help in unbelief. Preacher Thomas has his obvious prototype in Thomas the empiricist, one of the eleven, who came from his doubt, as Peter from his denial, to "My Lord and my God."

On Looking at Paintings

NICHOLAS WOLTERSTORFF   *February 1972*

Nobody just looks at paintings. Everybody always *looks for* something when he looks at paintings. And when we tug on what it is that a man looks for, a large part of his aesthetic will unravel. In his recent book *Modern Art and the Death of a Culture* (London: Inter-Varsity, 1970), Professor H. Rookmaaker of the Free University of Amsterdam attempts to develop a Christian perspective on contemporary art. It will benefit all of us who also wish to have a Christian perspective on art (not just visual art but the arts in general, and not just contemporary art but the art of the ages) to consider what it is that Rookmaaker looks for when he looks at contemporary paintings. . . .

Rookmaaker sees paintings as bearers of religious messages and it is those messages that he tries to discover. His strategy is to subject paintings to what might be called "a religious depth analysis" . . . [and] he suggests that *nothing more* than this is needed — that this gets at all that is really important in art. It is this suggestion that I especially want to discuss. But first we must see why he says this. And for this we must look at his underlying aesthetic, of which glimpses can be obtained here and there throughout the book.

Rookmaaker approaches art with the old distinction between form and content. He seems to identify the form of a work of art with the aesthetic element in the work, and this in turn he seems to identify with its sensory qualities (pp. 231f.). Furthermore, he regards excellence in the aesthetic element as consisting in the presence of *beauty*. As to what beauty is, he does not say. But he does hold a striking thesis concerning the connection between beauty of aesthetic element and truth of message. It is his view that if a work of art is an expression of belief, and if the form and content of the work are unified, then the work is beautiful just in so far as the message it conveys is true. A "pure" work of art, one bearing no message, may possibly also be beautiful (p. 232), though on his view "pure" works of art are exceedingly rare. And if the aesthetic element in a painting is not unified with the message that the painting is used to bear, the aesthetic element may be beautiful in spite of the falsity of the message. But apart from these exceptions the beauty of a work's aesthetic element and the truth of its message are intimately connected. . . .

There is one implication of Rookmaaker's thesis and his underlying aesthetic which should not escape notice. Rookmaaker sees the art of the last two centuries, with the exception of Rouault and a few others, as expressing false views of reality. He says, indeed, that they are never totally false; always the view expressed has *some* true implications. Thus in spite of the fact that he cannot agree with their overall views, Rookmaaker admires the work of the four great post-Impressionists: Van Gogh, Seurat, Gauguin, and Cézanne. Yet to study nineteenth- and twentieth-century art is, in the main, to conduct a study in falsehood. The implication, given Rookmaaker's principles, is that the art of these centuries is aesthetically poor. For, being false, it is not beautiful. And lacking beauty, it lacks aesthetic excellence. True, Rookmaaker seldom makes this judgment explicitly. Yet his principles lead to the conclusion that Jan Steen's art is greater than Picasso's, Jan van Goyen's than Matisse's (pp. 19-26). And Steen and van Goyen are scarcely among the luminaries of Western art. Yet Rookmaaker insists that the Christian community must not ignore contemporary art. Obviously, if he is to remain true to his underlying aesthetic, his reason cannot be that to ignore it would be to miss some excellent art. And in fact (if my reading has been accurate) he never does say this. His reason is rather that to understand the anti-Christian culture of our age we must be acquainted with its art. . . .

I cannot at this point restrain myself from confessing my profound suspicion of any aesthetic that leads to the conclusion that the art of Jan Steen is aesthetically greater than that of Picasso or Matisse or Cézanne or Gauguin. And when the aesthetic leads to the conclusion that the art of the twentieth century is *in general* aesthetically inferior, then I am persuaded that something is seriously wrong with the aesthetic. I am convinced that no century in the history of mankind has produced more aesthetically great art than the century from 1870-1970. And I am convinced that the Christian community should study this

art. Study it not just in order to discern its anti-Christian message —
though I agree that its message is in the main anti-Christian. Study it
for the positive reason that it is great art — aesthetically great, great
specimens of the aesthetic dimension of our created reality.

*   *   *

What went wrong? What is it in Rookmaaker's aesthetic that led to his
distorted evaluations? A couple of things, I think.

Characteristic of Rookmaaker's practice and partially justified by
his aesthetic is that he, as it were, looks right through the sensory qualities of the work of art in order to discern the message beyond. . . .
Thus in practice and in theory he has what might be called a gnostic
view of art. The message is what counts. The importance of the colors
is only that they bear the message. But at once it must be added, in ex-
tenuation, that Rookmaaker is not alone in holding this "gnostic" view
of the arts. The Protestant Christian community in general has tended
to adopt such a view. It has tended to regard works of art as religious
and philosophical tracts — artistically done up of course, but tracts
nonetheless.

We shall never arrive at a fully Christian approach to the arts until
such gnosticism is rooted out. For remember: this world of colors and
textures and shapes is good — good in that it pleased God its Maker,
good in that it gives to us men delight and satisfaction and fulfillment.
It was Plato — not the biblical writers — who said that we must avoid
the delights of the senses, take no joy in colors, long to flee the world of
textures. The strange thing is that Rookmaaker knows full well that the
Platonic vision is not the biblical one. . . . Yet by looking only for the
message, by giving no independent significance to the sensory qualities of paintings, he practices the very thing which in theory he repudi-
ates. Rookmaaker repeatedly argues that we must rid ourselves of the
notion that the painter copies, that in its place we must adopt the notion that the painter expresses his beliefs. What is striking is that both
views, the one repudiated and the one adopted, speak only of the relation of the work of art to what lies outside the work. . . .

But there is more askew in Rookmaaker's approach to art than his
failure to recognize the importance of sensory qualities. We can get at
some of this other by reminding ourselves that works of art are multi-
dimensioned things. Paintings, for example, have physical traits and

chemical traits; equally they function in the moral dimension and the economic dimension. And — what is of prime importance here — they participate in the aesthetic dimension. Correspondingly the norms for evaluating a painting with respect to, say, its moral qualities are distinct from those for evaluating it with respect to its aesthetic qualities. If we fail to keep sharply in mind that the aesthetic is one though only one of the many dimensions of a work of art, nothing but confusion and reductionism and aesthetic impoverishment can follow. . . .

Now Rookmaaker does in fact discern that the aesthetic is a distinct dimension in reality. Yet his understanding of it is seriously askew. . . . Rookmaaker makes *truth* the criterion for judging aesthetic excellence. He sees beauty as the norm for aesthetic excellence, but he makes truth in turn the criterion for beauty. The consequence for his evaluations is the same as if he had never noticed the aesthetic dimension at all: instead of giving works of art an independent aesthetic evaluation, he judges them wholly by reference to the truth or falsity of the message. And so, though his theory is slightly different, the result is the same as it is in the case of the eager evangelical who denounces a work of art just because it contains some obscenity, or the eager Marxist who denounces a work of art just because it fails to advance the proper class consciousness. In each case the aesthetic dimension is given no independent status and works of art are judged wholly by reference to something other than aesthetic norms. . . .

*   *   *

Once we acknowledge the aesthetic as a distinct dimension of reality, having its own unique norms for evaluation, then we will (I am convinced) be led to an assessment of twentieth-century art radically different from that found in Rookmaaker. With one proviso — provided we also give up the notion that beauty is the norm for aesthetic excellence. Rookmaaker does not say why he insists on beauty, and I cannot here discuss the matter in any detail. All I can really do is state my own conviction that aesthetic excellence does not depend on the presence of beauty. To make something beautiful is, I agree, one way of achieving aesthetic excellence; and there have been periods in the history of art when this way was prized above all others. But to insist that at all times and in all places the artist must seek beauty is mistakenly to impose on every artist one particular way of realizing aesthetic excel-

Nicholas Wolterstorff

lence. The great art of the twentieth century is often powerful, brutal, harsh, aggressive — seldom beautiful. Yet it is aesthetically great. I am, in fact, not even persuaded that the *Christian* artist should aim at beauty. I can understand, I think, why a Platonist would insist on beauty. But what is there in the Christian vision that would lead to such an insistence?

So, along with Rookmaaker I insist that we must extend to works of art the dignity of a religious depth analysis. But I part from him when, in practice and in theory, he suggests that this should be the whole of a Christian's approach to art. To make it the whole is once again — in line with the spiritualizing and moralistic tendencies of Western Christendom — to overlook the richness of that which is art.

Of Cynics and Hacks: Scorsese's *Taxi Driver*

MARLIN VAN ELDEREN   *May-June 1976*

This is a gripping but finally unsatisfying — even irritating — film.

Well aware of our contemporary willingness to absorb just about anything on screen, the filmmakers have chosen to exploit this freedom for the ultimately conventional reason — box office success. With consummate professionalism, they highlight the squalor of the setting and the moral emptiness of the characters with imaginative cinematography, brilliant acting, and dialogue which is appropriately devastating in its utter vacuity. All these elements are orchestrated to build to a final crescendo of violence which, as one critic has noted, matches anything heretofore seen in commercial films.

But therein lies the cynicism which finally vitiates *Taxi Driver*. It is difficult to avoid the impression that within the filmmakers' motivation for the two minutes of graphic horror at the end lurks the confidence that audiences will respond predictably, venting the primal urges that such heady bloodletting inspires. Thus the view of man which the film (with varying degrees of conviction) presupposes will be confirmed. Also — and more important — the film will become a *cause célèbre* (like *A Clockwork Orange, Last Tango in Paris, The Exorcist*). The turnstiles will click while the public moralists argue the issues.

Apparently the original version of *Taxi Driver* ended so violently as to earn an X rating, which — strange to say — still affixes some sort of stigma to commercial cinema and jeopardizes the financial investment. A revised version was therefore prepared, and it secured an R rating, which keeps it in its uncut form out of range of television while maintaining the respectability needed for it to run at your local theater.

Taxi Driver is the illustrated diary (except for two or three brief scenes) of "God's lonely man," ex-Marine Travis Bickle (Robert

DeNiro). Troubled by vague neurological complaints, insomnia, and a not-very-well-articulated revulsion at the moral cesspool that is New York City, he takes a job driving cab at night. A series of episodes demonstrates how rotten the Big Apple really is; Travis takes all of this in, numbly unable to get involved. Twelve, even fourteen hours on the streets do not suffice to cure his insomnia, and he becomes an habitue of pornographic movie houses.

In the midst of the swirling filth of his life arises the vision of "an angel of light," Betsy (Cybill Shepherd), a campaign worker for a presidential candidate — who provides the occasion, incidentally, for some fairly funny, though completely predictable, swipes at populism and contemporary American politics. Though it doesn't get very far, the relationship between Travis and Betsy manages to strain our credulity to the breaking point. On their second date her fascination with him wears thin after about two minutes of the pornographic film to which he takes her.

An encounter in his cab with a murder-minded cuckold (Director Scorsese himself indulgently overplays the part) eventuates in Travis's purchase of a small arsenal from a gun-runner. He shoots a black holdup man at a grocery store (the grocer finishes him off with a crowbar), then lays plans for assassinating the candidate. But the plan misfires before he has the chance to draw his gun. Eluding the Secret Service, he runs home, pops a couple pills, and goes off to shoot in cold blood the pimp who manages 12½-year-old hooker Iris Steensma (Jodie Foster), whom he has earlier befriended, even offering $500 to pay her way to a commune she has read about in Vermont. In the ensuing rampage he kills another pimp and a gangster who is one of Iris's regular clients. But his attempt at suicide fails because he has used up all his ammunition.

In an epilogue which is either a tired attempt at irony or an effort on the part of the filmmakers to thumb their collective nose at those who were horrified by the grisly violence, we learn that Iris has gone, not to Vermont, but back home to her grateful parents and back to school. Travis has been enshrined by the *Daily News* as a local celebrity for his contribution to the war on crime. He returns to cabdriving, suffering only a slight stiffness from his wounds. Betsy gets into his cab in front of a hotel, but he resists her overture at conversation. He drops her off at her destination. The movie ends.

I am led to some perhaps unfashionable observations.

The first is that the moral question raised by moviemaking like this is far deeper than the much-debated psychological one: whether violence such as that which this film climaxes in is salutary for people to watch. I wonder whether every obscenity is theoretically permissible (not in a First Amendment legal sense, but in a moral sense) in the pursuit of artistic ends. And while the jury is out on that question, I must confess that in any case the use of obscenity and violence in this movie seems to me to have little to do with art and a lot to do with shock value.

By obscenity I do not mean just the Four Letter Word. For me two years in the Army deprived that word, in any of its syntactical variations, of most of its force. But to hear "Nigger" on the screen still bothers me. And when *Taxi Driver*'s lowlight cabbies sit around in an all-night cafeteria and refer to Harlem as "f---ing Mau Mau land," and then the camera pans to two huge, nattily dressed blacks, tapping their fingers at another table, I think Scorsese is making a cynical effort to have it both ways: he is playing on our deepest racial anxieties and at the same time projecting them onto lower-class whites, thereby absolving us of guilt for them.

For like *All in the Family, Taxi Driver* never really threatens its prime viewing audience — the increasingly jaded middle class — with the evil within. The gore at the end may gag you, but you will probably recover in time to say, "Well, that's the way it is." On the seamy underside of life, blacks hold up grocery stores, Italians with brogues beat them to death with crowbars, and whores crawl like vermin. Of course they do. It's a jungle out there.

Out there. That's where *Taxi Driver* keeps the evil. But it doesn't hold it out there so as honestly, relentlessly to probe the mystery, the banality, of evil. That would be *too* repulsive, and drive audiences away. Instead, this movie contents itself with a lurid look at the phenomenology of evil. There is a morbid fascination with evil's manifestation, but agnostic incuriosity about its origin, growth, spread. Any impetus to examine these is thwarted by the intentionally fragmented way the picture of Travis is put together. The headaches are from Charles Whitman, the diary motif from Arthur Bremer, the Marine background from Lee Harvey Oswald. The inexplicability of the whole thing is taken for granted, justified by the only-partly-appropriate line from Kris Kristoffersen which Betsy applies to Travis: "He's a walkin' contradiction. . . ."

Marlin Van Elderen

It would not occur to me, I suppose, to fault this movie for not doing what it doesn't intend to do, except for screenwriter Schrader's recent willingness to nurture media hype about his lapsed Calvinist background. A number of reviewers have made much of the personal anguish behind this film; the *Detroit Free Press* (perhaps setting a new world record for stereotypes in one sentence) put it all in terms of the culture shock that moving to Los Angeles will induce in "a ramrod-straight, Calvinist divinity student from Grand Rapids."

*   *   *

However attractive as a myth, this will not wash as an explanation for *Taxi Driver*. It is not that Schrader is incapable of dealing reflectively with important issues: his film criticism (which he has virtually given up) demonstrates that he is, as do some tantalizing hints scattered throughout the dialogue of *Taxi Driver*. But for whatever reasons (and commercial acclaim seems to loom large among them), he has chosen a different route in this film.

An unkind sociologist might cite such success-orientation as evidence confirming Schrader's Calvinism. The rest of us may hope that, if he continues to tell interviewers about his theological background, he will reckon with the issues it raises in a searching fashion instead of an exercise in voyeurism. Perhaps his giving the character most calculated to shock audiences back home a Frisian last name is an antic hint that he will have more to say. Or perhaps it was just a cheap shot.

Fundamentalism & Political Rightism

Henry Stob   *January 1965*

One feature of the political scene in contemporary America is the alliance of conservative Christianity with political programs of the right. I am not in command of precise statistics, but I dare say that religion in the Bible-belt was — no doubt for a variety of reasons — on the side of Senator Goldwater in the recent election.

Why should this be? Why should conservative Christians range themselves in such numbers behind a candidate whose insignia, as I believe, was nothing so much as "Individualism" — the independence of the person from societal and governmental "control," or, as I should prefer to say, "involvement"?

One of the reasons is, I fear, not far to seek. It is a reason that is by no means flattering to a certain type of Christian orthodoxy. This reason lies in the unwitting alliance of religious conservatism — which in this country is usually called Fundamentalism — with the Spirit of Modernity.

Modernity

At the beginning of the modern era, under the influence of the nominalism which dominated the late Middle Ages and flowered in the Renaissance, Western man became an "Individualist." He became this by asserting his freedom, not "for" something, but "from" something; among other things "from" the Church, from the Bible, from Tradition, from History, from Society, from Religion, and even from God. Modern man, bred in the Renaissance, vaunted his freedom, celebrated his autonomy, and proclaimed individualism in very large letters.

It was this individualism, born out of a rejection of the historic Christian faith, and oriented to the pagan culture of the ancients, which set the pattern for much of occidental civilization after the sixteenth century. It came to classical expression in the eighteenth-century French Revolution, and it still dominates much of contemporary thought. The spirit of modernity, born in the Renaissance and come to maturity in the Revolution, spoke out for liberty and autonomy. Nothing, neither God, nor Creed, nor Church, nor Government, was to fence man in. In the liberty that was his by nature he could do as he pleased, and by nobody's leave. He was alone in the world and he had to make his own way.

One fruit of this modern spirit was the "rugged individualism" of nineteenth-century capitalism, which left economics to the impersonal workings of the market, and which lived by the slogan "get what you can get, and let the Devil take the hindmost." Another fruit of it was the evolutionistic ethics which proclaimed that only the strong — or the upright — deserved the "spoils," and that the weak — or the iniquitous — had better take the place that Nature — or God — had prepared for them: at the bottom of the heap. Still another fruit of it is contemporary Existentialism, which holds that man is bound by nothing; there is no tradition that can get a hold on him, there is no sovereign good that can engage his will, there is no objective reality that can regulate his intellect, there is no society that has a claim on his compassion, there is "Nothing" by which he can be regulated and controlled.

The effect of this individualism is to destroy community and to pulverize society. It breaks the community up into separate discrete particulars, each of which goes its own way. This does not mean that some sort of community is not desired; but it does mean that community is believed to issue "naturally," in an unplanned fashion, by each member of it going his independent way. But the belief is false. Individualism never yields community; it only rends the fabric of society and issues into nihilism. . . .

Fundamentalism

Fundamentalism is a somewhat amorphous thing, and it is not static. Being in process — happily toward improvement — it cannot be arrested and delineated in final terms. But in spite of its changing visage it can be roughly described. It is of course Christian. It is also basically orthodox and evangelical. But it has a typical fault. It has wedded its Christianity to the regnant individualism which characterizes modernity, and it has no uncompromised resources against the spirit of the age. For this reason it tends to be blind to the defects of Goldwaterism and to the current political conservatism which feeds on modernity. Evidence for fundamentalistic individualism lies on every hand.

Fundamentalistic Individualism

(1) Consider first the typical Fundamentalist view of man in relation to God. Is man, in the Fundamentalist view, "free" from, "loose" from God? I dare say he is. Fundamentalists are, as a class, Arminian in their theology. What does this mean in terms of individualism? It means that there are in the world a multitude of personal centers into which God cannot enter until man "sovereignly" opens the door to Him. God can knock at the door, but it will be opened to Him only when and if the individual autonomously decides it shall be opened. Man is "free." The human soul is "inviolable." No one may enter it — not even God — except by permission. The human soul is basically impervious to grace; it is "independent" of God. It is impregnable in its unqualified liberty and individuality. Man in this view, just as in modernity and Communism, is basically autonomous.

(2) The same individualism comes to expression in the Fundamentalist view of the Church.

    (a) In the first place the Church is here not a community of believing parents and their children; it is an aggregate of mature individuals usually plucked as a brand out of the burning. There is here no due appreciation of the continuity of God's people as it comes to expression in the doctrine of the covenant and in the practice of paedobaptism. Church membership stands in the token of discreteness and atomism; the Body of Christ is not a true organism but a sum of separate entities without history or lineage, a collection of people each of whom is of the order of Melchizedek.

    (b) Similarly, the order of the Church is individualistic. The typical church organization is congregational, undenominational, and sectarian. There is fear here of wholeness and inclusiveness, and a strong inclination toward separateness and autonomy. It is this same individualism which is in part responsible for the Fundamentalist resistance to ecumenical cooperation. In keeping with the dominant spirit of modernity the Fundamentalist wants above all to be "free" from, "loose" from, involvements and entanglements, and by that token from all super-individual responsibilities.

(c) For the same reason the typical Fundamentalist depreciates church creeds. The classical creeds are expressive of the massive and universal judgment of the Christian Church in its historic oneness and continuity. But subscription to these confessions places the particular church and the individual believer into a context. It insinuates these into an environing whole. And this goes counter to individualism. One is apt therefore to hear the Fundamentalist say, "No creed but Christ" — a slogan, significantly, which he shares with the typical modernist. This is of course not surprising. Both articulate, each in its own way, the theme of the Renaissance: individualism and autonomy — in this case, freedom from the church tradition.

(d) It is not irrelevant to mention in this connection the typically Fundamentalist understanding of the Reformation doctrine of the "private interpretation of the Bible." The Reformers never supposed that anyone at all was equipped to theologize, and they never supposed that biblical interpretation could be fruitfully carried on in independence of the history of interpretation, i.e., in isolation from the universal Church, in which the Spirit has been operative from the time of Pentecost. But in Fundamentalist circles any man with a Bible in his hand is presumed authorized to set himself up as a teacher. The individual interpreter is the court of last appeal.

(e) The dominant individualism characteristic of Fundamentalism is manifest also in the conception of church functions. Missions, for example, tend to be carried out by individuals without church sanction or control, or even without the church's financial support — whence arise the typical "faith missions" which are supported by an amorphous aggregate of individuals, missions which in their message and direction frequently bear the stamp, not of an organized and confessionally disciplined church, but of some particular "leader" or "leaders."

(3) But it is not only in relation to God, nor only in relation to the Church, but also in relation to the cosmos that the individualism of Fundamentalism appears. Also in reference to the "world" the slogan is separation, non-involvement, withdrawal, disengagement, non-participation. Salvation tends to mean the "rescuing" of the individual soul out of the world rather than the equipment of the whole man for beneficent and salvific activity in the world, in the company of the like-minded, the organism of believers. Also, whereas in the view of historic Christianity there is a solidarity of all men in sin by virtue of the fall in Paradise of man, there is in Fundamentalism a tendency to speak not of sin but of "sins," not of a disease that infects all men, but of discrete acts individually performed and separately numbered. By the same token there is little appreciation for the biblical conception of the cosmic Christ who is significant in one way and another not only for the whole race of men but for the whole of creation. There is consequently hardly any appreciation of the cultural mandate and of the world-encompassing tasks it imposes. Fundamentalism stands in the signature of individualistic world-flight and separatistic disaffiliation.

(4) By the same token there is in classical Fundamentalism — happily chastened by such messages as are contained in Carl Henry's book *The Uneasy Conscience of Fundamentalism* — a want of concern for social problems and a disinclination to elaborate a social ethic. Morals tend to be individualistically conceived. Emphasis is on personal purity and uprightness. There is little engagement with the structures of society, e.g., the structure of the state or of the economic order. It is supposed that all the ills of society can be cured if only the souls of individual men are "saved." Missions therefore become the preferred technique of social reform, to the virtual exclusion of legal enactments. It is not sufficiently understood that the external and environing "orders" of social existence must be fashioned and patterned in the image of the good, as well as the individual lives which are lived within these orders. And it is not sufficiently appreciated that this can happen only through the invigoration and implementation of the social will.

Politics

This review of the pattern of individualism which structures much of Fundamentalism discloses an inner connection between it and political rightism. Whatever other considerations may have influenced large sections of the conservative Christian community to support the Goldwater movement, this consideration was certainly present and effective. The two movements — the political and the religious — both betray an undue dependence upon a rugged individualism the source of which lies in the neo-pagan Renaissance and in the anarchic Revolution. It is for this reason that I, and many others in the Reformed community, felt obliged to decry Goldwaterism and to deplore the tendency of some theological conservatives to give it religious sanction.

I have said nothing in this piece about President Johnson and the Democratic Party. And such things as I have said about Modernity, Individualism, Fundamentalism, and Political Conservatism of the Goldwater type may not be interpreted as meaning that the present government is on the side of the angels. It does mean, however, that in my judgment the social and international involvements and concerns of the incumbents, whatever may be the "philosophy" underlying them, bear a closer resemblance to the sort of political program that would arise out of an authentic Christian vision than the social and international myopia and separatism of the Goldwater movement. In any case, Reformed Christianity has no inner connections with the autonomy and individualism of modernity and can ill afford to make an alliance with contemporary political rightism. Its practical affinity with historical Republicanism is of course another matter.

Graham and Hope

Richard J. Mouw   *September 1970*

Revolutions, it has been said, make strange bedfellows; and the same can be said, it seems, of counter-revolutions. The recent "Honor America" team of Billy Graham and Bob Hope deserves to be counted as one such curious alliance. Indeed, Carl McIntire was so taken by the unholiness of it all that he denounced it, citing Deuteronomy 22:10: "Thou shalt not plow with an ox and an ass together" — which is one of those lines which make one feel like Johnny Carson must feel when he grins and says, "I wouldn't touch that one with a ten-foot pole." . . .

Surely at some point in the past there has been a Bob Hope movie playing across the street from a Billy Graham rally, with the crowds on either side of the street eyeing each other suspiciously. One will never know, of course, but it makes one wonder what those same people were thinking, down deep beneath these infamously silent exteriors, when the lineup for July 4, 1970, was announced.

And what about the evangelist and the movie star? Did they feel any discomfort over the arrangement? Of course Billy Graham has been in the company of movie stars before, but usually ones who have gotten converted and have married ministers and who return to the limelight only for an occasional testimony at a Graham rally, or to appear in some Graham-sponsored movie about a movie star who gets converted and marries a minister and who returns to the limelight only for an occasional testimony at a Graham rally. And Bob Hope has undoubtedly had his liaisons with the clergy before — probably with a chaplain in Vietnam who stands on one of those outdoor stages and introduces Bob Hope to the boys and then inconspicuously steals off just before Bob Hope introduces some starlet with a name like "Cindy Graham."

Richard J. Mouw

Upon second thought, however, a case can be made for saying that Graham and Hope have quite a bit in common. For one thing, they get quite a few of their lines from the same material. For example, both Hope and Graham have made it their business to talk a lot about American sexual mores, although with very different goals in mind, it would seem: where Hope would try for laughs Graham would call for repentance. But on July 4 it almost seemed as if they had worked out a compromise that resulted in no laughs and no calls for national repentance, only "honor" for America. Although for this, too, there may be some precedent in their previous ministerings to the American public. In his particular brand of humor Hope is surely providing an *escape* from the frustrations that are caused by America's deepest flaws. And when Graham challenges the blacks in his congregations with: "If you accept Christ tonight you can go back to your ghetto with peace in your heart," and when he passes off student unrest as merely a desperate quest for a meaning that can only be found in Christ, isn't this too an attempt to deal with America's structural sins by providing an escape from the frustrations that they cause?

For whatever it is worth, Carl McIntire agrees that "Honor America Day" was an illegitimate escape from the real issues that confront America. He told his radio audience that Graham and Hope were trying to neutralize America; and that, he said, is no way to "honor" America. McIntire is surely correct on this score — the recognition of which makes one wonder what is happening to us. For when one finds oneself agreeing with Carl McIntire's criticisms of an unholy alliance between Bob Hope and Billy Graham, one gets the uneasy feeling that perhaps — just perhaps — we didn't really understand Candidate Nixon when we cynically laughed at his promise that he would bring us together.

The Pentagon Papers

Daniel H. Benson   *September 1971*

Does the phenomenon of the Pentagon Papers have a specific, unique meaning for us as Christians? I think so. It may be a bit difficult to get at it, but I deem the effort worthwhile because it seems to me that something very important and fundamental is involved. . . .

The ostensible purpose for concealing the Pentagon Papers, or trying to conceal the remainder of them after the *New York Times* began its series based upon them, was to protect the security of the United States itself. Significantly, no trial court involved in the ensuing legal struggles was persuaded that there was any evidence that the security of the United States would be damaged by publication of the Pentagon Papers. This is important, because it means that the decisions of the trial courts to allow the newspapers to continue publishing the Papers were not based upon what people fondly term "legal technicalities." The decisions of the trial courts were based squarely on the merits of the cases before them: the government simply failed to produce the proof. . . .

Accordingly, we must look elsewhere for the answer to the question of why there was such a frantic effort to keep the Papers secret. . . . The answer, I think, lies in something much deeper and more fundamental [than political or state-security motives]: the essential nature of man, and his vulnerability to the sin of pride. I think this accounts for the origin of the Pentagon Papers, the subsequent attempts to keep them secret, and the profound embarrassment that we have all felt upon having them revealed to the world at large. This explanation cuts across party lines, political considerations, and even individual self-interest. And it is less satisfying to us, personally, because it means that we are all to blame, and that we are all involved to a greater or lesser extent, and that we are all responsible for what has happened, and for what is now happening, in our nation.

Eugene McCarthy has pointed out that the published Papers have not revealed very much that is altogether new or different, but what they have shown is highly significant: "They have shown first that the executive branch, acting and speaking principally through the presidency and the State Department and the Pentagon, has been more devious and more deceptive than was suspected" (*The New Republic*, July 10, 1971, p. 14). McCarthy goes on to say that they also have shown that the administration was ready to mislead the country by withholding information, by telling only half-truths, and by positive misrepresentation. The Papers also show an arrogance and "a strong and almost frightening callousness and detachment" on the part of those who were managing the war (*ibid.*, p. 15).

What Mr. McCarthy does not say, but what is equally true, is that the American people have been content to accept such government. We have known that this kind of thing has been going on for a long time, and we have passively acquiesced in it. We are not as naïve as we pretend to be, with our current outrage over being deceived by our government. In a certain sense we *like* to be deceived by our government; it keeps us from being bothered about the important decisions at the time they are made, and it spares us from having to bear any responsibility for those decisions later — or so we imagine. What else was it but a lie when President Eisenhower said that it was not an American spy plane that had been shot down over Russia? And then later when he admitted to the truth, and stoutly insisted that he would send more U-2 planes if necessary on similar spy missions, were we not able to conclude that we had been tricked and misled by our own government? We were duped, in the first instance, because we knew nothing of such spy planes, and the pronouncements of our government were such as to cause us to believe that we did not engage in that kind of activity. We were misled, in the second place, or at least temporarily so, by our President's outright denial of the existence of such a spy plane and its mission. But what was done about it? What did *we* do about it, we who are so angry now that we have been lied to about Vietnam? Nothing.

We have allowed a system to develop in our government whereby there are some 20,000,000 classified documents in the hands of administrative officials which we may not see or examine. There are now approximately 38,000 employees of the Department of Defense who have direct or derivative authority to classify documents "confidential," and some 7,000 employees with original authority to classify documents "secret." This system of security did not spring up overnight. While the documents themselves may be classified, the fact of the security system itself is not classified, and has been widely known in and out of the government for years. In fact, the basis of the present security system is President Eisenhower's Executive Order 10501, issued in 1953. Of course, no government can conduct all of its business in public, and this is particularly true of military and diplomatic matters. But we have allowed our security system to develop out of all proportion to the legitimate needs of the government to keep certain of its operations confidential. . . .

The truth is that we will accept such deception by our leaders, and the systematic concealment of all of our mistakes through our security system, because of our pride. In discussing pride, C. S. Lewis noted that it is essentially competitive; pride gets no pleasure out of merely having something, only out of having more of it than the next man. This is true of our national pride no less than it is true of our individual pride. We want our country to be strong, but not merely strong: we want it to be stronger than any other country. We want our country to be clever in its diplomatic relations with other nations, but not merely clever: we want it to be more clever than any other country. We want our military and diplomatic ventures to be successful, but not merely successful: we want them to be more successful than the military and diplomatic ventures of any other country. In short, the sad truth is that through our pride we would like to be omnipotent.

Further, the Pentagon Papers support our proud belief that *we* are not to blame for what has happened regarding Vietnam; it was Kennedy, or Johnson, or now Nixon, or the men who advised and continue to advise them. The security system keeps us from being responsible for the mistakes that were made, for how could we do anything about all of it when we knew nothing because our government concealed the truth from us? These considerations motivate most of us as individual citizens, I think. And the frantic efforts by our present government officials to keep the Pentagon Papers secret were motivated by similar considerations. For their part, they did not want a public disclosure of the mistakes they (and their predecessors in the same offices) had made. The sum and substance of the matter is that we are all trying to use the Pentagon Papers, and the events arising from their public disclosure, to protect and bolster our pride.

If this is the central meaning of the Pentagon Papers, then as Christians we should be deeply troubled. In *The Children of Light and the Children of Darkness,* the late Reinhold Niebuhr said:

> . . . According to the Christian faith the pride which seeks to hide the conditioned and finite character of all human endeavor is the very quintessence of sin. Religious faith ought therefore to be a constant form of humility; for it ought to encourage men to moderate their natural pride and to achieve some decent consciousness of the relativity of their own statement of even the most ultimate truth (p. 135).

It should be one of our functions in society to contribute in some significant measure to the establishment and maintenance of the kind of religious humility described by Niebuhr. We ought to help our country to "achieve some decent consciousness of the relativity" of its political and military purposes in Vietnam and Indochina. The Pentagon Papers, and our reaction to them, both in and out of the government, indicate that as Christians we are failing in this task.

Niebuhr recognized that religious humility is "no simple moral or political achievement," and said: "It springs only from the depth of a religion which confronts the individual with a more ultimate majesty and purity than all human majesties and values, and persuades him to confess: 'Why callest thou me good? there is none good but one, that is, God'" (*ibid.,* p. 151). But does not our Christian faith confront us with just such majesty? Surely it is our opportunity, and our obligation, to give what leadership we can in these times, out of the depth of our Christian faith, and assist our fellow men in recognizing the consummate evil of pride when it dominates our national life. We cannot get very far in this until and unless, in Calvin's words, we contemplate the face of God, and come down after such contemplation to look into ourselves.

> For (such is our innate pride) we always seem to ourselves just, and upright, and wise, and holy, until we are convinced, by clear evidence, of our injustice, vileness, folly, and impurity. Convinced, however, we are not, if we look to ourselves only, and not to the Lord also — He being the only standard by the application of which

this conviction can be produced. For, since we are all naturally prone to hypocrisy, any empty semblance of righteousness is quite enough to satisfy us instead of righteousness itself (*Institutes*, I. i).

Watergate and the American Presidency

Ronald A. Wells   *November 1973*

For those who would make sense out of Watergate, *Some Presidents: Wilson to Nixon*, by William Appleton Williams, is essential reading. *Some Presidents* is not about Watergate: it does not mention the events and practices lumped under that name and was, indeed, written before these came to light. Nonetheless, it is a jewel of a book that glitters with possibilities of new approaches to understanding the contemporary situation. . . .

Williams' thesis is that the American presidency is in crisis because the American political and social system is in crisis. In suggesting this he offers, in brief outline, an interpretation of American history that he has developed in detail elsewhere. . . . [It] proceeds thus: The American revolution was essentially a democratic movement whose political ideals can be best seen in the Articles of Confederation, which stressed popular government and decentralized authority. The business-oriented upper-class leadership who "seized power" (Williams' phrase — I should have preferred another) in 1786-87 usurped the power of Congress, ignored their instructions merely to revise the Articles, and wrote a law-and-order, property-rights document called the Constitution.

Even though they were a minority, these conservatives might have succeeded in building among the lower and middle classes a social movement committed to an aristocratic republic, if they had been content to settle for half a continent as their domain. But westward expansion was part of the spirit of North American culture. The need to bring ever-increasing amounts of territory into one domain (Williams prefers "empire") is the root of our present trouble. Had American expansion been allowed to result in several related or unrelated commonwealths on this continent, the crisis today might not exist. Simply stated, if a continental and oceanic empire is to function effectively under one government, that government must have substantial centralized authority. It is the unsurprising abuse of centralized governmental power, and its unresponsiveness to the real needs of citizens, that lies at the base of our present malaise.

The question of a plurality of commonwealths in America was raised, of course, by the South in the Civil War. It was answered, not constitutionally, but militarily. When the South was defeated by force and the decentralizing principle thereby quashed, the power of the presidency under Lincoln began to expand to unprecedented dimensions. From Lincoln onwards, and especially in the twentieth century, we have witnessed the seemingly inexorable process of vesting ever-increasing power in the federal government and, concomitantly, in the presidency at the expense of the other branches of government.

All this leads Williams to what he calls "the central factor in the process: without a social movement based upon the recognition of limits, and upon the values that define a democratic community, there is no politics except special interest politics in an imperial economy." Special interest politics may function effectively for a while, but since it is based on the inherently corrosive factor of competitive individualism it can never result in the building up of a community (or communities) of shared values. Since the last quarter of the nineteenth century the large business corporations have become the predominant force in the marketplace. Their strategy was to construct a facade of community under the assumption that labor and capital could work together within the capitalist structure. . . .

The presidency became the crucial factor in the two-pronged struggle to maintain the newly created corporate state. It fought against the socialists on the one hand and against the traditional conservatives (the nineteenth-century liberals à la Smith and Locke), who believed in the individualism of the marketplace, on the other. Both William McKinley and Theodore Roosevelt understood this, and they were willing to see the presidency evolve into the "chairman of the board" of the corporate state. According to Williams, the course of American history in the twentieth century has been a working out of the realization that the new "corporate political economy could not function without intimate and extensive collaboration between corporation leaders and the President, or without subsidies supplied by the taxpayer." In the past sixty years the power of the Executive has been employed to maintain this system despite its failure (the Depression) and despite the fact that a majority of Americans may well have opposed it. Williams concludes most chillingly: "In that process, leadership steadily degenerated into manipulation. Dialogue was subverted by secrecy and evasion. Trust was undermined by lies. And the residue of confidence was further eroded by incompetence and failure." From there, the steps to Vietnam and Watergate were simple enough. . . .

*   *   *

Richard Nixon was elected in 1968 as a quasi-peace candidate. He had a "plan to end the war." What he meant was that, once in the White House, he would do all in his power to establish peace on the Wilson model: "We are now in a position to give the world all the good things that Britain offered in her Empire without any of the disadvantages of nineteenth-century colonialism." To the charge that this still means an American empire, Nixon responds that American colonialism is better than Communism. He is worried about America being "Number One" in the world; and he will never, in his own words, "cede U.S. influence in any part of the world where it exists."

The power and prerogatives of the President are bound up in all this. Realizing and accepting the fact that the post-Cambodia phase of the Indo-China war was his personal policy, Nixon justified it with an unintentionally accurate revelation: America must not be defeated, he said, because it would be a defeat for the presidency. In revitalizing "St. Woodrow's Crusade" Nixon has forged the final link of the chain that bound the vision of an America supreme in the world to a presidency supreme in the United States and perceived as such from abroad.

At the time of this writing (mid-September) much of the evidence surrounding Watergate remains to be heard. But (without prejudging the outcome) it now seems clear that a mentality pervaded the Nixon White House which caused or allowed what John Mitchell called "the White House horrors" to take place. While the break-in at the Democratic headquarters and other assorted buggings, burglary, and bungling were the deeds of Watergate, the "spirit of Watergate" is much more difficult to grasp. "The President's palace guard," wrote the *New York Times* (August 5, 1973), "feared every potential Democratic candidate, not as a challenger under the rules of the two-party system, but as a usurper of the power that had to belong to Richard Nixon for the nation's salvation."

In actuality the vision is far broader and far more frightening. Much more than the nation's salvation was at stake. The vision of the Nixon presidency was no less than the salvation of the world. An all-knowing and virtually all-powerful White House, acting in disregard of laws, the Constitution, and common decency, did so not out of vulgar desires for personal gain. Its actions sprang from a vision of the world and of America, and of the role of America's president in it. The alleged deeds of Watergate are perhaps Richard Nixon's own. The spirit of Watergate is part of an historic process that began in 1787, was accelerated during the twentieth century, and reached its apotheosis during Richard Nixon's tenure in the presidency. . . .

So it is that, in a study of the modern presidency by one of the fathers of the New Left movement in American historiography, the heroes are Herbert Hoover and Dwight Eisenhower. They (especially Hoover) are so because they recognized the dangers of the drift toward statism in general and toward the omnipotent, international presidency in particular. As Reinhold Niebuhr wrote, it is not the conservatives and pessimists ("the children of darkness") who have led us astray, but the liberals and optimists ("the children of light"). The corporate-liberal elite, with the President as chairman-of-the-board, conceived a myth of an efficient, corporate state at home and of a dominant, imperial state abroad. One must conclude with horror and sorrow that many Americans accept that myth as truth.

An alternative myth would have it that the structures of society can be changed to allow for a pluralist "mosaic" of communities of shared values to function within a national whole. But such a myth can be realized only when we recognize the bankruptcy of the corporate state and of its chief functionary, the presidency in its present form. As Williams writes, "a community offers the only viable technique of survival." Those redeemed by the grace of God want more than mere survival, of course: we want to do God's will. While gratefully acknowledging Williams' contribution in our reawakening as citizens, we must go beyond him. We who are united in the Body of Christ must make that unity the model for our community on this earth.

Readers of the *Journal* will perhaps disagree with Williams' viewpoints, as I do myself in some places. I regard what has been said in this

Ronald A. Wells

essay not as dogma but as talking points. I hope that Christians will debate these issues, because only out of such debate can full realization come of our Christian faith as presenting an alternative way of life.

The Palestinian Issue

Bert DeVries   *January 1975*

Perhaps the Palestinians' biggest tragedy of the past twenty-six years is that their plight has been ignored by most of the world. The wounds of humiliation and degradation have been allowed to fester with sufficient ointment to prevent death but not to effect a cure. The world allowed the refugees the shelter, food, and medicine necessary to enable them to dwell on their misery, but not to escape from the overcrowded camps. Numerous young Palestinians educated in the camps have been employed as teachers, engineers, and administrators in the oil countries, but they work with the knowledge that as soon as Kuwaitis and Saudis return from schools abroad they will be replaced.

The four wars between Israel and the Arab states were fought with Palestinians in mind, but not on their behalf. The United Nations General Assembly repeatedly passed resolutions affirming the right to return and the right to nationhood, but these recommendations were ignored by the statesmen who counted. Through it all the Palestinians have insisted that their plight has to be considered if a peace settlement is to be viable and that they should have a voice in the negotiations between the various parties in the conflict.

This was the message presented to the world by Yasir Arafat's selection as the spokesman for the Palestinians at Rabat and the subsequent UN General Assembly resolution reaffirming the Palestinians' right to national independence and sovereignty. Unfortunately, on this side of the Atlantic that message has been buried under a number of peripheral issues, with the result that the plight of the Palestinians seems once again fated to be ignored. These issues can be stated as criticism of the decisions of the Rabat conference and the UN General Assembly:

1. Arafat's Palestine Liberation Organization is a gang of terrorists. To elevate these criminals to diplomatic status is a travesty of human ideals of justice and opens up the floodgates of anarchy in the world.
2. Arafat and the PLO do not qualify as negotiator and representatives because their organization speaks for only a minority of Palestinians.
3. The General Assembly resolutions on Palestine reflect the degeneration of the UN into a tyranny of a majority of small, insignificant countries over the minority of large, powerful states.
4. With the PLO forming its government, a Palestinian state will become another small left-wing country that will threaten democracy in the area.
5. The foundation of a Palestinian state on Arafat's terms will mean the destruction of Israel.

To deal fully with each of these objections would require far more than this column. My purpose is merely to point out that preoccupation with them acts as a smokescreen that obscures the real issue: the need to solve the Palestine refugee problem and to rectify injustices done to the Palestinians as an integral part of a Middle East peace settlement.

As Christians we join most people in the world (including most Palestinians and Arafat himself) in condemning the indiscriminate killings of innocent victims in the international terrorist acts carried out by individuals and splinter groups. A discussion of terrorism in the context of conflict between Palestinians and Israelis, however, tends to become partisan. How does one weigh a commando raid on an Israeli village over against the shelling of a refugee camp in Southern Lebanon? What one calls a terrorist, the other calls a freedom fighter; what one calls aggression, the other calls liberation. As these judgments are made all of us tend to become partisan and from our one-sided position condemn or ignore the other side.

To say that Arafat does not qualify as a spokesman for the Palestinians amounts to saying that it is not possible for them to have a spokesman. The Palestinians are scattered in refugee camps and urban centers in a number of Middle East countries. There is no way for them to elect representatives to act as their spokesmen. This fragmentation is precisely one of the major problems they want solved. There is, of course, no way of determining whether Arafat has the support of a majority or not, but there are indications that most Palestinians, especially those in the refugee camps, are willing to be represented by him until national elections become possible. And his endorsement at Rabat has given him at least semi-official status which is recognized even by King Hussein of Jordan.

In a discussion of the degeneration of the UN it should be noted that between 1948 and 1974 the General Assembly passed resolutions affirming the Palestinians' right to return to their land twenty-one times, and between 1969 and 1974 passed resolutions affirming their right of self-determination four times. That Israel has simply ignored all of these resolutions may just be an indication that the ineffectiveness of the General Assembly in the world political arena is of rather long standing. Yet an overwhelming majority of the world's nations have, by means of proper democratic process, affirmed the Palestinians' right to self-determination.

The conflict over Palestine is not a conflict over political ideologies. Arafat has avoided political ideologies precisely because he wants to emphasize that his goal is the return of the Palestinians to their land. That some of the commando organizations have turned to a version of Marxism is in part a reaction to the consistent pro-Israeli policies of the US and other Western democracies. Although the question of a specific national ideology will have to be faced after independence, for the present most Palestinians find the content of their nationalism in the lament over exile and the desire to return. Distinctions between democracy, communism, and socialism are irrelevant. . . .

The PLO call for an end to the state of Israel does not mean the destruction of its Jews, but the destruction of its Jewishness. Arafat proposes to replace Israel with a state in which Muslim, Jew, and Christian will live together in "a democratic, humanistic, and progressive society." This is, of course, far too idealistic to fit the present situation, and Arafat may prove to be too uncompromising to achieve something less. Considered in the abstract, however, there seems to be something vaguely familiar about Arafat's ideals. His Palestine would not be the first nation in which people of various ethnic and religious backgrounds would attempt to live together in political and social harmony. And if Arafat's proposal for Palestine is unrealistic, so is the present Israeli situation. Israel has been able to exist only by means of secure borders as an armed fortress. It faces a future survival only as long as military superiority can be upheld. The need for this military way of life is due in large measure to the fact that Israel can maintain its uniqueness only at the expense of the Palestinians.

It is high time for Christians to become more aware of the Palestinians, not only as a key to Middle East peace, but also as individuals. A people humiliated, dislocated, and embittered needs our love and compassion. I pray that our love has the strength to rise above partisan Middle East politics so that our voices can cry out on behalf of Israelis and Palestinians for their reconciliation in peaceful ways rather than their mutual destruction in acts of war and terror. Even Arafat and the PLO figure in that.

The War Nobody Wants

LEWIS B. SMEDES   *February 1967*

Some people hate the war because they are sure it is immoral for us to fight it and doubly immoral to fight it the way we do. Others dislike it because we are not winning it fast enough. Those who hate it most are probably the young men who have to slough through the jungles in search of the enemy. But one ingredient that flows through all consideration of it is the ingredient of ignorance about it.

At the turn of the year I listened to correspondents summing up significant events, and especially the war, as they saw them. The only thread of agreement that stretched through all the TV year-end shows was unhappiness with the war and pessimism about its progress and end. We all suspect that we are not getting the "whole truth" — whatever that may be — about the war from Washington. What are we supposed to do when trained observers disagree on what has happened and what is happening? . . .

Never have the issues been so complex. Was the war at the beginning a civil conflict between the people and a military dictatorship which happened to be on our side of a struggle that the people in Viet Nam had no part in? Or was it a brutal invasion of one nation by another, an invasion that is part of a grand design of Communist conquest? Did we get into the war by a courageous and wise decision to protect the world from aggression? Or were we sucked in by a series of unwise decisions, the consequences of which we did not then foresee but which leave us now in what is really a problem of face-saving?

If there was an invasion — be it under the guise of a liberation movement — was the safety of the whole area so endangered as to leave us no other option than Hitler left us? And does whatever danger existed justify the kind of brutal force we are using in response to brutal force? Is the cure worse than the threatened disease? Do we have to burn villages? Do we have to bomb the North?

And even if the intervention per se was justified, can we win? That is, can we really keep the Vietnamese from going over to the Viet Cong? We are failing — and this everyone agrees — in the so-called pacification program. And this is only to say that we are failing to win over the people from the Viet Cong after we clear their villages of them. Why? Is it because of our color, our way of fighting — or, per-haps, is it because the people prefer the Viet Cong to the Saigon re-gime? Is it a victory for democracy if, after killing enough Viet Cong, we have to station soldiers there forever to keep the people on our side?

But, one might argue, all these questions are merely the qualms of timid souls in the presence of an enormous threat. The invasion of South Viet Nam is only one episode in a program of invasion without terminus. Aggression is aggression whether it occurs across the Rhine or across a north-south boundary fixed at Geneva in 1954. . . . Allowed to proceed, it will only lead us into a far worse war than we have now to put up with. Horrible as it is, the Viet Nam war is a moral necessity thrown on us by an enemy that has shown no willingness to revise his goals. If all of this is the case, then let us support the war to the hilt.

One thing we can do is demand that Washington level with us. If it is a just war, then it is our war — and we can take the bad news with the good, the mistakes with the right decisions, the failures with the successes. Another thing we have to do is remember Paul's word about prayer for national leaders. In our monstrously unclear situa-tion, we should remember that the President is neither infallible nor stupid, and we should be praying hard for him.

The War That Never Ends

LEWIS B. SMEDES   *November 1969*

Nobody knew when it began, or why. And nobody believed it would really ever end. And nobody seemed to know for sure what it was all about. This was the faraway war in the East that George Orwell talked about in *1984*. Our war is beginning to look more and more like that one.

A long time ago the Christian conscience of this country could have been brought to bear on Washington. A long time ago the Christian community could have spoken. But it was left for a few who saw things clearly and dared to say it like they saw it. Perhaps if we had seen then what we see now, and had had the courage to match the vision, we could have come down so hard on the Johnson people as to have prevented the endless summer of slaughter. But that is time now irrevocably past.

When we went into Vietnam in force almost five years ago, the South Vietnamese were fighting what we feared was a losing battle. Now, after we have dropped many more bombs on North Vietnam than we dropped in World War II, after nearly forty thousand American soldiers have perished, after who knows how many Vietnamese men, women, and children have been killed, we are still fighting in the suburbs of Saigon. The war is going no place except into infamy. And the Christian community is still not ready to ask what must be asked, to demand what must be demanded.

If we go on much longer, we will have forgotten when or why it began. And we will treat the weekly lists of dead the same casual way we treat the weekend traffic toll. The Vietnam War will become a way of life — our life and their death.

Things about this war are terribly complicated. Everything but death is complicated about it. The dying is being done for no good reason. And the fighting is being done with no reasonable chance for change in the situation there. No one expects victory, and few seem even to know what victory could mean. The power of decision resides finally at no place but the White House. One option for the man who has the power is to accept defeat for a cause that never was justifiable, to accept defeat and to pay its price in national humility. This, we contend, is the only right option.

Barry Goldwater said very recently that, as far as he could see, all Americans want the war to end now. The Christian community wants it to end no later. Would to God that the Christian community had seen five years ago that it should not have begun, and said so. Water over the dam? Not quite. We can still prevent the Orwellian vision from becoming the American reality: the war that never ends. And Christians must keep saying so.

We Are the Casualties

DANIEL H. BENSON   *May-June 1971*

A thin veneer of Anglo-American jurisprudence, applied through the medium of the Uniform Code of Military Justice, neither conceals nor alters the fact that modern American warfare is a brutal, vicious enterprise that tends to corrupt all who are involved in it. The recent trial of Lieutenant William Calley has brought this unavoidably to public attention.

Daniel Lang tells the story of another atrocity in his recent little book *Casualties of War* (McGraw-Hill, 1969). The conclusion of Lang's account of the kidnapping, rape, and murder of an innocent Vietnamese peasant girl by American soldiers ought to be that justice eventually triumphed. After all, there were several trials, appeals, and retrials. Some defendants went to prison. The prosecution's chief witness received a letter of commendation from an Army major general. But Lang is not telling us about the triumph of justice under wartime conditions. He is telling us that *there is no justice,* as that concept has been understood by civilized nations, in a modern war zone. . . . [A review of the processes followed by military courts follows.]

But the defects of military justice are not the heart of the problem raised by Lang's account. Lang drives home the point that modern warfare is almost the very antithesis of justice. Soldiers and civilians alike die at random, and for reasons that few can comprehend or control. Valor is largely immaterial, and the combatant/noncombatant dichotomy of former times is gone. Loyalty has become a meaningless shibboleth because there are so many conflicting and mutually inconsistent things to which an American soldier is exhorted to be loyal: his unit, his officers, his noncommissioned officers, his commander, his fellow soldiers, his country — and even, far down on the list, his God.

Mercy and decency are lost and forgotten amidst the claims of these conflicting official loyalties.

Thus, in this incident of modern warfare described by Lang, it is not the sanity of the rapists that is questioned, but that of the man who would not participate in the rape. It is not the gallantry of the murderers that is questioned, but that of the man who would not murder. Pity, in the war zone, was extended neither to the helpless girl who was kidnapped, raped, and murdered, nor to her family, but to the individuals who committed those crimes. And Lang's balanced account of the matter shows that these grotesquely twisted attitudes were shared by most American officers, noncommissioned officers, and rank-and-file soldiers as well.

It was only through the efforts of a chaplain that the case was finally forced upon the Army's criminal investigators, and initially even that chaplain was highly suspicious of a man who would "inform" on his fellow soldiers, regardless of whether they might be guilty of kidnapping, rape, and murder. And once the cumbersome machinery of military justice began to operate, it was plain that the Army was only reluctantly going through the motions in this one case because it had no other choice. There was no widespread horror, shock, or disgust about what had happened. It was happening all the time.

One recalls from the testimony presented at the court-martial of Lieutenant Calley that in modern American warfare one does not "kill" helpless noncombatant civilians, one "wastes" them. It is not murder to take the lives of the innocent in modern warfare as we practice it in Indochina; it is only "waste." When we invade another sovereign nation, it is now an "incursion" rather than an "invasion."

We have at last become the prisoners of our own American brand of Orwellian newspeak. What is worse, it may well be that we have finally become the prisoners of that kind of thinking, too. We are the casualties of war.

"Peace, Peace . . ."

RICHARD J. MOUW   *December 1972*

At the time of this writing there is not yet a negotiated peace in Vietnam, although there are signs that a settlement is in the offing. Perhaps one will have been secured by the time these words appear publicly. If so, and especially if the settlement means not only a cessation of the American military role but a genuine hope for healing and reconstruction for the peoples of Vietnam, this Christmas season will be an occasion for special rejoicing. But whatever happens, Americans must not quickly forget the issues that were involved in the war in Vietnam.

More specifically, evangelical Christians must continue to reflect on what the war meant, or should have meant, for a faithful evangelical witness to the full Lordship of Jesus Christ. Along these lines I want to register a complaint that no one — at least to my knowledge — has pointed out that the "peace with honor" theme that has been repeated continually by President Nixon is a case of theological heresy. Perhaps it is not surprising that no one has said it, since most of those who are critical of his policies are not very concerned about theological heresy, and those who are normally sensitive to heresies have not been very critical of the war. But in the interest of sound theology the point should be made.

The President's heresy can be illustrated by an analogy. Imagine that the following letter were to appear in Billy Graham's syndicated question-and-answer column: "Dear Billy Graham: I am a husband, a father, and a successful businessman, and I have a problem. I am involved in an extramarital sexual affair. It really began quite innocently, but one thing led to another and soon I was seriously involved. As the situation now stands I am caught between conflicting commitments and have perpetrated considerable deception. In a word, I want out. I am asking you for advice because I have heard that you have been able to help people who are involved in very difficult problems. I am willing to try anything. But there is one condition: I will only accept a solution which permits me to keep my honor intact. I have many friends who look to me for leadership, and also many enemies who would immediately capitalize on any sign of my weakness. My effectiveness would be severely reduced if my public image were tarnished. Please advise. . . ."

There can be no doubt as to what Graham, or any evangelical worth his salt, would say in such a case. The conditions on which the inquirer insists violate the heart of the Christian message. To find peace with God and men necessitates overcoming pride. It is to confess our sins to God and to our fellow men with the trust that God will not allow that to be applied to our ruin. It is to have our priorities reordered in such a way that the things which threaten our personal "honor" are not important in the light of those things which could stand in the way of obedience to our faithful Savior.

Well, what of President Nixon's "peace with honor" doctrine? If it is heresy to think that personal peace can be found while keeping one's honor intact, is it not just as heretical to think so with respect to the peace of nations? The Bible does not work with a double standard for peace, one set of principles applying to persons and another applying to nations. The call of 2 Chronicles 7:14 follows a pattern that applies to *both* individuals and nations: "If my people, which are called by my name, shall humble themselves, and pray, and seek my face, and turn from their wicked ways; then I will hear from heaven, and will forgive their sin, and will heal their land."

Some will reply, of course, that the biblical summons to national repentance deals with Israel, which occupied a special place before God not matched by the United States. This is true. But that does not mean that the way to national righteousness is any different for a modern nation than it was for Israel. Consider once again the individual case. Billy Graham does not have two different sets of answers for adulterers, one for Christian adulterers and another for unbelieving ones. The Christian wanderer must be told to remember what the Lord requires of him; the unbeliever must be told that an adequate solution to his problem can only be found in becoming a follower of Jesus Christ. Similarly, there is only one solution to the problem of international peace: it is the way of national discipleship that follows the path of humility, repentance, and trust in the Lordship of Christ. Nixon's quest for "peace with honor" is but a contemporary version of the ancient cry of "Peace, Peace" where there was no peace. The difference between the message to Israel and the message to America is one of context: for Israel there was needed a call to *return* to the vows that had been made with its covenant-God, but America must be told that it must first make those vows if it is to find the peace it seeks.

I am not speaking here to the full range of issues relating to American involvement in the Vietnam conflict; rather, I am commenting on the theology of peace which has recently been associated with our involvement. That theology, I submit, is heretical. If a popular speaker were traveling across the land instructing our people in false doctrines concerning grace or healing we would, I'm sure, speak out in the name of sound theology. We can do no less in the face of President Nixon's heresy. . . .

Who Needs Women's Lib?

KAREN HELDER DE VOS   *March 1971*

The women's liberation movement, although many may dislike its methods and its assumptions, has nonetheless had some good effect. For the first time in at least fifteen years, and possibly much longer, some orthodox Christians are trying to come seriously to grips with the effects of modern life on the role of women, both in society as a whole and in the church.

Two areas of conflict are becoming obvious, I think. The first is general in our society and is the result of our democratic statements about equality for all, and our practice of discrimination against women, particularly in jobs and wages. The second is the result of the orthodox churches' view of women's role; it affects married women, especially mothers, more radically than the unmarried. . . . [The author goes on to review the major discussion points on the question, in both church and society.]

What all of this comes down to, of course, is simply the question of whether women, especially wives and mothers, are equal to (though different from) or subordinate to men. Are they to develop their own lives and interests or are they to be *only* helpmeets for their husbands? May a married woman demand that her abilities and talents be used to the same degree her husband's are? May a mother who is a gifted scientist use that gift as fully as a man would? May a woman disagree with her husband and refuse to do what he asks (or demands) if she has good reason to think he is wrong? And here is where we get to those sticky Pauline texts: I Corinthians 14:34-35, "Let women keep silence in the churches . . ." and Ephesians 5:22, "Wives, be subject to your husbands, as to the Lord."

Oddly enough, the feelings of frustration among Christian women are largely the result of our failure to be consistent in applying these texts. Our grandmothers had no complaints about their place in society or in the church because they had never been led to expect anything other than a subordinate role. Younger generations have had a quite different experience. Not only do our political beliefs conflict with the concept of keeping almost half a population subordinate to the other half, but education, even in Christian schools, churches, and colleges, is ambiguous about women's role.

Any psychologist would tell us that if we expect subordination and subjection from women after marriage, we must not praise and reward them for being superior and self-assertive before marriage. Yet this is exactly what we do. All through school, girls are encouraged to compete with boys and win. We are not at all abashed if our daughter is valedictorian of her high school class or if, as editor of the school paper or class president, she is in a position to give orders to male contemporaries. But suddenly, upon leaving school, all that is changed. In high school, she may be chairman of a committee of which her future husband is a member; in college she may sit on committees that determine some matters for the entire college population, including males; but in middle age she may not even hold a seat on, much less be chairman of, the Christian school board that controls her children's education. At twenty, she may debate with her professor and prove him wrong, and he will (at least sometimes) be pleased; at forty, she may never prove any man wrong in an argument, and if she does, he'll certainly describe her as something other than "brilliant." She is rewarded and praised and encouraged when she does original and creative thinking in college; when her original thought leads her to disagree with her husband, she must "be subject to" him. She is told to develop her talents, to seek intellectual stimulation, in college; when her husband finds himself lonesome because she is out listening to music or discussing books, she must stay home to keep him company. It matters not that she may be better educated, better informed, or more objective than he; in a pinch, his decision must be her guide. . . .

There is a more important issue here than just what a couple should do when they reach an impasse. Such impasses seldom occur between two reasonable and reasonably loving people. What does occur, every day in every marriage, is the problem of who makes which decisions. I know of not a single marriage in which the husband is actually the ultimate authority in all areas. Contemporary marriages, it seems to me, exist by a division of responsibility for decision-making — the husband making those involving the car, the investment of money, and the children's education, for example; the wife those about furniture, food expenditures, and the children's social life. Why we refuse to recognize this fact and go on insisting that husbands must be the ultimate authority in all areas, I cannot imagine.

In other matters, too, our practice is clearly in conflict with our profession. If "Let women keep silence in the churches" is taken to mean that a woman cannot be an elder, for example, it should also surely mean that she cannot vote for elder. Women are permitted to teach Sunday School, but not catechism, a peculiar distinction to make under the authority of the command to "keep silence." Women may not preach — even permitting one to read the Bible from the pulpit brings unfavorable comment — yet they may, apparently, write articles telling us what they think Scripture says about thus and so and get them published in official church papers. Sometimes we take "in the churches" to mean "in the organized church program," as in our refusal to have women deacons or synodical delegates; sometimes we take it to mean "in the worship service," as when we let women speak at a congregational meeting or at the mission society but not in the service. And sometimes I suspect we extend it to mean that women should keep still about spiritual matters whenever men are present, as when we invariably ask a man to open with prayer at any meeting where both men and women are present.

I think that what really happens is that whenever we are faced with a challenge to tradition and a demand for change, we pull out our Pauline verses to support the *status quo,* regardless of the real intent of the text.

Whatever the theologians decide these texts must mean, however we interpret them, we have some hard analysis to do if we are to be fair to women. Besides being a vast waste of money and talent, it is unfair and cruel to encourage girls to develop talents and abilities and needs for intellectual and artistic stimulation, and then brusquely relegate them to their "place in the home" as soon as they have babies. It is amazing that a father will put out thousands of dollars for his daughter's college education and then be upset when she insists on continuing in the profession she prepared for. It is almost incredible, for example, that my own church, the Christian Reformed, subsidizes more than 1500 female students at Calvin College to develop to the highest possible level their creative and critical and spiritual capacities, and then expects them quietly to subordinate themselves to men the rest of their lives.

I believe that if we wish to avoid having more and more troubled women and, as a result, more and more conflict-ridden marriages, we must get busy. We must do some careful analysis of the biblical evidence to make sure it really does imply the rather sweeping things about women that we have always thought it does. (I rather suspect the first result of such a re-evaluation will be a demand that we stop being so suspicious of unmarried people.) If, after our analysis, we accept all or some of the traditional statements about women's role, we must restructure our churches and schools to bring the education of girls into line with what we really expect of them. If we decide that perhaps the biblical evidence for our beliefs about women is rather too scanty or too ambiguous to permit dogmatism, or that it does not support our traditional dogmas, we must stop putting pressure on women to be full-time homemakers, regardless of their needs and desires; we must open more opportunities for women to pursue challenging careers; and we must stop seeing women as inferiors or as adjuncts to their husbands and start treating them as individuals with valuable talents and ideas — people who can make important contributions in *all* areas of church and society.

Abortion: The Burden of Proof

Lewis B. Smedes   *July-August 1970*

With New York in the lead, the trend across the country is toward liberalized abortion laws. If the trend continues, the new laws are likely to embody the recommendations made almost a decade ago by the American Law Institute. This group of lawyers recommended that three grounds for abortion be permitted: the preservation of the mental and physical health of the mother, the conception of a child through rape or incest, and the prognosis of deformation in the child. The question is whether we will stop there. The Civil Liberties Union wants to get the law out of abortion altogether, leaving every woman free to decide for herself whether she shall carry a fetus to term. What should the Christian community say? Ought anyone to decide for herself whether she should keep or destroy a fetus?

As everyone knows, the entire question hinges on the status of the fetus. Is a fetus at any particular time a *thing?* Or is it from conception a *person?* If a fetus is a thing, the question of abortion and the law is a simple matter of whether to allow a woman to dispose of unwanted flesh. But no one is sure whether a fetus is a person or a thing at a given day on the calendar. And here is the rub. Who has the burden of proof, the pro-abortion or the anti-abortion people?

At some point in the muddled debate about abortion the burden of proof has gotten misplaced. In their gibes at theologians who used to think they could pinpoint the time when a fetus was invested with a soul, and thus became a human being, pro-abortionists seemed to suggest that our ignorance — or imprecision — about when a fetus becomes a person lent support to their position. It is as though one must now be able to prove that a fetus *is* a human being, at least in the (vaguely defined) earlier stages of pregnancy. A potential human being, it would seem, is not an actual human being. And therefore it is morally and therefore, of course, legally permissible to abort the existence of the fetus-thing.

But, of course, being a potential human being is not unique to a fetus. What about a newborn infant? What about a boy walking frightened to his first day at kindergarten? What about a young lady taking her college diploma? What about a brand new PhD? Are these all fully actualized human beings? Potential humanity is the best any of us can claim. And where is the line to be drawn? Does a fetus, at some miraculous moment, spring from sheer potentiality to potential-actual humanity?

We cannot say. We do not know. But we do know that when we abort a fetus we are destroying what no one has demonstrated and probably no one can demonstrate to be a mere thing. And since there is a constant mixture of potentiality and actuality in human life, ought we not to assume that this combination is present from its conception — unless it can be proved otherwise? And if it cannot be proved otherwise, have we a right to legalize the destruction of what we must assume to be human life?

Many old ways of marking the leap from fetus-status to child are unworkable, we agree. Viability — the ability of the fetus to live outside the womb — surely is an artificial construct; is a man who cannot live free from an iron lung less than human? Quickening — the moment when the mother first feels movement — is even less indicative of humanity; is a man in a coma less than human? But the fading away of clear-cut dates for the change from thingness to personhood only makes the pro-abortion case harder to maintain. The dynamic and unpredictable way that physical and spiritual life waxes and wanes between potentiality and actuality suggests a continuous line of humanity leading back to the moment of conception. Any other conclusion must be, and has not been, and can hardly be, proved.

Perhaps the crucial difference between a fetus and a child after birth is its visibility — and therefore a difference primarily in the eyes (and heart) of the beholder. We cannot see a fetus. We cannot hold it in our arms. We cannot feed it at our breast. And so we do not feel the same way about a fetus that we do about a visible child. Especially in the early stages, a pregnant woman can abort a child without ever sensing that it is real, her own real child. Abortion can then be in a class with our feelings about the death of a Chinese peasant, old and feeble, away off in some obscure village in the remote interior of China. We don't *feel* moved, offended, hurt, bereaved by his death; but our feelings have nothing at all to do with his right to live.

The current demand from many quarters for liberalized abortion laws is consistent with a violent, egotistical stance toward life. It is consistent with a demand for anxiety-free, tragedy-free, trouble-free existence. The movement for legalized abortion is consistent with the approval of legalized slavery; did not slavery rest on the assumption that slaves were *things* because less than human? Could it be that the pro-abortion movement, contrary to all the propaganda, is really a facet of the violence of our time? And ought the Christian community not insist on the *rights* of *all* people — including the unborn? At any rate, let it be clear that the anti-abortion people are pro-life.

We ought to add one more note. The Christian community may campaign for life in our present situation only in painful sensitivity to the insufferable offense to humanity that illegal abortion frequently causes. It may campaign for life, not in callous self-righteousness over against the pro-abortionists, but only in anxious acceptance of the priority of life over death. It may campaign for life only in sensitive love for those poor women whose pregnancy is either the result of or involves others in tragedy. Finally, it may campaign for life only as it keeps itself open to the unusual case, the extraordinary conflict, which, in view of the demands of love, as well as the dictates of law, oblige a parent to abort the pregnancy. All these things should be said. But, as its prevailing conviction, the Christian community ought, in my judgment, to be for life — and against abortion.

Navel Theology

James Daane   *March 1974*

A recent *Los Angeles Times* editorial presented a case for abortion that is widely held and thus worth a comment or two. The *Times* told its readers that the question of abortion should not be decided by government rule but by the free choice of the individual. The individual in mind here is of course the pregnant woman. But is a pregnant woman an individual? The term "individual" literally means "that which is not subject to division." On linguistic grounds alone, then, a person subject to abortion is not a mere individual.

But language can be debased, and people can play games with words. Biological fact is another matter. Biological truth will out, if given a nine-month, undisturbed chance. Allowed to take its course, nature will in due time present the noisy evidence that a pregnant woman is no mere individual.

In the English of the King James Version, a pregnant woman was a woman "with child." That phrase is loaded with biblical teaching about the nature of our humanity. It denies that humanity can be defined in terms of individualism. No person in biblical thought is a mere individual. Every person (regardless of the spatial distance between us) is a part of humanity, of the human race.

We can deny the truth of this. The unborn dead will not break silence to challenge us. We may attempt through the choice of abortion to destroy the evidence. But the evidence will not go away. Every bikini and hip-hugger puts the evidence on public display. Advocates of abortion by free individual choice apparently do not recognize the significance of what they see. In these days of black theology, political theology, ecological theology, someone should write a navel theology. It could say much about the nature of our humanity.

The argument for abortion on the ground of free individual choice is a phony argument. When our choices touch people, they are never merely individual, never free of consequences for others.

The pro-abortion forces have won a sudden and quick victory. Yesterday they had no chance. Today it is all over. They received some help from the Supreme Court, but nothing abetted their sudden triumph so much as the widely held and rarely challenged view of our society that individuality is the most characteristic feature of what it means to be human. No man, said John Donne, is an island. Most Americans think him wrong. And it is sad but true that large sectors of the American church endorse and even promote this individualistic but wholly unbiblical view of the nature of man. When the mind and heart of our society defines humanity in terms of the individual and then makes this the ground on which abortion is permissible if the pregnant woman so chooses, all that the word *humane* has meant in the past slips through our fingers.

Perhaps what we now need is a Christian Art Buchwald to relate our folly in the language of satire. Someone to explain why we still need Humane Societies to insure that animals will be treated properly. Someone to explain why a pregnant woman is free to choose to deny an unborn child the right to life, liberty, and the pursuit of happiness, but has no right, on pain of fine or jail, to be less than humane in her treatment of her dog. Such a satirist would remind us of Erasmus, who wrote *In Praise of Folly*. The Christian community would find such a writer hilarious and, God willing, an unofficial means of grace.

The Right-to-Life Amendment

Henry Stob   *March 1976*

In 1973 the Supreme Court of the United States made a far-reaching decision on abortion. It declared, among other things, that in the first three months of pregnancy a woman may legally seek, and a physician legally perform, an abortion on no other ground than that it is desired. This decision was applauded by many — not least by the radical wing of the women's liberation movement — but it startled and aggrieved many others, especially those whose consciences had been formed under the influence of the gospel.

What offended the latter — and what offends me — is that the decision fails to pay sufficient respect to the emerging human life which is present in the womb. Such life is precious and should not be terminated without due cause. The simple desire of the prospective mother (and father) to be rid of the fetus is not a sufficient reason to effect its destruction. Abortion "on demand" suffers from arbitrariness and is on this account morally unacceptable. There must be grounds for the "demand" before abortion can be ethically justified. The fetus, not being the "property" of the mother but a relatively independent being in the process of becoming human, may not be disposed of at will.

It is therefore understandable that, hard upon the court's decision, concerned citizens marshaled their forces in behalf of the fetus and set up Right-to-Life movements across the country. The movement has done much good. By way of education it has called attention to the sacredness of human life and to the legitimate claims upon protection that accrue to the innocent and defenseless. More than that, it has supplemented education with political action. It is currently sponsoring a Right-to-Life amendment to the US Constitution.

The amendment — introduced in Congress by Senator James

Buckley and Representative James Oberstein — provides for a definition and extension of the word "person" as this appears in the 5th and 14th Amendments of the Constitution. The proposal is that the word "person" shall henceforth be understood to denominate not only the post-partum individuals which the Supreme Court adjudged to be in the purview of the Constitution, but also all unborn embryos and fetuses "at every stage of their biological development" — presumably even at the point of conception.

I have observed that many fellow Christians with whom I sit around the communion table, some colleagues, and a significant number of the seminary students with whom I am still associated, are ardent supporters of this proposal. I regret that on this issue I find it hard to join their company.

My first difficulty arises out of the language game that my friends are playing. There is an established vocabulary in the area of genetics and obstetrics, but a revisionist tendency is undermining the linguistic establishment. In recent years the descriptive word "abortion" has too often and too quickly been taken as a synonym of the valuative word "murder." It is now proposed that the biological words "blastocyst," "embryo," and "fetus" be equated with the philosophical and theological word "person." I find this language shift too facile and not a little confusing. Analysis is impeded and issues are obscured when verbal conventions are unnecessarily violated. We normally speak in straightforward and understandable language. No one that I know is in the habit of saying that he had chicken for breakfast when it was an egg he ate; nor do any of my acquaintances declare that they have eaten sturgeon when it was caviar they had. It is also odd to say that squirrels bury oaks when it is acorns that they store. I think it similarly odd to call a fertilized ovum, simply as such, a veritable though microscopic person.

It is possible, even probable, that at least some supporters of the proposed constitutional amendment are not wanting by the use of the word "person" to make an ontological or theological judgment about the status of an embryo in the hierarchy of being, but only pragmatically attaching themselves to the existing language of the Constitution in order to secure for the embryo the legal status and protection accorded by our fundamental law to all individuals born of human parents. If this be the case, the move is not in itself an improper political maneuver, but it has a number of questionable scientific, social, and moral entailments.

As already indicated, the proposed amendment would legally oblige us to adopt the term "unborn person" to name a fertilized ovum even before implantation, i.e., before it meets one of the necessary (indispensable) conditions for ever becoming a baby or even an embryo. This is scientifically inadmissible.

The proposed amendment is socially unmanageable, for it would incorporate into the basic law of the land a religiously oriented view of man and his origins not shared by the general populace nor likely to be translated by it into behavioral patterns.

If the amendment is adopted and implemented by the states it would also have serious moral consequences. The amendment provides that "no unborn person shall be deprived of life by any person . . . except to prevent the death of the mother." This provision should by itself give pause to the Protestant and Roman Catholic sponsors of the amendment. Will Catholics now, in contravention of their ethical tradition, allow the fetus to die in order to save the life of the mother? And why should Protestants, in accordance with their ethical tradition, prefer to save the mother rather than the fetus? Must not the tradition at least be rethought, inasmuch as now the issue of death is between two persons, and one of them is innocent besides?

But there is more. If a fertilized ovum and no more is a person, and always to be so regarded, then a DNC performed by a physician upon a woman after criminal rape may itself be adjudged a criminal act, it being, or possibly being, the deliberate killing of an innocent person. It would appear, in addition, that backed by the amended Constitution, states would be able legally to proscribe the use of intra-uterine devices to prevent pregnancy, or punish a woman for taking a morning-after pill. This is hardly the sort of legislation which is to be recommended or authorized.

The proposed amendment, though well intentioned, carries too much unacceptable freight, and should not be adopted.

Sexism: A Random (House) Sampling

KATHRYN LINDSKOOG   *September 1975*

I am a random housekeeper who happens to keep a Random House Unabridged Dictionary open in my house for daily use. I was in love with my dictionary for seven years. It was my authority, my support, my helper, and my friend. Then one day I noticed it sneering at me. I wouldn't mind my dictionary sneering at me because I am an uncertain speller. But because I am female?

It all started the day I got interested in the cryptic little stories that show how words are used. There were six stories on page 929. Four were about men: "He became a monument in his own lifetime." "He certainly was in a mellow mood today." "The president tried to gauge the mood of the country before proposing the bill." "He was in a receptive mood." The other two were about women: "She was mooning about all day." "She spent the day mooning about her lost love." It sounded to me as if she were anemic.

Undaunted, I tried page 179. It told only three little stories: "He is thinking of opening another restaurant in the suburbs." "He refused to prepare for the exam but counted on being able to pick his roommate's brains" (the clever scoundrel). "She beat her brains out studying, but couldn't keep up with the rest of the class." This time I suspect that her trouble is low thyroid. Perhaps she could get a job as a waitress at his new restaurant in the suburbs.

The last page of short stories that I bothered to read straight through, page 1561, included seventeen different men: one unqualified for the presidency, Dante the master poet, one who felt unquiet and alone, Jack who never wore a hat, a man who disliked books, a multimillionaire who was unread, a brilliant literary critic ignorant of nuclear physics, a man whose scrawl was almost unreadable, one who was emotionally unready for success, one who found himself uneasy in awkward situations, one who dressed his unreal conclusions in rhetoric, one who lived in a world of unrealities, one whose dream of military glory was unrealizable, a general who was unreasoned by a devious plot, a man who was unreasonable, one who was Bohemian, and, finally, an unreflecting, self-satisfied man. No wonder their accomplishments were uneven; the words on that page all begin with *un-*. But every man sounded like an interesting individual. There was only one female account on that page: "The cackling of unquiet women."

I turned directly to the noun "woman" to see what better female stories it would tell. "There's not much of the woman about her." "The woman will be in to clean today." "Woman is fickle." (Would you want your son to marry one of those?) In contrast, the noun "man," meaning male, gave six cheerful accounts: "Be a man." "The army will make a man of you." "Now, now, my good man, please calm down." "Now that he has a business he is his own man." "After a refreshing nap he was again his own man." "He's been working that farm, man and boy, for more than 50 years."

On a hunch I turned to the word "uppity." There she was! Cleaning tools discarded, "The uppity dowager stared superciliously from her limousine." Now I ask you, would Random House have called an old duke uppity? They claim that "uppity" simply means "affecting an attitude of inflated self-esteem, haughty, snobbish." But I say their uppity had to be a woman. At this point I notice that "woman-hater" is a word in the dictionary and "man-hater" is not.

How about manpower and womanpower? It seems that men *exert* and women *endeavor.* Manpower is power supplied by the physical exertions of men; womanpower is power from the endeavors of women, as in "the utilization of womanpower during a great national emergency." So much for equal employment. I see that women's rights are "the rights claimed for women, equal to those of men, with respect to suffrage, property, professional fields, etc." I would compare this morally noncommittal definition with the one for men's rights, but there is no such entry.

It's good to know the distinctions between woman, female, and lady. Woman is the general term, as in "a woman nearing middle age." (That's a story in itself.) Female refers especially to sex and can be used in place of woman but sometimes has a contemptuous implication, as in "a strong-minded female." (Would "weak-minded woman" be less contemptuous?) Lady used to imply high status, as in "a highborn lady; the appearance of a lady," but now it is used courteously for any woman, as in "a scrub lady." Somehow I find these distinctions rather depressing.

Manly is used as a boy's name, and "manly" means having the qualities usually considered desirable in a man: strong, brave, honorable, resolute, and virile; possessing dignity, honesty, and directness. In contrast, womanly only means like or befitting a woman, as in "womanly decorum or modesty." It seems to me that the Random House antonyms for manly — servility, insincerity, and underhandedness — are the slimy underside of too much decorum and modesty. No wonder we don't name our girls Womanly.

The second pair of adjectives in this set is "manful" and "womanlike." "Manful" stresses courage, strength, and industry. "Womanlike" may express mild disapproval or disgust, as in "Womanlike, she (he) burst into tears." Not "Womanlike, she (he) worked courageously." The final pair of adjectives is "womanish" and "mannish." "Womanish" suggests weakness or effeminacy as in "womanish petulance." "Mannish" means resembling a man — fine so long as it modifies a boy. But applied to a woman it is derogatory, suggesting the aberrant possession of masculine characteristics. She's wrong if she does and she's wrong if she doesn't.

So "manly," "manful," and "mannish" are compliments for men and boys. "Womanlike" and "womanish" are insults for anyone, and "womanly" doesn't mean much. I guess that when a woman is strong, brave, honorable, and resolute, with dignity, honesty, and directness, we don't sum it up sexually as we do for men in manly; we have to spell it out.

Goodness knows it isn't the fault of Random House that adjectives mean what they mean. As editor Jess Stein stated in the preface, "In man's language is to be found the true mirror of man himself. His lexicon is an index to his ideas and passions, his inventions and achievements, his history and hopes. . . ." But for short stories I'm returning to Flannery O'Connor. She's a better writer anyway.

A Word of Thanks for a Friend

LEWIS B. SMEDES   *February 1972*

That Cal Bulthuis was for so long Managing Editor — and, too lately, Editor-in-Chief — of the *Journal* was never the key to our friendship. None of us on the staff knew him only as a colleague. Each of us, in his own way, had a friendship with Cal that went beyond the *Journal* associations. He and I were close friends when the editors of this *Journal* were still our teachers and, in their way, our private saints. And during these years when we worked together on the *Journal,* our friendship undergirded everything. So, while we all are going to hurt badly, journalistically, without him, what we are going to miss most is a good and gracious friend. . . . Today, the day before Christmas, the day Cal went to God, I hate death more than I have ever hated it in my life. Yet, my tears mostly spent, what I feel more strongly is an urge to thank God for the delicately indestructible gift of Cal's friendship.

We first met one morning on the front porch of Calvin College, where we used to go for a quick smoke between classes. It was right after World War II, and Cal was one of the matured GIs who crowded the campus those days. We happened to find ourselves standing next to each other, so we lit up and started some small talk. Somehow, I think, we both had a quick sense that we could understand each other. We became friends right away, to remain closest friends until today.

Cal had an uncommon grace for burden-bearing, and it won him an uncommonly large number of friends. How many people, through the years, have driven or walked over to the Bulthuis house whenever they had problems and hurts, we cannot guess. He was a kind of unappointed burden-sharer to most of his friends and colleagues. Many of them, as they read this, will rehearse their own debt to Cal's wise, and never judgmental, counsel.

Alvin Toffler *(Future Shock)* warns us that we shall have to be content with *ad hoc* friendships in the future. *Ad hoc* friendships are built on the transient projects and tasks that we share for a while with others: they are not built on human relations, but on job relations. In the mobile life of the future, no job or project will last long for anyone, and friendships based on them will last no longer. As we consume disposable products, we will increasingly have to settle for disposable friendships. This strikes me now as an unbearably sad thought. Will this really be the style for the future? Can there be no room for a Cal and Lew, Cal and Dirk, Cal and Henry, and all the other abiding relations that Cal created and sustained with real people apart from specific tasks? If not, I want to turn my back on the future.

Still, there may be something to it. Maybe the only place where real friendships will endure is within the Christian community. I cannot conceive of my friendship with Cal outside of a Christian context. Here was a person, a real person, who, quietly, through my times of sadness, insecurity, indecision, stupidity, and minor victories, was willing to digest all of my ambiguity within his own soul. Both of us assumed the Christian framework we live in; he always practiced it. . . . We were kept together by a power working inside each of us, a power not ours, and yet very much a part of us. Friendship is not the same as Christian love, I know. One loves people who are not his friends. Yet, friendship these days is getting harder and harder to keep alive through the years without the substratum of Christian love. If the futurists are right, the Christian community may be the last place where persons can be friends as persons.

But I suspect the pinch may be getting even tighter. For Christians too are victims of the new style of life; they are, as a whole, part of the "disposability" syndrome. I work presently among as fine a group of Christian people as can, I think, be found anywhere. But we all were shaped within differing traditions, come from very different spiritual experiences, and are thrown (or led) together mostly by vocational concerns. We "happen" to teach at the same school. Friendship for the most part is *ad hoc*. And it is hard to create something deeper. I am truly grateful for the friends I have come to have here. But there is a difference. What is it?

As I ask the question, an episode in my friendship with Cal springs to mind. In our college days, a group of us, students, took on ourselves to address our church broadside. We published a little booklet called *Youth Speaks on Calvinism.* Each of us wrote an essay in it that summoned the church to relevance and realism as we saw them. What strikes me now is that even then all of us, critical as we were of our church, made our pitch on the basis of an implicit commitment to that church. At the time, our booklet was something of a sensation. Those of us who wrote it took some minor bruises from the establishment. But to my knowledge not a single member of the group, to this day, has left the denomination for another. Most of us, in fact, are involved, in one way or another, in the ministry of the same church. What this tells me is that, maybe, the gift of friendship needs more than a common Christian commitment. As Christian people are swept up in the same cultural revolution that is changing the life-style of almost everybody, it may be that only in the context of a Christian subculture, a definable community where tradition and mission and life-perspective all merge into a communal experience, will authentic friendships be possible.

We had this, Cal and I. And so did several others who were his friends. . . . I cannot remember our talking much about our friendship. Nor did we talk about how our relationship was getting on. We would have felt clumsy had we moved away from just being friends, in our setting, and started introspecting on the friendship. I don't think either of us ever gave much thought to how we were relating to each other. I guess people need the sort of interpersonal analysis that goes on these days. The *ad hoc* character of friendships in our society leaves people's need for a secure friendship unsatisfied. So they have to keep asking and wondering about their relationships with people. But I thank the implicit background of common trust and understanding that our community gave us for the kind of secure friendship Cal gave to me.

Now that I have said this about our not talking about our friendship much, I remember our last days together and must take back some of what I just said. And I have to admit some regret mixed in with the very thing I am thankful for. We *did* talk about our friendship. During the three days I was with him, in the hospital, the week before he died, we told each other of our gratitude for each other. We wept together, and thanked God for what we had together. And we admitted that maybe we had held back too much on our emotions in times past, and maybe kept our friendship too implicit. I am immeasurably grateful for those last hours we had together, that our friendship on earth did not end without this intense, direct expression to each other. But it could have been different. Not every person is given the opportunity to face his own imminent death with clarity and profundity, as Cal did. And not every friend of such a man is given the privilege of sharing some of his last thoughts. Maybe we who have friends should not wait so long or take the chance. Maybe we should bring our friendship up to talking level now and then. Not very often, of course, and then with delicacy. But now and then it ought to be done. I know I would be very sorry now if I had not had this last opportunity to say to Cal that I loved him and thanked the Lord for his friendship to me.

I admit that my feelings are not pure gratitude. I want to fight this one out with God. I cannot understand why, and I deeply resent that a good man has to die at so unripe, so unseasonable a time. [Cal's wife] Joan will have to grope her way somehow into the discovery that God is nonetheless gracious. I and his other friends can find our infinitely easier way. I know that death is indiscriminate; it strikes down babies and stays away while some men grow very old. And many other men die in their prime. My own father died when he was barely thirty. None of us has a claim on life. Still, for all that, it makes no sense to me now, in Cal's case.

But what I feel most, just now, is not resentment at the loss, but gratitude for the gift. Now that I have written all these things down, I suspect my focus has not been clear. And I wish for profounder insights. But what I have been feeling is thankfulness. My wife and children aside, nothing seems to matter much right now next to this: I have had in my life a good friend. For that I want to say, Thanks be to God.

Confessions of an Ex-WASP

STANLEY WIERSMA   *April 1973*

Attending an organ program in a WASP church recently, I remembered that I had last been in that church as a college student, fresh from a farm in Iowa. A quarter of a century ago that vaulted ceiling and those gothic arches were to me the most noble architecture I could imagine. Because I knew the tradition of the church to be evangelical, the divided chancel with the candlesticks on the altar struck me as elegant and daring. The sound of the organ overwhelmed me and brought a tear to the eye. How civilized it seemed to sit next to a stained-glass window and hear such music! The memorial insets in the windows impressed me most of all: simple, prestigious names like *Hancock, Richards,* and *Worth.* A name like *Wiersma* would look all wrong on a pane like it. (For some time as a college student I considered what I might change my name to: *Wilder, Winston,* or simply *Wier.*)

But now I was again in the same church, and it all looked different. The Midwestern gothic was at once a pretentious and puny attempt to get the effect of Westminster Cathedral, which is neither pretentious nor puny. The divided chancel brought back dismal memories of the creeping episcopalitis of the Army's "General Protestant Service." (The more evangelical the tradition of the chaplain, I found, the more candles he is likely to burn, and the more likely he is to be addicted to the divided chancel; Catholic chaplains are content to burn a discreet pair of candles and are able to function comfortably when the chancel is not divided.) The sound of the organ had only loudness to recommend it; it lacked the brightness for Bach's "In Thee Is Gladness," which was being played. The memorial windows were expensive but ugly; I was comforted that a name like *Wiersma,* so awkward on the WASP ear, is a guarantee that no such monstrosity will be built in my memory.

Community   179

Stanley Wiersma

As I reflected afterward on my change of attitude toward that church interior, it occurred to me that I had also changed my ideas about the most significant controversy in my home church: *"De taal zaak."* The Middleburg Church in northwest Iowa went through "the language crisis" considerably after the rest of my Christian Reformed denomination. I remember when all the preaching and catechizing at Middleburg was done in Dutch, though equal time for Dutch and English began when I was in first grade and continued until I left for college in 1947. Not until the early fifties did English services replace Dutch ones.

So I remember very well the polarities of the debate as they revealed themselves in my parents' living room during after-service coffee with fellow Middleburgers. Translated into English from Dutch, the debates ran something like this:

> *Liberals:* We're not going to change our religion. Only the language of it.
> *Conservatives:* You can't change just the language. Our way of life and our religion will change too.
> *Liberals:* Then we must be open to the leading of the Spirit. He has led us here where the language is English.
> *Conservatives:* What you call the freedom of the Spirit is already bondage to the English tradition. First some English tunes before church, then some English words to the tunes during the service, then English Bibles, then English theology, and finally English order of service.
> *Liberals:* But how are we to exert an influence on the religion of America when we speak a foreign language?
> *Conservatives:* We influence the religion of America best when we preserve our own identity. What you call the freedom of the Spirit is following the path of least resistance, being conformed to the world. You are too lazy to assert yourself against a trend!
> *Liberals:* You're too lazy to learn English!

Conversations regularly involved some name-calling on both sides, but sooner or later the liberals would bring up the argument for which the conservatives had no answer:

> *Liberals*: Our children are speaking more English than Dutch. Soon, they will understand no Dutch at all. It is our covenant responsibility to translate our heritage into English.

And so the liberal side won, and they were right.

But issues are never simple, and the conservatives were right too. They had said, "You never change just the language," and no sooner had we dumped the Dutch Psalter than we were singing "Gracious Lord, Remember David" to the tune of Fanny Crosby's "All the Way My Savior Leads Me"; anyone who knows the tune for Psalm 132 in the Dutch Psalter does not see that change as progress. Yet the unquestioned assumption of the liberals was that anything Anglo-Saxon is better than anything Dutch. Incidentally, that assumption still operates in churches where hymnals clap shut whenever the minister announces one of the few translated Dutch psalms or, worse, where ministers never choose those psalms at all.

The assumption that anything Anglo-Saxon is better than anything Dutch worked its way out culturally as well as religiously. What perversity made our Dutch teachers insist that we learn "Ride a Cock-horse to Banbury Cross," when even they did not know what *cockhorse* and *Banbury Cross* meant? Would it not have been more sensible to teach us *"Schuitje varen, theetje drinken/Varen wij naar de Overtoom"*? But I did not learn *"Schuitje varen"* until a Fulbright year in Amsterdam, though it is as charming as anything in Mother Goose. Vondel and Da Costa were on our shelves at home, but we never read them; instead, our parents sent us off to college at considerable expense to themselves, and there we learned to read Milton and Cowper, English contemporaries to Vondel and Da Costa respectively. Even the sensible Dutch division of *Sinterklaasfeest* from *Kerstmis* gave way to the hodgepodge of the Anglo-American Christmas. The conservatives saw it all and no doubt wondered whether the word *free* in "home of the free" was to be glossed "free to be Anglo-Saxon."

Meanwhile, we winning liberals were losing our Dutchness and disguising ourselves as WASPs. Our victory was historical necessity more than superior argument, but no sooner did we see that we were winning than we forgot all the persuasive arguments on the losing side. Compromise gave way to caricature: "Those conservatives think Dutch is going to be the language spoken in the New Jerusalem." We liberals who accused the conservatives of absolutizing Dutch had ourselves already absolutized the Anglo-Saxonism of the American way. And so Middleburg rejected one provincialism in favor of another; Middleburg felt uncomfortable remaining creatively open-ended; and Middleburg is a microcosm of America.

In spite of being on the losing conservative side, the van Oordts and the vande Griends were really arguing in favor of an open-ended, free America. If English needs to be the language of business and education, they asked in effect, why cannot second languages and dialects be encouraged and taught as well? Is America really the land of the free? Or is it the land of the melting pot: everybody melted down under compulsion into a uniform mass of Anglo-Saxonism, and fake Anglo-Saxonism at that? The very arguments that Black Power has brought to the American consciousness with such urgency were first articulated for me by the conservative side of *"de taal zaak"* in the 1930s.

To be non-Anglo-Saxon in America is the same *kind* of handicap — though not as great a one — as being black or Catholic. America intimidates all her minorities into conformity to the Anglo-Saxon pattern. A decade of violence in our inner cities has dramatized the black man's frustration. He has given notice that, if he contributes to American civilization at all, it will be in his own style. He will simply be what three centuries of explicit and implicit slaveries have made him, and he refuses to subject himself to any more WASP discipline than serves his needs. Why does a black child need "Little Boy Blue" in order to be a complete American?

Black Power has given us all more courage to be ourselves. When I attended that WASP church a quarter of a century ago, wanting its elegance and hating my own Dutchness, I had a punier sense of what it means to be a Dutch American than I have now. Sitting in that WASP church now with — I confess it — a little contempt for its shabby pretentiousness, I have a prouder sense of what it means to be Dutch, and also a prouder sense of what it means to be an American pluralist. I can even tolerate a WASP, provided he knows his place as a fellow immigrant with the rest of us. Why, some of my best friends are WASPs.

Though English literature has become my specialty, I am doing my best to regard it as a foreign literature. I'm afraid that WASP prejudices made me choose it in the first place. Perhaps I would have been more honest — both to myself and to the plurality which is the noblest America — to have chosen Dutch literature as my specialty instead.

But language and literature were never the profoundest issue in *"de taal zaak."* The basic issue was the question of American freedom: Freedom to be ourselves or freedom to be Anglo-Saxon? And though the conservative side lost the battle of *"de taal zaak,"* that same side won the war on a parallel and vastly more important issue: When the liberal Anglo-Saxon mentality argued that education ought to be made religiously neutral, then the conservatives argued that education couldn't be neutralized religiously, no matter how hard you tried.

The National Union of Christian Schools would be unthinkable in England, and hence many people feel that the National Union is somehow out of step with the rest of Anglo-Saxon America. During that time when I so much admired the WASP church and all it stood for, I thought of my diploma from Western Christian High as a blemish, of that school itself as a symptom of un-Americanness, and of the National Union as a useless vestige of a Dutch past. All through high school I wondered why we bothered to fly the American flag on our schoolyard; my friends in public schools had called Christian schools un-American for so long that I believed them. But I know now that the National Union of Christian Schools is as American as Black Power.

The losing conservatives in *"de taal zaak"* should have argued their position with Black Power's urgency until our liberal consciences finally awoke. If even this more vigorous debate had failed, perhaps the conservatives should have marched in solemn procession to the Middleburg Church and set it on fire. If the conservatives had burned down the church and had gone to jail in the name of a more pluralistic America, and if a response of equal vigor had existed in Dutch communities elsewhere (and in Polish, Scandinavian, and Italian communities too, in every part of our land), perhaps we would be closer to a genuinely pluralistic America today. If conservatives had fought harder then for a pluralistic America, we might now find it easier to convince American society that it needs Black America and the National Union of Christian Schools.

The conservatives in *"de taal zaak"* cared, but they didn't care quite enough.

Babe Ruth and the National Pastime

JOHN J. TIMMERMAN   *July-August 1975*

During the first quarter of this century baseball was the national pas-
time in attendance, public interest, and consummate skill. Many think
it has been slipping ever since.

The game of sheer strategy, the John McGraw, New York Giants
type of game, is as dead as the baseball it was played with. Today a low-
scoring game is usually unintentional. The old game of a sharp single,
stolen base, well-executed bunt, and sacrifice fly, ensuring a one-run
lead which was made to hold up through superb fielding and tricky
pitching is almost obsolete. George Herman Ruth, who already as an
all-star pitcher with the Red Sox was blasting the dead ball over the lon-
gest fences, together with the cork-center ball changed the game permanently in the early 1920s. With the Yankees Ruth hit more and longer
home runs in a dozen years than any other player, with accompanying
batting averages from .300 to .393. The day of the classic, lean beauty of
the old game was over, and after 1920 not only Ruth but most of the bat-
ters were swinging for the stands. The old, tricky pitches were out-
lawed; attendance ballooned; and baseball entered its greatest age.

At the center of the dramatic revolution in the nature of baseball
was the raucous, illiterate, and superbly coordinated son of a German
saloonkeeper in Baltimore. A troublesome lad, he was at an early age
put into the care of St. Mary's Industrial School, where he was saved
from a sinister future by Brother Matthias — "THE GREATEST MAN I
ever knew," as Ruth said — who transformed the seedy boy from the
waterfront into a vividly exciting baseball player. The life of Ruth,
gaudy, uninhibited, and often vulgar, moving from indigence and bar-
keeping to national prominence, drawing bigger crowds than presidents and glamorous Hollywood stars, exalted into a hero by boyhood

America, is a saga in success and snuffed-out sunlight. He was cheered and hooted for twenty years, experiencing unparalleled acclaim and bitter frustration. He was the symbol of a dazzling era even when he stood at home plate in Yankee Stadium — sick, suffering, and near death — to receive a last tumultuous hurrah. Beaten down by cancer, he croakily mumbled thanks from his ravished throat, and then after hobbling to the dugout said to old friend Dugan, "I'm gone, Joe. I'm gone, Joe." A few days later he died. The famous number 3 uniform was retired, and baseball never saw his like again.

Mr. Robert W. Creamer, senior editor of *Sports Illustrated*, in his biography *Babe* (1974) has written a first-rate life about Ruth. It is a popular, unsentimental, and highly skilful narrative. Creamer effectively uses all the resources of biography: the meticulous statistics with which baseball is almost obsessively concerned, newspaper accounts, an enormous range of interviews, substantially accurate conversations, and the physical data of ball parks. In all the multifarious data, we never lose sight of Babe and the sharply etched portrait that is constantly emerging. There is little waste and little pointless repetition. The style is lively, fresh, and easy, and the character of Ruth becomes luminously alive.

Ruth was a character, an extraordinary human being in whom the purely physical reached an excellence and intensity seldom seen. His personality forces an ambivalence from admiration to disgust. At twenty, fame stoked his natural exhibitionism into flame for over a decade. Ruth did things with resonance. Everything about him was gargantuan: his size, which he constantly fueled with prodigious meals, beer, whisky, and interminable hot dogs; his pursuit of women in every American League port; his grotesque social ineptitude; his madcap driving; his mammoth home runs and the crowd-pleasing élan with which he struck out; even his proneness to injury and the exciting ritual of a dramatic exit from the stadium on a stretcher. . . .

The fact remains that no player ever did what Ruth did. For three years he was the best pitcher, or at least the best left-handed pitcher, in the American League. In 1916 he won twenty-three games, had nine shutouts, and the lowest earned run average in the league. He won twenty or more games a year for three years, but his overwhelmingly impressive batting turned him into an outfielder in 1920, when he was sold to the New York Yankees, in whose employ he accumulated the most astonishing batting record ever compiled in a similar span of years. It is wholly unlikely that any single player will duplicate his dual achievement.

Ruth's enormous appeal says something about American culture and human nature. He was the epitome of the Horatio Alger hero in his rise from rags to riches through pluck, industry, and ability, although he was no prim moral model as Ragged Dick and the other Alger heroes were. An unruly bartender's son rose from snitching beers to handing out hundred dollar tips to waitresses. He offered vicarious satisfaction to the man tied to a weaver's shuttle hour after hour. He was the day-dream come true of a home run in the last of the ninth with two out and the score tied. His uninhibited vulgarity tallied with the freewheeling morality of the era. Ruth meant power and Americans liked power. His geniality and largesse attracted people. He would autograph scorecards long after other players had wearied of it, and he would serve the little kids first; he never forgot St. Mary's Industrial School. He would put a five dollar tip on the table while Lou Gehrig sneaked in a dime. He seemed to justify the whole American inflation of sports. Finally, after the betrayal of the White Sox in the World Series, Ruth restored integrity to the game. Nobody doubted the validity of his swing. Finally, he gave his best to the game even when he was as taped and bruised as Mantle. Ruth never quit; he was mowed down by cancer.

Some are no doubt thinking, "But it's all just a game." Indeed it is, and I am not confusing it with much more important forms of effort and excellence. But what a game it was! A major league park was a happy place years ago with the flags streaming, the vivid green of nat-ural grass, the graceful, geometric design of the diamond, with its pre-cise chalk-white lines, the traditional and exacting ritual of the action. The hum and stir of the big crowd, the sense of steady action punctu-ated by sudden drama all made for pleasure. Many of us have happy memories of great plays. I have seen Ruth hit his long home runs, and I once saw Lefty Grove shut out the tremendous Yankees of 1928. I saw Detroit play when they had Cochrane, Gehringer, and a major league team. However, the best catch I ever saw occurred in a game at River-side oval in Paterson, when a centerfielder called Murphy ran at top speed into the farthest reaches of left-center field and caught the ball with his bare right hand. There were no important consequences; it was simply a marvelous piece of judgment and coordination as pleas-ing in its own way as a well-executed sonnet. There is something memorable about excellence wherever it occurs.

Cemetery

Jon Pott   *December 1974*

Like many farming communities, the one where I lived for several years as a boy, and where my father was minister of the only church, had its own small cemetery. I have always been touched by the place and have occasionally gone back to see it. The first — and perhaps the saddest — funeral I can remember was for a classmate killed by an auto and buried there.

Unlike some rural cemeteries, this one was not adjacent to the church. The living did not worship in the shadow of the dead — a contiguity I have always thought to have its own value as a reminder to the Christian of the seriousness and transitoriness of life and at the same time of his bond with those who have gone before.

The cemetery I knew stood apart, on a wooded knoll about a mile away, accessible by a single dirt road. Yet the relation between church and cemetery was profound and nearly complete. To my knowledge, all members of the church, except perhaps the very first, were buried on that knoll. And with few exceptions, only members of that church were buried there. In fact, I recall being disturbed when a young man in the community, whose family had become embittered with the church, was buried elsewhere, which I took to be vaguely symbolic of his apostasy. When one stood on that knoll and looked eastward toward the church — the two separated and yet very much connected by open fields — one had his own small picture of Christendom in both its parts. There, across the field, was the church still militant; here, that same church triumphant.

What this cemetery represented unforgettably was wholeness and solidarity, in itself and in its continuity with the ongoing community. Entire families are buried together there in family plots reaching back

Jon Pott

through several generations. But the ties go further than this. Like other Dutch settlements, the entire community had originally come across intact as a congregation from the Netherlands. And through its history, most of these various families had known each other intimately in life. They built barns together, they threshed grain together, they hunted together, they brought food to each other, they worshipped together. And to an extent that is hardly possible anymore, the communion of their worship together had its roots in the communion of their life and work together. The church functioned not only to promote the fellowship of the saints, but as much to recognize and express a fellowship already existing in the field.

The community has changed since I moved away some twenty years ago. The sons no longer automatically assume the farms of their fathers but move away or build ranch homes along the road and pay off the mortgage with jobs in neighboring towns. The parents have sold their land to outsiders and live out their lives in quiet retirement in the farmhouses they've been allowed to keep. And the old wooden church, though it still stands, has recently been abandoned in favor of a new structure without alarming problems in maintenance but also without history.

But the final blow to the provincial integrity I knew as a youth will come some time this month, when a new expressway is opened which cuts the community apart. In its course, it also slices between the cemetery and the church. For most people this thoroughfare will simply shorten the distance between cities. For me it will widen immeasurably the distance between the present and the past.

God With Us

R. DIRK JELLEMA   *December 1976*

Against the pattern of routine come shocks
Of miracles we'd thought were past, absurd —
Those speaking asses, waterspouting rocks
Are things we rather wish had not occurred:

The patient shepherds circling their flocks,
Called to see the child no father fathered,
Might understandably have been excused
(their sensibilities and ours infused)
If they had said they'd rather not be bothered.

But here again the miracle of birth,
The fatherhood of son, the living word
Among us lives. In birth we find his death,
In death discover birth, and every breath
Of every creature signals through the earth

His presence. This is the consequential hour,
This earth the place we keep; and in it lies
Our work, his love made real. We see his power,
God with us in the Christ-crossed skies.

There Were These Shepherds, Abiding . . .

Roderick Jellema   *January 1974*

Every Christmas morning I used to walk to church early through the squeaking snow, flapping my bathrobe behind on a hanger. I always had to be a shepherd in the Christmas play. Some of the good kids (mostly girls) were Angels, and a few kids who weren't afraid were Joseph and Mary and the innkeeper and Gabriel. The best thing I could shoot for was to be a Wise Man: the Wise Men got long shiny robes and turbans, like the man on the red and yellow coffee can. But you had to be almost as good all year in Sunday School to be a Wise Man as to be an Angel, so I always took my bathrobe to church and joined the shepherds.

We always felt funny at first, standing around the darkwood high-raftered church in our bathrobes. Some of us had canes, and that made us feel like old men on the porch of the hospital. We used to wear those flannel robes — soft plaids, usually, or runny colors, with silky braided cords around the middle, and they didn't look at all like the Bethlehem styles in the pictures. And they were always getting too short. But pretty soon, in all the confusion of trying to act like we were in the hills of Judea, we forgot that we were facing backward through the 14th Street Christian Reformed Church in Holland, Michigan. We forgot the parents and the older kids and the grandparents who were out there smiling and laughing.

The Christmas story is really simple. I always thought it would work best if we could just watch our sheep and talk like shepherds a while, and then see the star and the angels and walk to the stable to see the baby savior. But I guess it all happened in a more complicated way than that. We had to clatter off into the consistory room a few times while other things happened. I remember a long, polished table and very heavy books. Sometimes for a few minutes the Angels were out there with us, showing off a little and checking each other's wings.

Some of us had to say some lines that we had learned and practiced, and of course we all knew how to sing Christmas songs when the piano came in. In between we just had to make up things to say. Shepherd talk. And through it all we would lean on canes or pet our fake sheep or rub our hands over fake fires. We were told to keep looking up as though looking for something — though I don't think the *first* shepherds did that. But we shielded our eyes as though from the stars and scanned the horizon like sailors and looked up into the fat shafts of the gilt organ pipes that looked like Christmas-wrapped cigars with dove-holes in them.

We rubbed our hands and looked up and talked, and worked in the lines that some of us had learned.

1st shepherd: Well, it sure is cold!

2nd shepherd: Yeh.

3rd shepherd: I don't see anything yet.

1st shepherd: I mean, it's *really* cold!

4th shepherd: YEH!

2nd shepherd: We are nigh unto Bethlehem, the city of David, where the Messiah is to be born, that the Scriptures concerning him might be fulfilled.

3rd shepherd: How are your sheep doing?

1st shepherd: He shall be the consolation of Israel.

5th shepherd: Fine. How are *your* sheep doing?

3rd shepherd: He who was foretold of old. For. . . .

4th shepherd: I hope my sheep aren't getting too cold.

5th shepherd: Me too. Hark.

1st shepherd: Well, it sure does get cold here in Bethlehem of Ju—

5th shepherd: HARK!

. . . and in came Miss Velzinga on the piano with "While Shepherds Watched Their Flocks by Night," and we all sat down to match what the words said, All Seated on the Ground (which was maroon carpet), tugging bathrobes over our knees, singing. And then one of the few boy-Angels came with the Tidings of Great Joy and we scurried around looking Sore Afraid and all the Angels came in (some of them giggling to see us in our bathrobes), and the Angels sang two songs that we weren't supposed to sing with them. And then we filed off to the consistory room again.

But we got to come back at the end — to look at the Baby Jesus and Joseph and Mary and to kneel and bring gifts. The three Wise Men came with big fancy packages, wrapped by their mothers, but I didn't care much. They got to say only one line, all together — "We have seen his star in the east and have come to worship him" — while we got to talk it up a little before the piano cut in and got us all singing.

There is never actually anything in the box in front of Joseph and Mary except some straw. You can see that up close. Our church doesn't go much for images. But I remember when we were in third grade Lester Ver Steeg looked in carefully, drew back, and said *"Wow!"* very loud, and nobody laughed.

Mostly we would come into the quiet scene talking about how the Angels were *right*, here *was* this new baby, and we would set little gifts near the box. One year I had to bring him the wooden collection plate. I didn't feel right about it because there was a churchy, dark-red velvet bottom that reminded me of communion, and the plate was empty anyway. I didn't think Jesus would like it to play with. And once one of the shepherds, a first-grader, gave him a green car out of his bath-robe pocket. I thought Jesus would have liked it, but the teacher gave it back afterward and said it wasn't appropriate.

At the finish we always sang another song or two, right along with the others, and then we all got the box of candy and the orange from the teachers. Nobody clapped of course, because this was in church.

I used to wish that at the end we could mix in with the Angels and join hands for the last song — but maybe that's because I liked Ruthie, who was always an Angel. They kept us shepherds in our bathrobes mostly by ourselves, off to one side.

Christmas nights, after the presents and turkey and skating, with the Christmas voices of aunts and uncles going dim, I would try to think about it in bed, about being a shepherd. I knew that if I really worked at it I could switch to being an Angel. I wouldn't have to walk around as a public spectacle in my bathrobe. But I never did switch, and I'm glad now — not just because the Angels were mostly girls and sissies, but because they could only sing the same old songs, just tell-ing about what was going to happen and what was happening. The thing about us shepherds was, we were the ones the story happens to.

Maybe it's wrong, not wanting to be an Angel. When I was little,

Christmas nights, I used to worry about it. But I could never think it through because always on those nights, thinking about it, something warm and soft like cloth and starlight and distant singing would make me drowsy and drop me deep asleep. It was probably only carolers starting down State Street hill. It didn't matter who. I knew it was shepherds they sang to first.

PART III   1978-1990

By the end of the 1970s many Christian Reformed people had become so thoroughly enmeshed in North American society that denominational loyalty was but one piece of their identity, no longer its center. If that fulfilled an original *Journal* dream of engaging the outside world, the actual engagement made was not, so to speak, the parents' dream for their child. The birth of the Moral Majority in 1979 followed by Ronald Reagan's election to the presidency in 1980 signaled the triumph of the reactionary-nationalist, Sunbelt, and Pentecostal side of evangelicalism over the progressive Midwestern type that the *Journal* favored. The magazine's old defense of political activism against fundamentalist tendencies toward world-flight was now engaged for causes the *Journal* decried. From the grave or from retirement its founders might have been heard crying, "This is not what we meant at all!"

Accordingly, the *Journal* devoted a good deal of effort over the third phase of its career to coming to terms with the evangelical phenomenon. Strong leaders of Reformed conviction drew particular attention: J. Gresham Machen, a real — and apolitical — intellectual from the original fundamentalist wars; and Francis Schaeffer, a putative intellectual and real holy warrior (yet also a Machen descendant), from the current scene. The critique of Schaeffer printed here by (later a *Journal* editor) Ronald Wells, "Francis Schaeffer's Jeremiad," caused quite a stir in evangelical circles. The *Journal*'s range of tone and style broadened further in this era, and a good thing too, given the depths it had to plumb. The eminent American religious historian and *Journal* editor George Marsden caught the syndrome well: the '80s contretemps of assorted Bakkers, Falwells, Robertses, Swaggarts, and Schullers amounted to "Star Wars in Beulah Land."

Traditional *Journal* concerns persisted, now extended to new topics. More women appeared in its pages as writers, and more articles on gender by men and women alike. The dimensions and implications of ecological consciousness registered in some of the best quality writing that the *Journal* ever published. The level of book and movie reviews stayed high, and its range expanded. The injustices consequent upon apartheid and Zionism received more attention than ever. The successful conclusion finally reached in South Africa was witnessed in moving articles written by Allan Boesak and Leonard Sweetman; the Palestinians' plight remains unresolved and largely unremediated at this writing. The crisis and eventual demise of the Soviet Union was tracked especially by *Journal* editor and Calvin College English professor Edward Ericson, Jr., an authority on Aleksandr Solzhenitsyn and the magazine's house conservative. Non-Reformed interlocutors found their way into its pages, as represented by essays from Anabaptist historian James Juhnke and eminent Methodist theologian Stanley Hauerwas.

Through it all, a theme that had been present but often underplayed from the start of the *Reformed Journal* emerged more boldly — a frank confessional tone of spiritual encounter. It is evident in Nicholas Wolterstorff's recounting of a conversation he had with an exiled Palestinian bishop, in Roy Anker's review of *Tender Mercies*, in Richard Mouw's "Prayer to Mary," and in what only can be described as a conversion narrative in Howard Rienstra's encounter with impending death, vividly captured in "Who's in Control?" All these writers were for long stretches Calvin College faculty members, a species notably wary of religious effusions. Perhaps this registered the mood of the times (Oprah went national in 1986), perhaps a recovery of old Dutch piety, perhaps even some evangelical influence. Or perhaps, as the brilliant concluding story by Hungarian-American writer Lawrence Dorr would have it, it spells an essential trait of the faith — Reformed, but finally Christian.

Au Revoir

MARLIN VAN ELDEREN   *October 1982*

"Let us not be daintie of leave-taking," says Malcolm to Donalbain in one of those charming and memorable lines from Shakespeare's *Macbeth* that stick ever after in the mind of the high school English student. Extended farewells are like the conclusion of Rossini's *William Tell* overture.

With such cautions to mute my expressions of regret, I am this month terminating a regular association with the *Reformed Journal* which dates back to the early 1970s. In October I shall be assuming the editorship of *One World*, the monthly magazine of the World Council of Churches in Geneva.

The *Journal* will continue to thrive, I believe, because and as long as it continues to tap a rich vein of dedicated volunteers. From the publisher who subsidizes it to the writers who are willing to see their hours of work paid for by intangibles, from the editors who steal hours from more-than-full-time jobs to review manuscripts to the subscribers who are loyal enough to take seriously a magazine whose circulation is as small as that of the *Journal* — the 31-odd years of this periodical have been more a saga of conviction and commitment than a publishing success story.

Yet it is not too much to say that the *Journal* has thrived. To be sure, the "profile" of the readers to whom the magazine speaks now is not the same as that of the readers whom Harry Boer, Jim Daane, George Stob, Henry Stob, and the late Henry Zylstra wanted primarily to reach in the winter of 1951. On the surface, the "big issues" have changed, too. But the pledge which the editors made in that first issue remains firm: ". . . as servants of Christ and of his church, we shall endeavor in all our writing to serve the church and her communion. . . . It is our resolve to write with the honesty, courage, and love that serve the well-being of the church."

My sincere hope and conviction is that, in leaving the editorship of the *Journal*, I shall not be abandoning my own identification with those words of resolution.

Editing even a small periodical like the *Reformed Journal* is an endless sequence of relying on and being helped by other people. Leaving the editorship is thus an occasion mostly for deep and heartfelt gratitude. Readers will not, I trust, take it ill if here I single out for specific mention only three individuals from the numerous people who have made this work possible and even enjoyable over the years: Bill Eerdmans, whose support for the magazine as publisher is perhaps most eloquently attested by his insistence on not seeing an issue until it is published; the late Cal Bulthuis, my predecessor, during whose all-too-brief tenure as *Journal* editor I learned as much as I have from any teacher; and Jon Pott, the new editor-in-chief of the *Journal*, indispensable colleague and close friend.

A Tradition Unbroken

Jon Pott   *November 1982*

A magazine of sturdy Calvinist propriety has no business, it would seem, indulging in long public declarations of where it presumes to have been and where it hopes to go. Better to get on with the job and conduct one's self-examination discreetly behind the scenes. But perhaps at this point of quiet transition it would be useful to address a concern voiced by some readers who have been with us for a very long time.

The Reformed Journal began in 1951 with the pledge "to serve the church and her communion" and in doing so "to address itself, not only to ecclesiastical matters but as well to other things that belong to the scope of Christian life and thought." But if it is true that from the outset articles on Christian education, on the arts in the Christian community, and on the Christian's responsibility to the social order were positioned firmly beside essays on the policies and deliberations of the church, it is also true that the magazine then had a far more vivid denominational cast than it does today. The December index to the *Journal* for 1951 lists no fewer than five articles in the category "Synod of the Christian Reformed Church." And as if this weren't enough, an addendum to the category points the reader further to "Worldly Amusements" and (in the kind of primly fastidious wording that sets librarians aglow) to "Divorce, The Problem of." If the synodical delegate or any other theologically interested pastor or parishioner wanted help in sorting out the denominational issues for that year, he or she could count on a word from the *Journal* to embrace or rail against.

That this is no longer invariably the case seems to some a pity, even a kind of broken trust. But we believe that what has happened is less a break with tradition than a natural extension of it. Even our founding editors, having acknowledged what would be the "household character" of their magazine, went on to stress the importance of relating the issues it raised to the broader church: "We shall discuss them in the focus of our denominational experience, but we shall endeavor to do so in terms of the wider need and interests of the whole Church of Christ." If it was once possible, given the parochialism of our own denomination, not to insist too rigorously on meeting that idealistic standard, it would seem strange and irresponsible for us not to try to do so now, when our denomination itself has become more ecumenically aware and a number of our finest scholars are taking their place in discussions in the larger evangelical and mainline world.

"It is our conviction," wrote the founding editors, "that in the Reformed tradition we have a vital heritage to which our thinking must be oriented, and in terms of which our thinking must grow and become more dynamic." This conviction, we believe, remains today as firm as ever; but we also believe that our thinking and our heritage must be tested and tempered — perhaps more often than they once were — in the crucible of the broader church experience. We have things to say to the larger Calvinist and non-Calvinist world; we also have important things to learn, as historian Mark Noll eloquently insisted in these pages some months ago. So if this magazine in its basic character remains Reformed, it will also continue to welcome enthusiastically to its pages writers of other Christian perspectives. And if we address matters specifically facing the Christian Reformed Church, as we expect to do, we will also try to keep one eye steadily fixed beyond.

It is in this ecumenical spirit that we relinquish our colleague Marlin Van Elderen to the World Council of Churches, keenly aware of our loss but immensely pleased that he was chosen. It pleases us, too, that his name will continue to appear on our masthead as an editor and in our pages as often as he is able to contribute. Those close to this office know well that Marlin and I have long enjoyed a partnership that would be the envy of many people considerably more willing to emote about friendship than either of us has ever been. Marlin will understand if in tribute I offer simply a paraphrase of Dryden: "Words, once my stock, are wanting to commend, so fine an editor and so good a friend."

Like a Shot to the Heart

CORNELIUS PLANTINGA, JR.   *January 1988*

A friend recently told of hearing a sermon that began roughly like this: "Have you ever seen . . . a *train?* Have you ever *seen* a train? Have *you* ever . . . ?" And so on.

Because he was harried, or lazy, or merely unaware, this preacher had tried a greasy old recipe. You ask an outstandingly uninteresting question. Then, using a pattern of alternating emphases — the homilist's hamburger helper — you ask it repeatedly till you enrage all listeners not already numb.

Preachers err when they suppose such devices charm everybody but snobs. My grandfather was a devout farmer who loved the church and the things of faith. One Sunday noon he complained angrily of a sermon he found insulting. Jesus, the preacher assured the congregation, had healed a blind man: "He was *blind,* beloved! He could not see. His eyes were dark. Things were hard for him to spot. His optic nerves were shot. Blind, beloved!"

I know that a preacher can sabotage his own sermons in ways beyond meaningless repetition. Some sermons run on tangents to their texts. Many lack point or force, even if adorned with cute alliterations or blusteringly delivered. Some suffer from predictability more in concept than in language:

> A man was born two thousand years ago. He preached and worked miracles and went around doing good. But his followers abandoned him in the end, and when he went to his death he nearly despaired. But three days later an astonishing thing happened that changed the course of history. Perhaps by now you've guessed that . . .

Cornelius Plantinga, Jr.

Oddly, pretentious sermons often pack the same sedative power as humbler ones. In my own tradition, the three-points-and-a-poem variety has often appeared in the sort of heavy, Latinate language that rises to an almost genius level in its ability to fetch a yawn:

> The Prodigal Son: Three points, beloved, under the general heading, "Election of Guilty Sinners." First, election's predestinate origin in the eternal decree. Second, its forensic accentuation in the justification of sinners. Third, its vindication in eschatological glorification. First, then, its predestinate origin. . . .

Whatever happened to the *story*? Where's that heartbroken word *lost* ("My son was lost and is found again")? Why can't we see the *picture* of grace — a parent running out like some finishing sprinter, arms splayed, robe flapping, beard crushed against that familiar rebel who is sheepishly trying to recall his memorized confession?

Pulpit language undisciplined by apt reading, good models, and careful preparation tends to become flat or puffy. In either case it may suffer from terminal banality. Given how much preaching matters, the struggle for cure is worth trying.

My own reflections on pulpit language have recently had two sources. First, I've been noticing my own pastor's mastery of it. His sermons are lean and meaty, full of insights into Scripture and outsights onto human life. But what especially impresses is how much gets said in twenty minutes. The style is so efficient as to be almost epigrammatic.

Second, a few years ago I wrestled with an assignment to write a doctrine book for thirteen-year-olds. This is a difficult audience not only because their interest in, say, the Second Coming is typically mild, but also because an author cannot hope even to arouse interest unless he uses a particular voice. The language has to be right. On the one hand, theological jargon would be worse than useless, smothering whatever low fires got kindled. On the other hand, patronizing simplicity ("He was blind, beloved; he could not see") is just as insulting to teens as to grandfathers.

So where's the middle of the fairway? C. S. Lewis once said it exactly: "Any fool can write learned jargon; the test is the vernacular." And Lewis had in mind a certain sort of vernacular — the sort of artful, sparkling vernacular that, at least as he used it, never thinned down to routine prose. Lewis, in fact, passed his test of the vernacular so transcendently that his place as the best Christian writer of the twentieth century is probably forever secure. As nearly everyone knows, Lewis's vernacular could often be so tight, spare, and evocative that, like a change in a Mozart score, the replacement of only a few words would mean diminishment:

> Many people are deterred from seriously attempting Christian chastity because they think (before trying) that it is impossible. But when a thing has to be attempted, one must never think about possibility or impossibility. Faced with an optional question in an examination paper, one considers whether one can do it or not: faced with a compulsory question, one must do the best one can. . . .

The quoted passage is from *Mere Christianity* and was written for adults. But Lewis's children's literature is probably an even purer recording of this simple and yet redolent voice that at once instructs and delights:

> They say Aslan is on the move — perhaps has already landed.

> Aslan isn't *safe,* but he's good. He's good and terrible at the same time.

> "And now," said Aslan, "to business. I feel I am going to roar. You had better put your fingers in your ears."

Of course none of us who preach will ever be as good as Lewis. We are all Salieri to his Mozart. But we can learn from him and others. One of the most important lessons I myself learned from trying to write for teens is that the kind of language you want — Anglo-Saxon nouns, vivid, active verbs, sparing use of adjectives — is exactly the kind of language needed in the pulpit. Educated pulpit language is not that of *The New York Times Magazine;* it's the language of *The Wind in the Willows.*

After all, why (apart from length) are adults more interested in their preacher's children's sermons than in his regular ones? They are delighted by images instead of arguments, by plots instead of outlines, by crisp language instead of some other kind.

Thus two suggestions. First, all preachers should steep themselves in good children's literature (Lewis, Tolkien, Madeleine L'Engle, E. B. White, Kenneth Graham, A. A. Milne, Ursula Le Guin, Katherine Paterson, Paula Fox, etc.). The best children's literature has a quality of language that is equally potent for adults and that therefore transfers naturally to sermons. I mean, especially, a kind of deceptive simplicity. In between flat and puffy banality is the sort of simplicity that sets off depth charges in us.

You can often find it in music. As one of my friends likes to point out, the five-note descending motif in the slow movement of the Mozart *Clarinet Concerto* is eloquent not just because, harmonically and thematically, it is perfectly set up. The eloquence comes just as much from the sheer simplicity of the motif itself. There it is: just five notes going down a scale, and yet the notes seem to be struck "at a depth not of years, but of centuries."

In great children's literature one finds this same deceptive simplicity. The words look ordinary, and yet they are freighted. It's a simplicity of essence, of concentrate, of distillate. In a wonderful little book *(How to Read the Bible as Literature)*, Leland Ryken makes a similar observation about biblical poetry. For example, on God's care, the earnest, but uninspired, authors of the Westminster Confession instruct us thusly: "God the Creator of all things doth uphold, direct, dispose, and govern all creatures, actions, and things, from the greatest even to the least, by his wise and most holy providence. . . ." Inspired poets say this: "The Lord is my shepherd. I shall not want."

Second, where necessary, church councils ought to take quality control of their pulpits by writing a reading requirement into their preacher's job description. Then they ought to appoint a small, friendly committee (including, perhaps, a librarian and an English teacher) whose task is, twice a year, to furnish their preacher with a thoughtful list of recommended reading. Moreover, twice a year this committee would report to Council on the minister's conquests in the field of reading.

For preachers the test is always the vernacular. The supreme test is the dignified and deceptive vernacular — terse, spare, apparently simple, but cocked and loaded and ready to pierce the people of God like a shot to the heart.

Getting God's Joke [On Frederick Buechner]

Roy M. Anker   *December 1978*

This new book by clergyman-novelist Frederick Buechner is about the necessity of preaching from the guts. *Telling the Truth: The Gospel as Tragedy, Comedy, and Fairy Tale* sets forth the notion that for preaching to be preaching it need not be "what we ought to say about the Gospel" or "just what it would appear to be in the interests of the Gospel for us to say" (p. 7). A more useful wellspring for its doing lies in that deep and silent region of the self that shapes who we are as we encounter the world and the Word. It is Buechner's feeling, I suspect, that most pulpiteering, ensconced in moral niceties and ecclesiastical polity, never gets around to the messy facts of what it is like to live in a human skin, which is the place the gospel comes to.

Buechner's exposition passes over tips on three-point sermons and homiletic sideshows to dwell on what seems to be preaching's crucial task — how it can be the medium of grace, a flame for hope, courage, and charity. Much of Buechner's gospel-talk is not new or different, but Buechner puts it all together in one neat and compact place in adept, lively, and sensitive writing. In effect, Buechner wittily recites what he takes to be the gist of the gospel, and it amounts to a nice refresher or first-timer for would-be prophets and exegetes. His rendition follows the literary scheme summarized in the book's subtitle: the gospel as tragedy, comedy, and fairy tale. These imaginative modes indicate the central dramatic structure and narrative movement of biblical history. To say that the Bible contains, even relies on, what are now usually seen to be secular dramatic apparatuses does not demean or diminish its revelatory stature, though some conservative folk would contend that it does. We can venture that secular literature constitutes in fact only a footnote to the chief modes of Scripture's storytelling —

and not the other way around. We can also speculate that these narrative categories in Scripture can be seen as God's concession to meet his usually obtuse creatures where they hurt, rejoice, and dream. . . . Most of the time we live unaware of the very patterns Buechner spells out, and he should be congratulated for showing us their persistence throughout the Bible and in contemporary life. . . .

[Their worst shortcoming,] perhaps, is the failure of preachers to know people, including themselves, in their lostness, torpor, nakedness — as lecher, beater, cheater, and quisling. Before we can proclaim "this past-all-grasp God," we have to know the world the gospel comes to and how the gospel itself responds to our sorely ambiguous existence (p. 46). Good preaching points to the fact that the gospel's primary datum is that "the news is bad before it is good," showing forth our common and immense vulnerability; "stripping us naked is part of what preaching is about, the tragic part" (pp. 33, 31). Christ knew the question well, with Lazarus and with prostitutes and on the cross: "My God, where the Hell are you, meaning if thou art our Father who art in Heaven, be thou also our Father who art in Hell because Hell is where the action is . . . where I am and the cross is. It is where the pitiless storm is" (p. 39). This is, after all, a place of "human tragedy," where God "is often more conspicuous by his absence than by his presence," and where "men can at best see God only dimly and from afar" (p. 43). Preachers worth their breath should be "willing to appall and bless us with their tragic word — to speak out of the darkness and weep as Jesus wept because maybe only then can the reality of the other word become real to us . . . the divine comedy," from darkness to light (p. 47).

When Buechner does turn to treat comedy, he means it in the fundamental sense of happy endings and gut-busting laughter. Sarah: "laughing because she is pushing ninety-one hard and has just been told she is going to have a baby" (p. 49). David: "stripping down to his fig leaf and to the unmixed horror of his aristocratic wife dancing before the ark of the Lord because more than most he got the wonderful joke of it" (p. 57). Or Job, Jacob, Noah, Moses, the prophets — all looking a little like a hopeful Charlie Chaplin, after the pie in the face. Or the parables: "jokes about God in the sense that what they are essentially about is the outlandishness of a God who does impossible things with impossible people" (p. 66). After the tragic journey which we all sooner or later take and which "barely fails to swallow us up," then comes the "I will give you rest," which "breaks into their darkness, something so unexpected and preposterous and glad that they can only laugh at it in astonishment" (p. 57).

The gospel as fairy tale is here because the child's gullibility before fantasy is the closest approximation we have to the childlike credulity the gospel's "hilarious unexpectedness" demands of the believer (p. 61). There lies in fantasy as well the too neat resolutions and happy endings that evidence "our deep hunger for the wholeness that lies east of the sun and west of the moon" (p. 85).

What Buechner gives us in effect in this beguiling and forceful book is a rendition of the moment, shape, and texture of grace, a primer on how we might know the fire and the balm when we come across them. A Presbyterian (explaining in part his concern for preaching), Buechner displays a thoroughly Calvinistic rigor in his insistence on humankind's disposition to mess things up, the tendency to bend the self, others, and God to a tawdry perversion of God's intentions. As an antidote to this egoism, he posits always the unexpected and shadowy Agent who heals and makes anew. The result rips apart our palorous shroud, cracks the dark glass, and lights a new path with hope and love to some incredible and festive end. In recounting this movement, Buechner does no less than lay out the basic pattern of grace spelled out in Scripture . . . : "Sin and grace, absence and presence, tragedy and comedy, they divide the world between them and where they meet head on, the Gospel happens. Let the preacher preach the gospel of their preposterous meeting as the high, unbidden, hilarious thing it is" (p. 71).

On Being a Reformed Catholic

HOWARD G. HAGEMAN   *May 1978*

The other day there came to my desk a rather ambitious German volume entitled *Die Reformierten Kirchen der Welt*, containing historical and theological descriptions of Reformed Churches in Switzerland, the Netherlands, Scotland, Germany, France, Hungary, America, and various African countries. Much as I enjoyed the book, I was struck by one fact. In their theological descriptions of their churches very few of the authors had anything to say about their liturgical or sacramental life. In terms of the headlines of the Creed, theology stops with the coming of the Holy Spirit.

I am afraid that has been typical of Reformed theology for a long time. Liturgy, church, sacraments — these have not been very lively topics for discussion among us. In fact, from the days of the Reformation till the twentieth century one could almost count on the fingers of one hand the serious discussion of these questions by Reformed theologians. One of the most significant took place in the nineteenth century in the German Reformed Church in the USA. But even then the Mercersburg theologians, as they came to be known, were dismissed by Charles Hodge, that classic representative of Princeton orthodoxy, as "crypto-Romanists."

The strange thing is how sharply this neglect is in contrast with Reformed theology and practice in the sixteenth century. Who could look at Articles 27 through 35 of the Belgic Confession (virtually one-quarter of the whole document), or Questions 65 through 79 of the Heidelberg Catechism, and assert that church and sacraments were of little interest to our fathers in the faith? Who could read through the Palatine Liturgy (the companion of the Heidelberg Catechism and the direct ancestor of the Dutch liturgical forms) and maintain that the liturgical life and integrity of the congregation was a matter of no interest in Reformed tradition?

To be sure, between 1563 and the 1970s stretches a long period of Reformed pietism and Reformed scholastic orthodoxy, neither of which had much time for church, liturgy, or sacraments. I sometimes think that we are much more the creation of these later developments than we are of the Reformation. Certainly because of them it is not possible to go back to 1563 and pick up our tradition as though these developments had never taken place. But it ought to be possible to take the headlines which were developed in the early days of the Reformed Reformation and make them speak to the church in our part of the twentieth century.

I see some encouraging signs that the long-neglected Catholic side of our Reformed tradition has begun once again to be recognized. There seems to be an increasing awareness that the liturgical integrity of the congregation ought to be as much a concern as its theological integrity; indeed, that the liturgical integrity has far more to do with theological integrity than we have been willing to admit.

I should like to assert, at least for discussion, that the Reformed tradition may have come into the kingdom for just such a time as this. Given the theological inadequacy (to say nothing of the theological frivolity) of much of what has passed for liturgical renewal and creativity in the past decade or so, the Christian world could well be ready for a serious Reformed Catholicism. Long neglected it may be, but there is more in our tradition than most of us realize to argue that concern for church and ministry, liturgy and sacraments, is not the sole interest of Rome, Wittenberg, or Canterbury. Geneva and Heidelberg also have something significant to say.

Calvinist Links

RONALD A. WELLS   *October 1986*

Readers of this venerable journal have been treated over the years to Reformed comment and opinion on a wide variety of subjects. Our world-and-life view demands as much. Under the heading of sports, however, the record is somewhat thinner, excepting, of course, learned articles on "homo ludens" and the rhapsodic articles on baseball by John J. Timmerman. But to my knowledge no one has offered an explicit Calvinist commentary on baseball and golf. It is into this unaccountable gap that I would bunt and chip.

For nearly twenty years, this émigré from Calvinist New England has lived among the practical and hopeful people of the Midwest. My open loyalty to the Boston Red Sox has been ridiculed by the many fans of the Detroit Tigers and Chicago White Sox and by all three fans of the Chicago Cubs. This past summer I visited my family in Massachusetts, glad, among other things, to be with people who had their priorities straight. Moreover, since the Red Sox had led the American League for most of the season, my visit back home could be anticipated as one of celebration of the boys of Fenway, led by the great Clemens and the incomparable Boggs.

Soon after I arrived, I sensed a different spirit. An old friend replied to my "How about the Sox this year?" with "It's over." My feet not yet fully planted on New England's rocky soil, I misunderstood, and said, cautiously, "No, it's not quite over, they still have to win another thirty games." My friend gave that wan smile reserved for dealing with innocence, and sighed resignedly, "No, I mean they've lost it."

What was the cause of this pessimism? Why, our heroes had a sizeable lead (eight games then, though down to four games at this early September writing). The answer was not long in coming. The August 14 edition of the *Boston Globe* shocked even this resident of Calvinist Grand Rapids, because the front-page story on that day had the headline, "Is it Calvinism or Realism?" And, beneath the headline, pictures of no less than John Calvin and Babe Ruth (surely a first in the history of American journalism). The headline story discussed what most Bostonians seemed to believe — that the Red Sox would find a way to lose — and there remained only the task of explaining why. The presidents of Yale and Tufts universities offered differing explanations of the Sox's sure demise. Yale's A. Bartlett Giamatti (now, indeed, president of baseball's National League) saw the roots of this pessimism in New England's Calvinist theology. He pointed to the feeling of guilt about success, "that we must re-enact the Garden of Eden again and again." Further, Giamatti wrote, "there's a sense that things will turn out poorly no matter how hard we work. Somehow the Sox fulfill the notion that we live in a fallen world. It's as though we assume they're here to provide us with more pain."

Sol Gittleman, of Tufts University, agrees with Giamatti and everyone else that the Sox will fold, but disagrees that this dismal view has to do with Calvinism. Realism, he suggests, is the answer, because Sox fans know that their hopes have been dashed so many times. If it were Calvinism in the culture, asks Gittleman, why do Bostonians believe that the Celtics will win, as they usually do? The *Globe* went on to discuss whether the Red Sox are among the elect or the reprobate, and the article concluded with comments by C. Allyn Russell, a noted scholar of fundamentalist evangelicalism at Boston University. Russell, a theological Arminian, ended the argument by stating his firm belief in free will. The fate of the Red Sox was in the team's own hands and is not predestined; it's all a matter of more consistent play from shortstop, center field, and the bullpen.

As I came back to the Midwest, I wondered if the *Detroit Free Press* or the *Chicago Tribune* would ever discuss the Tigers, White Sox, or Cubs in such terms. Even in Calvinist Grand Rapids the analyses always seem to be Arminian. Calvinist theologians, please take note!

Comments on golf from a Calvinist viewpoint are also lacking among us — this all the more surprising given the number of clergy and theologians who play on Mondays. For this we must turn to another Eastern newspaper, the *New York Times*. Alistair Cooke wrote that, while golf is the national game of Calvinist Scotland, its origins are in the Calvinist Netherlands. The essentials of golf, and its terminology, are of Dutch origin: the mound from which one hits is a *tuitje* (tee); the hole is a *put;* the game itself *Het Kolven.* But the Dutch gave up the game in the 17th century when they saw where it was leading — "to paranoia and the paralysis of their empire."

The Scots picked up the game, but monarch James II saw that its popularity was diminishing the national defense. It seems that archery practice declined as golf's popularity rose. But the royal proscription of golf in Scotland was no more successful than royal attempts to ban the wearing of the kilt in the highlands and the speaking of the Gaelic language.

Cooke believes that golf is dear to the Scottish soul because it is "a method of self-torture, disguised as a game, which would entrap irreligious youth into the principles of what was to become known first as Calvinism, and then, through *het kolvenism,* as 'golf.' The main tenets of this faith are that life is grim and uncomfortable, and that human vanity cannot prevail." Is it any wonder, Cooke muses, that the symbol of the St. Andrews Golf Club — the Geneva of golf — is that of St. Andrew himself carrying the cross on which he was to be crucified at Patras? No golfer would think this a morbid symbol, because the golfer's credo is that "man should expect very little here below and strive to get it." Idealists, of course, never play golf, because who could imagine them sallying forth on a weekend afternoon to subject the ego publicly to the facts of life?

Humiliation is essential to golf, a game whose aim is, in Winston Churchill's memorable definition, "to hit a small ball into a smaller hole with weapons singularly ill-designed for the purpose." Nor is the human body designed to play golf. The swing involves sixty-four muscles in a continuous and subtle series of unnatural movements lasting all of two seconds. Cooke believes that the lure of golf "has to do with a unique brand of companionship possible only to a psychological type that unites the little boy aching to be king with the sensible adult who knows he'll never make it." Other games can be faked, but golf cannot. To play golf with friends is to enter a worldwide secret society that revels in the mutual display of human frailty.

During this past summer, your correspondent walked the links with the esteemed Editor of this journal, the Professor of American Religious History at Duke University Divinity School, the Director of Evangelism of the Christian Reformed Church, the Professor of Old Testament Languages at Calvin Theological Seminary, and my younger son. At the end of our rounds, we all knew vividly again what it meant to be a Calvinist.

Intimations

Jon Pott   *March 1988*

Consider three pictures, at first seemingly unconnected.

It is late winter, and you are a freshman at some college in the Midwest, though home is in California or Nova Scotia. Thanks to the distance, you haven't been back for the entire school year, except for Christmas. Spring break is too short for you to make the trip and you're eager for the coming summer. Truth to tell — though you might not tell the truth in broad daylight — you sometimes ache for home. Then summer finally comes and you do get home — only to find that two days into your homecoming all the warm atmosphere of your welcome has dissipated as your father blows up for the first time and your mother closes in with her first list of demands.

The more you reflect on your disillusionment, the more you realize that, in one way or another, this is what has always happened when you've gone away and returned — from summer camp, from weeklong vacations with teenage friends. Not only, as Thomas Wolfe said, can you not go home again; you never really could. Not to the home of your sweet imaginings.

Another sketch. You are a businessman travelling through a snowstorm from Grand Rapids to Chicago, alone and by train and thus not preoccupied with conversation or staying on the road. (If I make this trip, as I frequently do — Amtrak No. 371, "The Pere Marquette" — I happen to traverse the precise geography of my life, though not precisely in the right sequence.) As you glide over the countryside, you gaze vacantly out of the window. Suddenly, across a distant field, you spot an ancient, rusted haymower, the kind you knew as a boy on the farm but haven't seen or even thought of for forty years — and the recognition floods you with a vague melancholy yearning.

For what, you ask yourself. For all those years, surely, that are so swiftly receding into the past, like the telephone poles outside your window. But the pang goes deeper, and you realize that what saddens you is not just that the past is gone, but that what is gone, that world of forty years ago, seems somehow a world more innocent and idyllic than the hectic world you inhabit now, racing along to attend yet another meeting.

And then you reflect still further, and you are able in your mind's eye to see yourself as an eight-year-old boy trudging resolutely across this same snow-blown field, three muskrat traps slung manfully across your shoulder, imagining that each one-foot drift you encounter is six feet deep and that the barking of dogs in the distant barnyard is nothing less than the howl of a pack of wolves. Forty years ago, in other words, our intrepid dreamer, instead of enjoying his idyllic landscape, was in search of something else. The worlds we seek seem always to lie further on and deeper in.

A final scene — briefly. You are listening to music, and there comes a passage of such fresh and radiant loveliness — the second movement of Mozart's Third Violin Concerto will do — that it breaks your heart. Why such sadness at such joy?

The most eloquent and convincing description of all this that I know occurs in a famous sermon by C. S. Lewis:

> In speaking of this desire for our own far-off country, which we find in ourselves even now, I feel a certain shyness. I am almost committing an indecency. I am trying to rip open the inconsolable secret in each one of you — the secret which hurts so much that you take your revenge on it by calling it names like Nostalgia and Romanticism and Adolescence. . . . Wordsworth's expedient was to identify it with certain moments in his own past. But all this is a cheat. If Wordsworth had gone back to those moments in the past, he would not have found the thing itself but only the reminder of it; what he remembered would turn out to be itself a remembering. The books or music in which we thought the beauty was located will betray us if we trust to them; it was not in them, it only came through them, and what came through them was longing. These things — the beauty, the memory of our own past — are good images of what we really desire; but if they are mistaken for the thing itself they turn into dumb idols, breaking the hearts of their worshippers. For they

are not the thing itself; they are only the scent of a flower we have not found, the echo of a tune we have not heard, news from a country we have never yet visited.

The point, then, that links our three vignettes is this: we seem to be creatures of deep and ineffable yearnings which attach to one thing or another — whether home or art or the life of our dreams — which never fully satisfy but point us ever on. What we ultimately long for, says Lewis, is Glory, when the music we hear is no echo but the tune itself, when our hopeful trek across long fields is ended, and when we have arrived at last at our own true home.

He Leadeth Me

R. Dirk Jellema   *February 1980*

I guess I'm a Christian of little faith. Students come to me from time to time, flinty of eye, claiming that God has led them to this or that. One told me God had led him to believe that his Word was sufficient and it was up to me to convince him that the text in my literature course was worth reading. I chose the coward's way (not wishing to be pitted against God) and asked the youth why he needed his Physical Chemistry text.

Youth, of course, will be swerved. But lately I've heard from mature people whom I respect an easy access to God's leading that causes me to wonder. How do we know that it's God, not Satan, whose map we follow?

The first was one who had taken a job in a better area, closer to home, at higher pay, and among friends. "God led us here," he said, including his family. The second had wondered about leaving a job, decided that he'd leave it to the Lord: if he got a promotion, it would be God's way of telling him to stay; if not, he would leave. He got the promotion and stayed.

I like to ask God to lead me, too. I'd be happy if his wisdom would get around to recognizing the raise and promotion I could use. But the more serious I get about being led, the seamier the conditions into which he leads me. Unlike Gideon I've never thrown out a sheepskin, but an old 40% cashmere sweater did once follow the dewpoint exactly — and besides, the cats got at it. Signs ain't what they used to be in my neighborhood.

In his essay "Commencement Address," Milton Mayer warns his audience that while God works in mysterious ways, the devil is no fool; he comes at us in all the disguises of virtue. Mayer was, by my limited lights, accurate.

From what I can tell — and there's even a good deal of biblical evidence — the Lord seldom leads his children from a path of lesser advantage to one of greater, from a post of great sacrifice to one of great comfort. It's usually the other way around.

He doesn't ask us to be stupid, I think. Fools, clowns maybe, in his service; but not stupid. Those who are led to power and riches tend almost always to be absorbed in the system that perpetuates power and riches.

There should be something in the Beatitudes about those who get led up the ladder of success — that they should inherit the pollen, maybe. Or the whitewash concession.

Evangelicalism — A Fantasy

Lewis B. Smedes   *February 1980*

Among the "end-of-the-1970s" wrap-up articles filling the pages of periodicals a few months ago was one by Harold O. J. Brown in *Christianity Today*, called "The Church of the 1970s." What struck me about this piece was that, while it was about the 1970s, it was not at all about the church. What Brown talked about instead was something called evangelicalism. Maybe for Brown — and for others who see things the way he does — evangelicalism is the church. When he speaks of church divisions, for instance, he does not talk about a divided body; he talks about competing ism's: liberalism, conservatism, and of course evangelicalism. Belonging to a church comes down pretty much to espousing the right ism.

Evangelicalism, as Brown writes about it, is not just a system of evangelical beliefs. The ism is a kind of power structure. It has a hierarchy — somewhere — that can say to the faithful "Go" and expect them to go. There are evidently people in the top offices of evangelicalism that can depose leaders and excommunicate followers. No one has ever told me who these powerful folk are by name, though I have some hunches.

Francis Schaeffer knows, and he is not satisfied. Brown reports that Schaeffer, winding up one of his current rallies, calls his audience to a radical curial reform — including, "if necessary, even removing our leaders." He also wonders whether "evangelicalism can tolerate in its fellowship" people who will not condemn abortion. Schaeffer must then see evangelicalism as a kind of authoritarian church, which can remove leaders and decide no longer even to tolerate people "in its fellowship." Schaeffer is not alone. Brown says that the "inerrancy group" is "asking whether [evangelicalism] can tolerate within its leadership those who will not affirm inerrancy." Here, again, somebody must have power to determine the limits of evangelical tolerance for dissenters.

But leaving abortion and inerrancy to the side, let us focus on this image of evangelicalism as a kind of hierarchical church. How does it make its decisions? When does its quasi-papal curia meet? Where? Who gets to participate?

I can imagine a scenario. I see a grim theologian, in a vested pin-striped suit, armed with a bulging initialed briefcase heavy with the latest Carl Henry volumes, arriving alone at O'Hare Airport. Fighting his way past the Moonies, he joins a few other theologians, identically uniformed, at a hot dog stand. From there the small group is driven in a donated microbus to Wheaton, Illinois. After checking in at the desk and washing up, they are brought to evangelicalism's rented curial chamber in the local Holiday Inn, where about fifteen more members of the ruling circle are waiting.

After an opening litany the evangelical College of Cardinals begins to discuss, in alphabetical order, this year's doubtful leaders. The discussion is somber, frank, and manifestly painful for everyone. Finally, as things must, it comes to a vote. Each ballot has one name at the top, and two squares — one labeled "Tolerated," the other "Non-tolerated." The ballots are collected and counted, and only the names of the non-tolerated are announced. The secretary first declares — with a trace of unction — *"Non est tolerandus,"* and then gives the name of the fallen leader.

Their solemn work done, the cardinals bow for "a word of prayer," shake hands, wish each other God's blessing, pick up their briefcases, sign out, climb back into the shuttle bus to O'Hare, arriving in time to catch their flights back to their respective headquarters.

What will happen to the persons whose heads fall under the sharp-edged sword of evangelicalism's official *Non est tolerandus?* Will they be fired from their jobs at the seminary? Will their articles now always be rejected by *Christianity Today?* Will they be taken to court if they continue to use the word "evangelical" in resumes? I just don't know. I know what it used to mean for the church to excommunicate people: to bar them from the sacraments. But when evangelicalism excommunicates a person from its fellowship or removes him from leadership, the effects must be more subtle and more spiritual.

Evangelicalism as a power structure, with hierarchy and all, is probably a fantasy. I suspect that people like Brown tend to imagine the Christian enterprise in terms of a kind of political party in which people jockey for position and power — and to see this party as the real church. This is a dangerous fantasy because it leads evangelicals to act it out, and this means that they ignore the real church and invest their energy only in the quasi-church called evangelical*ism*. Such a portrait of the Body of Christ is illicit from the point of view of biblical Christianity.

Evangelical people need to be protected from evangelicalism and its hierarchy. Evangelical theology needs to be free from power plays called by party leaders. Evangelical theology needs to be the theology of and for the church. All the cracks in the earthen vessel notwithstanding, it is the church — and not an *ism* — which Jesus Christ founded to be the carrier of his great treasure. And it is in the church, not an ism, where the evangel, evangelists, and evangelicals find their true home. Evangelicalism is a fantasy — acted out perhaps, but still a fantasy. The church is still real.

Star Wars in Beulah Land

George M. Marsden   *April 1987*

Jimmy Swaggart, who knows a lot about entertainment, called it a soap opera. It was also a comedy. "The world is laughing at us," he observed. "I mean they are making fun of us and I don't blame them." Indeed, the script seemed to be something out of *Saturday Night Live.* Only weeks after Jim and Tammy Bakker had announced that Tammy was seeking rehabilitation from drug addiction (*Saturday Night Live* in fact suggested that the over-the-counter drug involved was Maybelline), Jim confessed to an illicit sexual encounter; but no sooner had he done this than he was blaming his troubles on a takeover attempt by Swaggart.

Oral Roberts, who during the winter had kept the readers of *Doonesbury* entertained with his claim that God had threatened him with death unless his supporters sent more money, was calling Bakker "a young prophet of God." Just at the same hour that Swaggart was denouncing his rivals, Roberts received his 1.3 million dollar check from the racetrack owner who said that Roberts should seek psychiatric help (which makes one think that Roberts is not the only one). Son Richard Roberts cheerily noted that they had intended to have the receiving of the check broadcast live the day before but that a thunderstorm had knocked out their TV transmission. This was a "technical" difficulty, Richard explained, thus avoiding the interpretation of both insurance companies and charismatics of such events as "acts of God." Meanwhile Swaggart, deploring both Roberts' fund-raising tactics ("We've got a dear brother perched up in a prayer tower telling people that if they don't send him money God is going to kill him") and Bakker's theme-park commercialism ("I am not in the waterslide business"),

George M. Marsden

concluded: "I'm ashamed. . . . The Gospel of Jesus Christ has never sunk to such a level as it is today."

In a way, the open warfare among the big-time evangelists might have been predicted just because of the way their ministries are structured. American evangelists have virtually ignored the organized churches and simply built their own empires. Their organization has been more or less like that of the medieval feudal system. Each evangelist has his own fiefdom in which he is the absolute ruler. Nominally, these domains are supposed to be allied as kindred parts of Christendom. In fact, however, they are competitors for loyalties and funds. From a more contemporary perspective, we might say that they are organized as big business in a free-enterprise system. They are turning over huge amounts of money (several of the biggest evangelists bring in over two million dollars per week) . . . so it is not surprising that there are fierce underlying animosities, takeover threats, and so forth. On the one hand these organizations are evangelistic agencies, on the other hand they are competitive businesses. The latter has been obvious enough to anyone who would look; now that side has been exposed in a particularly sordid way. Everyone involved is likely to be sullied. One of the wonderful ironies here is that Pat Robertson may prove to stand above the fray, having moved from evangelism to the cleaner field of politics!

In terms of American religious development these machinations reveal a more subtle trend than just the exposure of perennial human frailty, lust, and greed. Two ethics in big-time American evangelism are clashing. Jimmy Swaggart represents the old style of American revivalism. Unlike most other TV evangelists, he still preaches about sin. His ethic still sounds like the old 19th-century American evangelical ethic of austerity and discipline. To be a Christian one needs to give up some things, especially some of the indulgences of the flesh. The war on liquor has been an apt focus of this style of revivalism. . . . Although the individualism and oversimplifications of this style, as well as its compromises with commercialism, are hardly above criticism, the message does involve some rigor. Swaggart is a pentecostal, but he does not emphasize the crass exploitation of charismatic gifts and has been openly critical of evangelists such as Robertson, Roberts, and Bakker who claim "words of knowledge" from God and miraculous powers to control the weather and to perform healings at a distance, and who promise prosperity to anyone who contributes to their programs.

The new-style revivalism of these latter evangelists (and also the sinless Reformed style of Robert Schuller) reflects a typically 20th-century American ethic just as much as Swaggart's reflects the dominant 19th-century style. This is the ethic of consumption. While the discipline and rigor of the 19th-century Protestant work ethic was appropriate to an emerging industrial society, we now have a society that thrives on consumption. So through the 20th century the typical American value system has emphasized the importance of the self and of its satisfaction. Bakker, Robertson, Roberts, and Schuller all endorse this outlook. Sin has almost disappeared from their outlooks, except perhaps talk of the sins of liberals and secularists whom they deplore. No need to give up anything to be a Christian — the emphasis is on what you get. The culture of consumption emphasizes a therapeutic style in which ethical issues are questions about relationships and fulfillment rather than about rules. Grace is cheap and forgiveness is little more than good manners.

Within the evangelical world these two ethics have been quietly coexisting and competing for some time. Despite the revolutionary nature of the change involved, the two have seldom come into open conflict. Many evangelical, fundamentalist, and pentecostal groups manage to combine the two, preserving a few of the old rules of the ethics of austerity, but also reassuring their affluent congregations that almost unlimited consumption is simply a sign of God's blessing. Jerry Falwell represents this combination of the two ethics about as well as anyone. A noncharismatic, he has avoided some of the crasser commercialism of Bakker, Robertson, and Roberts; at the same time his gospel is entirely reassuring to the prosperous.

But while the two opposed ethics have usually blended more often than they have confronted each other directly, the Bakker case has brought the issues directly into the open. One important reason for this is that a denomination has been involved. Ordinarily, evangelists have been able to ignore their denominations, but in this case both Bakker and Swaggart happen to belong to the Assemblies of God. One of the classic pentecostal groups, the Assemblies is becoming one of the important denominations in America. Several generations ago, pentecostals were socially marginal in America. Now they are arriving. Often they are well-to-do, and they are beginning to get close to the centers of power. James Watt, former Secretary of the Interior, is a case in point. Although Pat Robertson is not a member of the Assemblies, the presidential bid of someone with views so similar to theirs suggests how far pentecostals have come in American life.

The question for the Assemblies is what will happen to them as they enter the mainstream of American life. They are a sect becoming a church. Swaggart represents at least a part of the old ethic of the days when they were still a sect; the lifestyle Bakker promoted (aside from the sexual indulgence) represents the new ethic of a culturally influential American church — that is, it is an ethic that challenges the dominant lifestyle of the culture only in superficial ways. In the Assemblies of God there are parties that stand for each of these outlooks, and no doubt some of the denomination's conservatives are more consistent and more mature than Swaggart on these issues. The Bakker case has exposed the conflict of these two ethics to public view. The question for the Assemblies, as they arrive as a significant force near the centers of American life, will be whether they are moving toward maturity or simply toward success. Most other American evangelicals should be asking themselves the same question.

Commemorating a Warrior
[On J. Gresham Machen]

Mark A. Noll   *January 1987*

January 1, 1987, marked the 50th anniversary of the death of J. Gresham Machen, the "scholarly fundamentalist" who founded Westminster Theological Seminary and who was the central figure in the beginning of the Orthodox Presbyterian Church. . . . From almost every angle, Machen's life was intriguing. An accomplished student of the New Testament, he produced books of technical scholarship (*The Origin of Paul's Religion* [1921] and *The Virgin Birth of Christ* [1930]) that were taken seriously by biblical scholars and theologians and read by both professionals and the laity. Even unbelievers like H. L. Mencken and Walter Lippmann respected Machen's efforts to defend the traditional Christian faith, especially his *Christianity and Liberalism* (1923) and *What Is Faith?* (1925). And although Machen had been an indifferent churchman as a young scholar, he eventually became a passionate advocate of a truly Presbyterian church, an advocacy which led to the creation of Westminster and the OPC.

By the standards of his life, however, the circumstances of Machen's death were decidedly incongruous. He died far from home in Bismarck, North Dakota, more than half a continent removed from his regular environs — the pulpits, classrooms, libraries, and hotels of New York, Philadelphia, Princeton, or his native Baltimore. Although he was suffering from a cold and knew that he was overextended, Machen had gone immediately at the end of the fall semester from teaching duties at Westminster to North Dakota (and its -20 degree temperatures). There, at the request of a minister friend, Machen was rallying support for the new denomination. Machen inspired intense loyalty among a wide circle of younger ministers and intense dislike from denominational opponents; yet he died in a city where almost no one knew who he was.

The incongruities were more than simply geographical. Machen was a determined champion of Reformed Protestantism, but he spent his last hours in a Catholic hospital. He was a dignified individual who had enjoyed inherited wealth, a superb classical education in America and Germany, and respect from the intellectual elite of the Northeast, but he succumbed while on a speaking tour to very small groups of people who probably did not have a firm grasp on the complicated ecclesiastical proceedings in the distant East.

Machen was a man of great physical energy (he had played a lot of tennis, and climbed in the Canadian Rockies during the summer of 1936), but he had come to North Dakota physically spent. An exhausting round of activities on behalf of the new denomination had taken its toll. Even in America, it still takes a lot of work to form a new denomination, especially if one insists, as Machen did, that the new group come up to Old World Presbyterian standards.

Even more enervating was the crushing strife among the separated Presbyterians. Only days before he left for North Dakota, the Independent Mission Board, which Machen himself had formed for the support of only those Presbyterian missionaries entirely faithful to the Westminster Confession, had ousted Machen as its head in favor of J. Oliver Buswell, president of Wheaton College. This meant that an agency which Machen hoped would promote a genuinely Reformed Presbyterianism was now captured by more separatistic and fundamentalistic Presbyterians who were also threatening to divide the infant denomination itself. (That division occurred later in 1937 with the formation of Carl McIntire's Bible Presbyterian Church as a split from the OPC.)

In one thing, however, Machen's last hours were fully consistent with his life. The story is told by members of Machen's family that a local minister stopped by his hospital room, perhaps not even knowing who was there, sometime immediately before his death. As it happens, this minister pastored a congregation of the Presbyterian Church of the United States of America, the denomination which had unfrocked Machen the preceding spring and from which the OPC had "come out" in June. The Sisters at the Bismarck hospital of course did not know what they were introducing into their patient's room. And so they were greatly surprised when, returning after a few minutes, they found the gravely ill Machen out of his bed, energetically upbraiding this minister for not fleeing the perils of liberalism in the Presbyterian church.

And so in one respect at least, Machen died as he had lived. Theological combat was his métier, theological combat of a very high order — combat informed by education, driven by piety, carefully articulated, almost never vindictive or spiteful — but combat still. The surviving young men who left the Northern Presbyterian church with Machen are now old men. Perhaps in the repose of retirement they sometimes wonder what was gained and lost by Machen's combativeness.

It is certain that Machen's biblical work kept alive a tradition of intelligent evangelical scholarship when the world was being sundered by liberal academics and fundamentalist anti-intellectuals. Just as certainly his defense of historic Calvinism was altogether laudatory, especially set against the great anthropocentricism of 20th-century America. In addition, Machen's willingness to invite Dutch and Scottish Calvinists, who seemed to fear Arminians and dispensationalists more than modernists, to join him at Westminster Seminary was far-sighted and broad-minded.

Viewed from other angles, however, the cost for Machen's combativeness was large. By reading controversies within Princeton Seminary, Presbyterian missions, and eventually the Presbyterian denomination as battles between two separate religions, "Christianity and liberalism," Machen undermined the effectiveness of those Reformed and evangelical individuals who chose to remain at Princeton Seminary, with the Presbyterian mission board, and in the Northern Presbyterian Church. By committing himself so strongly to *theological* and *ecclesiastical* combat, Machen left successors who were ill-equipped to deal with the more practical matters of evangelism, social outreach, and devotional nurture. By pursuing the virtues of confessional integrity, he opened the door to sectarian pettiness.

Future generations of Reformed Christians will want to continue reflecting on Machen and his influence. . . . A careful sifting of Machen's role in the early 20th century is a worthy task. Such study will not make it fully clear where in our day we should decide to fight and where we should decide to get along by going along, but it will show how important such decisions are.

Francis Schaeffer's Jeremiad

RONALD A. WELLS   *May 1982*

I first heard Francis Schaeffer lecture while I was a graduate student in Boston in the mid-1960s. He had not yet published anything of note, and I saw him plot his now-famous "line of despair" on the chalkboard. Hearing *Escape from Reason* in lecture form was a marvelously stimulating experience for those of us (perhaps pretentiously) styling ourselves as "a new generation of evangelicals." Schaeffer had been brought to Harvard and Boston by Harold O. J. Brown, then minister to students at Park Street Church, later professor of theology at Trinity Evangelical Divinity School. Brown had persuaded some well-endowed New England evangelicals to fund a "Christian Contemporary Thought" lecture series in which a leading Christian intellectual of evangelical commitment would be brought in for a week of lectures once a year. The first year was launched by the American university debut of Herman Dooyeweerd. Francis Schaeffer was the second year's lecturer. Now, nearly twenty years later, I see significance in that juxtaposition: Dooyeweerd the leader and path breaker, Schaeffer the follower and popularizer.

What Schaeffer has popularized in his successful publication campaign (nearly a million copies of his various books have now been sold) is a notion which at first hearing would seem like an academic nuance: *the antithesis*. . . . Readers familiar with Schaeffer's works already know the outline of the argument: humanism has become the dominant mode of thinking and acting in modern society; and in founding institutions on an anthropocentric world-view, society has effectively abolished truth. On this view, Schaeffer suggests the theocentric world-view of Christianity has been totally obliterated in nations like the USSR, where "humanism" is said to reign supreme.

228   *1978-1990*

The United States is almost a similarly totalitarian state because the basis for behavior and belief is similarly founded on a world-view which systematically excludes God-consciousness and upholds the "secular religion" that the world is "in reality" only material plus energy, shaped by impersonal chance. As Schaeffer said in one of his earlier books, "the gulf is fixed" between these two world-views, and therefore between the types of social and political institutions required by Christians and non-Christians. While Schaeffer realizes that most Christians already understand this in their purely "religious" lives, he encourages them to extend that understanding to all aspects of life.

Within this framework Schaeffer illustrates the depth to which modern society has fallen because of the "humanist religion." Given his prior interest in abortion it is unsurprising that many of the examples given have to do with the Supreme Court and "right to life" issues. But there are other areas of concern as well, most notably the place of Christian schools in secular society, and especially the teaching of evolution or creation in them and in the public schools. Readers might wonder if, on Schaeffer's view, the cause is not already lost. The answer is that it is almost lost to the dominance of humanism, but that victory might be snatched from the jaws of defeat if Christians were to act now. It is in this context that he lays out the Calvinist-Reformational notions of God-given law, and the responsibility of Christians to resist the state, to reform it, even to overthrow it if society diverges too far from the requirements set down in God's law.

*　　*　　*

Shifting now from description to analysis, we must ask if Schaeffer's characterizations of modern society and his remedies are to be accepted and followed. My answer to both is a qualified no. While I laud Schaeffer's attempt to encourage Christians to realize that ideas have consequences, and that religion is related to life, he has offered his work with such careless bombast and simplicity that it is very difficult to endorse his characterizations of modern society, much less the remedies he offers. . . . [It is especially important to] question Schaeffer on the meaning of humanism and on the meaning of America.

If humanism be the enemy, it would be helpful to delineate just what humanism is. Yet here is exactly the point: no historian will accept an ahistorical, propositional definition. This has been Schaeffer's

Ronald A. Wells

difficulty throughout his work, although most notable in *How Should We Then Live?* When "humanism" arose in the context of the Renaissance it offered a methodology by which persons could challenge "authority" in any realm of life. First artists, then literary critics, then historians, then theologians, and finally political thinkers used a method whereby they could rebel against the authority of the "medieval synthesis." Whether in art, literature, history, theology, or statecraft, persons acted "humanistically" if they asserted the right of private conscience over an authority which prescribed a way of doing things. (Schaefferites would do well to read Crane Brinton's *The Shaping of Modern Thought* on this point.)

The religious authorities in the sacral medieval society of Christendom realized what a threat "humanism" was. The church saw the potential danger of the freedom of conscience, and wondered where it would all lead. I suppose it has led to the sorry state of things which Schaeffer illustrates. So, what is my critique of Schaeffer? His confusion rests on his inability to see Protestantism as the religious form of Renaissance humanism. To be sure, Protestants *said* that their consciences were informed by the Bible, on which authority alone rested *("sola scriptura")*. Yet we all know of Protestant inability to agree on what the Bible said, or even on what kind of book it is.

In his triumphalism, Schaeffer cannot see the ironic and tragic in the Protestant movement, because he refuses to see it as an aspect of the humanist movement itself. In his various works Schaeffer repeatedly invokes the Reformation as the answer to the problem of humanism, when in reality it is part of the problem. I do not say that these religious humanists were "wrong" in invoking the primacy of private conscience, but I accept that when they did so they, among others, loosed a methodology on the world which results in modernity.

Schaeffer is half-right, but half-truths are sometimes more dangerous than falsehoods. What Schaeffer must come to grips with is the tragic and ironic entrapment of Protestantism's development at a time when a new methodology was developing for other reasons in other aspects of culture. He cannot have it both ways: he cannot lament the excesses of a methodology and at the same time offer a critique on the basis of the religious formulation of that methodology.

*   *   *

Throughout *A Christian Manifesto* Schaeffer implicitly endorses what historiographers call "the Whig theory of history." This view of history has had several incarnations, and the details vary, but in general it means that right religion and liberty are on the same side against wrong religion and tyranny. The Anglo-Saxon peoples are especially blessed in this regard, and it is the Protestant nations of northwest Europe and their overseas extensions which are cited as the righteous nations. . . . It is for the United States that the superlatives are reserved in this view of history, and Schaeffer seems to have swallowed the theory whole. . . .

As is well known, Calvinists came to the New World early in the seventeenth century. Winthrop's sermon, "The Model of Christian Charity," offers the interpretative paradigm for American history; the meaning of America was to consist in "building the city on the hill," in which the light to the Gentiles would shine, and in respect of which all would one day turn and be converted. With this model of early American development clearly in mind, Schaeffer turns to the American Revolution. True to the Whig theory, right religion and liberty were arrayed against wrong religion and tyranny. Schaeffer correctly notes the evangelical impetus behind the Revolution, and he endorses it. But should it be endorsed? As Nathan Hatch has written in *The Sacred Cause of Liberty*, many evangelicals did believe that there was a British conspiracy against liberty, especially after the passage of the Quebec Act in 1774. While we might have empathy for these evangelical revolutionaries in their context, surely they were deluded if they believed that an "absolute tyranny" was about to be imposed. . . . Surely the Americans acted on a pretentious view of themselves and their cause if they believed that they alone were protecting the right view of society.

As to the Declaration of Independence and the Constitution . . . Schaeffer's argument is substantially flawed by suggesting a moral-legal consensus among "the Founding Fathers." There were two sets of Founding Fathers, because there were two factions in the revolutionary party, advocating quite different visions of society. As John Adams said in writing the Massachusetts state constitution, the question was whether or not the government would be "a government of law or of men." While Adams clearly advocated "law," for Jefferson the meaning of America and of its revolution was that it would be "a government of men." It will come as no surprise that the one main sign of hope Schaeffer sees (an "open window," in his terms) is the present-day conservative successes in American politics. One of the founding principles of the neo-conservative faith is the doctrine of return to the principles of the Founding Fathers. What this simplistic view of past reality cannot accept is that the same divisions which bedevil our society were there then too. Nostalgia will not help us out of our present malaise, nor will rewriting American history.

*   *   *

In fact, Schaeffer's book stands in a long tradition of American history, and is a good example of a literary form which Sacvan Bercovitch calls "the jeremiad," in his brilliant book, *The American Jeremiad.* There is a long history of Calvinists preaching the doctrine of return to the vision of Winthrop. Already in the seventeenth century this form was well developed. The theme is familiar: the people had betrayed the faith, had fallen from grace, but there was still time to return and recapture the vision. This theme was reasserted in the Revolution, and at regular intervals throughout the nineteenth and twentieth centuries.

Schaeffer conforms to one important aspect of the genre of the latter-day jeremiad: the enemy within. All the vision that Schaeffer sees as "the base" of American society was founded by immigrants from Protestant countries. The story begins to turn wrong when substantial Catholic immigration begins in the 1840s. While he does not name the Irish specifically, he suggests that 1848 is a turning year, a year in which (of course) the migration from famine-ridden Ireland began. He returns to this theme in the conclusion. Here we have a vestigial remain of that virulent Protestant disease: Anglo-Saxon anti-Catholicism. I am appalled to see Francis Schaeffer appearing to endorse this. Surely a person like Schaeffer, who knows that ideas have consequences, must know that in endorsing such views he is endorsing by extension some of the most undemocratic acts of intolerance in American history, acts of which Protestants must be ashamed. It is too late to be nostalgic about an Anglo-Saxon America.

In the 1950s, when political and religious conservatism had its last revival, several scholars took note of it and some important books were written which give an analytical perspective on such conservatism in America. Richard Hofstadter wrote of "the paranoid style" in American history (neither Hofstadter, nor I in mentioning it, means to accuse anyone of the clinical phenomenon called paranoia). One nevertheless observes that there have been many movements — ideologically centered on evangelical Protestantism — which fit the typology of social paranoia. The argument proceeds as follows: the precious heritage is about to be lost, both because of the indifference of the brethren but also because of enemies within. While happily falling short of an accusation of "conspiracy" (which would have fit the paranoid style perfectly), Schaeffer nevertheless believes that institutions which specialize in the collection and dissemination of information (universities and the media) are in an informal league with the courts to foist the secular-humanist mind onto the American people.

I do not endorse American social behavior and belief as it is. As a committed Christian, I believe that my religious principles require me to assert that there is something quite wrong with American society. I share Francis Schaeffer's sense of urgency about matters as diverse as "right to life" and "the battle for the mind." Yet Schaeffer's outrage does not mention much at all about what I believe to be equally important questions, i.e., the arms race, institutional racism, the inequities of industrial capitalism. Schaeffer's outrage, and his willingness to be civilly disobedient, seems to be rather shallow in not taking these important matters into account.

Rather than "A Christian Manifesto" Schaeffer's book should have been called "A Fundamentalist Manifesto," because it bears all the marks of that unfortunate movement. Writing in this journal on the "new fundamentalism" (February 1982), George Marsden suggested, in a memorable phrase, that "the Moral Majority turns out to be something of Dooyeweerdianism gone to seed." If that be true, a reading of evangelical fundamentalism's leading thinker will help us to understand why. It is cruelly ironic that evangelicalism's philosopher, who spent so much time on "the antithesis," winds up a synthesizer after all. In this book we have a vintage blend of evangelical orthodoxy and the lore of one version of American history.

This is a bitter recognition for some of us who, fifteen years ago, thought that Francis Schaeffer was a leading light of a new movement in evangelicalism. With his atrophied view of "the antithesis" and his chauvinistic Americanism, Francis Schaeffer becomes less appealing the more he writes.

Francis A. Schaeffer (1912-1984)

GEORGE M. MARSDEN   *June 1984*

Once at an after-dinner session, when I visited L'Abri in the late 1960s, Francis Schaeffer offered to answer any questions students might have had after a week of listening to tapes of his lectures. One student, saying that he was in engineering and had not studied philosophy, observed that he was greatly helped by Schaeffer's expositions of Western thought, but that he could not quite understand Hegel yet. "So, could you explain Hegel?" were, I believe, his exact words. Schaeffer did not miss a beat. He did not hesitate, smile, or preface his reply by allowing that Hegel was a deep subject. He launched into his answer with a bold "Yes." Up until Hegel truth was a matter of antithesis. "A" could not be "not A." With Hegel truth in the Western world became a matter of synthesis. For the modern person, truth was no longer a question of one thing being right and its opposite wrong. Synthesis meant that the truth lay somewhere in the middle. So twentieth-century intellectuals no longer talked about absolute rights and wrongs.

This episode stayed with me as epitomizing both the strengths and the weaknesses of Schaeffer's ministry. Many Christian academic friends of mine have been so appalled by Schaeffer's cavalier digests of Western thought that they have wondered why anyone would give him serious attention. The fact that he has been touted, especially in recent years, as a great evangelical philosopher has added to their conviction that he was an intellectual fraud. Yet his two-minute summary of Hegel illustrates some important virtues as well. For one thing, Schaeffer had interested the young engineer in philosophy and its relation to Christianity, a feat that Christian academics often fail at, even with their captive audiences. Second, although what Schaeffer did was outrageous as an explanation of Hegel's philosophy, he was using Hegel plausibly as a symbol for an immensely important change in the structures of dominant Western thought during the past two centuries. As he often did in his writings, Schaeffer was penetrating to the heart of an issue, even if his account of the details fell short of any academic standards.

Most importantly, this whole conversation was taking place not in a classroom, but in an evangelistic setting. Francis Schaeffer was first of all an evangelist, one of the finest evangelists of his generation. Unlike most American evangelists, he took the trouble to learn a good bit about the history of Western thought and culture, and he explored, often with insight, the implications of that history for presenting the gospel message. He was not a philosopher, except perhaps in the way that Benjamin Franklin was a philosopher. But he did embody an important, if largely faded, tradition of the preacher cum amateur-philosopher who brought wide learning to bear on his message. So his combination of thought and fervor accomplished what few of his academically more sophisticated Reformed contemporaries did. In the 1960s he conducted at his Swiss mountain retreat a remarkable mission to many disillusioned young people of that era. The church continues to benefit from the ministries of many who were touched by his work.

Perhaps most importantly, Schaeffer's evangelism took place in the context of a vital Christian community where prayer and compassion were two outstanding traits. Schaeffer had begun his ministry under the aegis of Carl McIntire and into the early 1950s had been one of the spokespersons for McIntire's polemical message of ecclesiastical separatism, anti-Romanism, and anti-Communism. Gradually, however, he became alienated from the mean tone and tactics of the McIntire style, and finally he helped lead the break from McIntire that brought about the Evangelical Presbyterian Church (eventually part of the Presbyterian Church of America). His writings condemned "ugly orthodoxy," and in his last book he acknowledged that bitter attacks on fellow Christians in those polemical days had left scars for generations. At L'Abri the benefits of these lessons were manifested. There the power of Christian love and community was evident. Schaeffer, his wife Edith, and those who worked with them were willing to take sinners seriously, to listen to them without immediate condemnation, to present the radical demands of the gospel firmly but with compassion for individuals.

George M. Marsden

One of the ironies of Schaeffer's career was that during his last de-cade this compassionate work with individuals at the L'Abri commu-nity was subordinated to the bright lights of slick media productions and promotions. At the same time his message became more and more oriented toward the Moral Majority, a constituency among whom he now found his most enthusiastic receptions. Whereas in the 1960s he had stressed those elements of his message that coincided with coun-terculture critiques of the emptiness of technological society and middle-class lifestyles, now he sounded themes that resonated best with the political right.

Even so, Schaeffer provided some important qualifications to the self-serving middle-class-first superpatriotism that characterizes some of Christian political conservatism. His influence in that community has unquestionably been a healthy one, and we can only hope it will not be immediately vitiated by imitators who lack both his theological sensitivities and his loving character. Francis Schaeffer always lived close to controversy; often he precipitated it. Nonetheless, he was a man of high principle who was willing to follow those principles wherever they led. He was unpredictable just because his vision was so broad. Though he was a partisan, he also found that the gospel did not point exactly the ways that any one party among twentieth-century Christians advocated. Especially he found that true spiritual-ity demands charity toward each person God has made, whether an ecclesiastical opponent or a down-and-out sinner. Even those who may not agree with all the distinctives of Schaeffer's message can learn from his life and ministry.

With Jews in a Hot Tub

Ronald A. Wells   *January 1981*

I had been on the verge of writing a letter of resignation from the evangelical movement, but now that I have discovered a special identity in it, I will not resign. So upset have I been with the political activism of the Moral Majority and their kind that I wanted to make some public gesture of disassociation of myself from them. But to whom would I resign — to someone like Harold Lindsell, the self-appointed arbiter of the movement?

Inactive in my dilemma, I was delighted to see a resolution when the November issue of *Eternity* magazine reached me. In surveying evangelical intellectuals, an article there touched on many institutions, publications, and persons. I was delighted to see that the college at which I teach, the journal I edit, and the publisher of my books were given favorable mention. A particularly incisive and delightful paragraph read as follows:

> Christian Reformed people, concentrated in Michigan, function as our Jews: they tend to be bright, well-educated, and self-confident. They are ethnic, affluent, a bit clannish, and prolific. Indeed, *The Reformed Journal*, with a modest circulation of 3100, is the closest to a hot tub available for the intellectually inclined evangelicals.

At last I know where I stand — or sit. With this evangelical identity, I now have no need to resign from the movement. Having been raised in a largely Jewish town (Brookline, Massachusetts), I take it to be a great compliment to be likened to the Jews, a people for whom both education and theological literacy are important. I am not always pleased by the clannishness of the Dutch Reformed community, but I realize that the solidarity of the community affords a framework in which good thinking, teaching, and writing are valued.

Still, if evangelicals think we are necessary and even to be respected, we want them to know that we can exist in their movement only on its fringes, more often an embarrassment than an asset. I have heard some evangelical leaders wonder if Calvin College, *The Reformed Journal*, etc. are "evangelical." Well — perhaps. Never quite adversaries, we are never quite allies either.

Whether or not this journal is a "hot tub" for evangelicals I cannot judge. If it be true, I can say only that it offers a pleasurable experience, almost addictive. But evangelicals should realize that if they choose to plunge in with us, they may see and experience things for which their personal histories have not prepared them.

Does God Listen to Girls?
Women in Society and the Church

MARY STEWART VAN LEEUWEN   *June 1986*

When it comes to accepting women as leaders, evangelical churches
and parachurch organizations have historically spanned the entire
range of attitudes from hostility through indifference to enthusiastic
endorsement. Each of these groups has had its preferred hermeneutic
and favorite biblical proof-texts to support its position. But in their
roles as ordinary citizens, workers, and consumers, Christians are no
longer permitted the luxury of choosing from such a wide range of re-
actions towards the idea of women in leadership. Like it or not, they
are having to deal with women in positions of power and authority
rarely dreamed of a decade or so ago. As a result of changing legislation and changing cultural attitudes, women are more and more likely
to be found practicing law or medicine, assuming executive positions
in corporations, presiding over school boards and city councils, doing
research in universities, training to become military officers and astro-
nauts, and even running as vice-presidential candidates.

Such examples, taken from the more publicized range of middle-
and upper-middle-class jobs, represent only the tip of a much larger
iceberg. According to a recent national poll, 50 percent of all American
women are gainfully employed, with another five percent unem-
ployed but actively seeking work. Only 21 percent classify themselves
as homemakers, and a total of 63 percent of all the women polled say
that they would *prefer* to work outside the home in the future, even if
they are financially secure enough to live comfortably without doing
so. For although almost 60 percent of women originally seek paid employment purely to balance the family budget, once on the job close to
50 percent report that the most important thing about their work is
"the sense of accomplishment" it gives them.

Mary Stewart Van Leeuwen

. . . Many feminists point out that none of this has decreased the average wage gap between men and women (which has hovered around 40 percent for most of the past century), or prevented the "feminization of poverty," or reduced the incidence of violence towards women by direct and indirect means. By this reading, American society still has a long way to go before justice between the sexes is achieved. But to the average person on the street — including the average evangelical Christian — the pace at which women are entering the salaried work force at all levels is little short of dizzying. Almost overnight, it seems, the full-time homemaker has become a historical oddity. And in the wake of her return to the *paid* labor force, we are seeing a rapid shrinkage of the *volunteer* work force that used to sustain the activities of the church, raise money for charities, run the local P.T.A., and promote the city symphony, ballet, art gallery, and other cultural endeavors. It seems that things are definitely not what they used to be — and, judging by the letters sent to the editors of Christian periodicals on this topic, a high percentage of evangelicals view these changes as alarmingly anti-biblical.

I want to argue, however, that this apparent shift in women's roles is not nearly as unbiblical or unprecedented as it may seem to many Christians. I don't mean simply to point back to the days of World War II, when masses of women placed their children in government-supported nurseries and went off to factories and offices in support of the war effort. Wars, after all, are atypical emergency situations in the history of most nations, and it could be said that what women do during such periods is not to be taken as standard. What I mean is that if we examine the nature of women's roles throughout the entire scope of Western history, we find that it is the middle-class family pattern of the recent past which is in fact atypical.

*   *   *

Before the beginnings of the industrial revolution almost all work — whether done by young or old, men or women — took place in or around the home. There was a sexual division of labor, to be sure, but not a separation of men and women in terms of *where* each worked. Men and their young apprentices handled the heavier crafts such as barrel-making, carpentry, blacksmithing, and stonecutting; at the same time, and never very far away, adult women and their younger helpers were responsible for a formidable roster of equally essential jobs. Dorothy Sayers, in her provocative essay "Are Women Human?," lists these responsibilities as follows:

> The whole of the spinning industry, the whole of the weaving industry, the whole of the catering industry, the whole of the nation's brewing and distilling, all the preserving, pickling and bottling industry, all the bacon-curing . . . and a very large share in the management of landed estates.

We can see from this that life in medieval times was more *socially organic*. In other words, the generations and the sexes were less compartmentalized from each other, and work activities were less atomized. And what was true then was largely true of biblical times as well: families were more extended, the work of men and women was less polarized and less separate in terms of location and economic status, and the rearing of children took place in the context of daily adult industry, rather than being separate from it. (Indeed, this pattern is one that many of us can recall as being still typical of our grandparents or great-grandparents in rural America.)

Only in the 17th century, when the rhetoric of modern science and technology began to pit mind against nature, reason against feeling, masculine against feminine, and public against private life did all of this start to change — and not always for the better. True, science and technology have brought us advancements in medicine and food production, more and cheaper consumer goods, and the necessary media tools for mass education. But we have paid a heavy price in social and sex-role fragmentation: in the wake of the industrial revolution, families became nuclear rather than extended; men began to work away from the home in factories and offices. As a result, women were not only isolated from adult contact at home, but stripped by mechanization of their traditional and economically essential crafts. They were forced, by default, to turn housekeeping (with the aid of progressively more appliances) and childrearing (of progressively smaller numbers of children) into full-time occupations. At the same time, single adults of both sexes became more and more socially marginal, rather than remaining essential members of the extended family and its economic activity.

Now it is true that not very many of us would like to turn back the clock to medieval times: most of us — men and women alike — would rather have our vehicles and at least the bulk of our bread produced on the assembly line. But in Dorothy Sayers's memorable words, "it is perfectly idiotic to take away a woman's traditional occupations and then complain because she looks for new ones." Some have argued that by relinquishing their traditional roles in the communal economy women have been left with the privilege of specializing in the highest task of all, that of raising children. And no Christian is going to deny the value of every child that is born, nor the importance of training children in the ways of the Lord. But children, while they do need a lot of individualized attention, also need *varied* patterns of social and cognitive stimulation for optimal development. In addition, current psychological research indicates more and more that children of *both* sexes need regular, involved interaction with adult caretakers of both sexes.

It has aptly been said that in our society, mothering has been a job, while fathering has been merely a hobby — and a largely optional one at that. It could also be added that earning the family's money has been a full-time job for men and, at most, an occasional hobby for their wives — at least according to the middle-class ideal most of us have been taught to value. The result of such polarization in *both* areas has been humanly unhealthy for everyone involved. Men have had to carry almost the entire burden of breadwinning, and with it the constant worry that if anything happened to them, their family's lifestyle would change suddenly and drastically for the worse. Conversely, women have had to carry almost the entire burden of childrearing, and with it frequent feelings of claustrophobia and isolation from adult social and mental stimulation. Finally, all family members have suffered from the problems which arise (and which current psychology is documenting) when children of both sexes are reared largely in the psychological if not physical absence of fathers and other adult male role-models.

*   *   *

Where has the church been in all of this? I think we can say that, at its best, the church has cushioned the worst effects of the negative social changes I have been describing. At its best, the church has operated as an extended family, not only to its own offspring, but also to those drawn into the covenant through evangelization. In its diaconal task, the church at its best has provided a safety net for widows, orphans, and disabled persons of both sexes, and reminded its members that worth in God's sight is not a matter of one's social class or one's earning power. At its best the church has discouraged men from idolizing their jobs and encouraged them to be actively involved in the nurture of their children. It has also encouraged women to have active ministries outside the home, and to continue their education, however informally, both in the Word of God and in many other areas that might further their capacities for Christian service.

For many Christians — women as well as men — this pattern is both personally satisfying and worth retaining, and this is not an attitude any of us should hasten to discourage. A recent study of North American family patterns concluded that there are, in fact, *two* family life-styles which seem to be both psychologically healthy and personally satisfying for all the family members involved. The first is what most of us would label the more traditional pattern, with the father as the primary breadwinner and the mother the primary homemaker and nurturer. But for this to be a satisfying pattern, it was discovered, the father has to be very actively involved in family life, supportive and proud of his wife's and children's accomplishments, and nonauthoritarian in his parental style. The other pattern is the less traditional one, with both parents equally active as wage-earners, domestic coordinators, and child-rearers. The qualifiers here are that *both* husband and wife must have chosen this pattern willingly and both must be satisfied with the resulting shifts in earning power and domestic and childcare responsibility.

In light of all this, what recommendations might be made to evangelical churches and their members as they enter — or more accurately, re-enter — an era characterized by the more equal involvement of men and women on both the domestic and the wage-earning fronts? Here is my preliminary list of three:

1. Churches can become more creative and flexible in their definition of ministry and outreach. . . .
2. Christians can try to avoid the mistake of labeling any single family life-style as the only biblically normative one. . . .
3. It is important for churches and other Christian organizations to encourage and use women's gifts in largely the same range as men's. . . .

I will end with an anecdote which comes to me from the parents of a three-year-old girl named Jessica. Sitting in church with her parents and sisters one Sunday, Jessica seemed quite alert to the fact that every person participating in the liturgy was a man. Having followed each of these in turn with her eyes (the priest, the servers, the readers, the deacons), she finally turned to her parents with an abrupt question: "Does God listen to girls?"

When the Scriptures speak of discipling, an oft-repeated theme is the importance of setting an appropriate example for those being nurtured in the faith. Today, social learning theorists who study the dynamics of role-modeling tell us that, other things being equal, children are more likely to imitate adults who are seen as nurturing, successful, and similar to themselves. What this means is that most young women will remain hesitant to use the full range of gifts God has given them until they see substantial numbers of other women doing likewise in positions where they are respected, content, and willing to enter into a mentoring relationship with younger women. Churches and Christian organizations can fulfill a central role in this process as they make more visible and frequent use of the leadership talents of women. In so doing, they will be affirming the most important message of all to Jessica and her peers — that the parable of the talents is not qualified by sex, and that God does indeed "listen to girls."

A Prayer to Mary

Richard J. Mouw   *February 1989*

Recently I read another evangelical critique of Roman Catholicism's Marian doctrines. I was in basic agreement with the points that were made. I find it difficult to know why Roman Catholics say what they do about the status of Mary. But I do wish that the tone of the criticisms had been a little gentler. While my theological convictions on this topic are still firm, my mood has gotten a little softer in the last year or so. Ever since the afternoon when I found myself breathing a short but heartfelt prayer to the Holy Mother.

It was in a cathedral in northern France, on a lazy summer day in July of 1987. As a way of giving some focus to our vacation wanderings, my wife and I were making a point of visiting Gothic cathedrals.

As we approached this particular cathedral, a young couple on a motorcycle pulled up. They were in their late teens. They were decked out in a style that was very punk: both were dressed in black; his hair was spiked, hers was dyed orange; her face was heavily painted in white and black.

I was curious about why they were visiting a cathedral. So while my wife studied the art, I followed this couple at a discreet distance as they walked around. Actually, they swaggered. I caught nothing of their conversation, but their insolence was unmistakable. She would point at something derisively, and he would snort. Then he would point and she would snort. Whatever the purpose of their visit, I decided, it had nothing to do with either a spiritual or an aesthetic appreciation for the contents of Gothic cathedrals.

I lingered longer than they did at the high altar, so I don't know how the change of mood occurred. But when I came upon them again, she was standing near a statue of the Virgin Mary in a side chapel, while he was a little ways off, looking at a painting. The young woman was staring directly into the Holy Mother's face. Mary's eyes were directed toward a little kneeling bench at her feet, and her hands were outstretched.

Suddenly the young woman lurched toward the bench and knelt before the Virgin. Face buried in her arms, she began to sob uncontrollably. Her companion turned and saw her. His face registered shock.

I moved on. Many minutes later, I slowly made my way back to the side chapel. The young woman was just standing up from the kneeling bench. She looked into the Virgin's face, then turned to her friend. Her punk makeup was almost all washed away, and her eyes were very red. She held out her hand, and he took it. Slowly, and without a word, they walked away.

I don't really understand what happened to that young woman that afternoon, and I probably never will. But I'm glad that she knelt before the Virgin. My hunch is that it was very good for her to shed those tears. I hope so. I think about that young woman often. And when I remember her, I pray to God on her behalf.

On that afternoon, though, I prayed to the Holy Mother. After the couple left, I sat in a pew in the side chapel, and looked into the face of the statue. "Mary," I asked, "please don't let her wander far. Keep her safe, and lead her to your Son."

That is the only time I have ever addressed a petition to the Virgin Mary. I don't know whether that one prayer makes me guilty of "Mariolatry" or not. Nor has the question troubled me much.

The theology that I instinctively operated with on that summer afternoon may have been confused. But I still sense that my prayer arrived at the right destination; which means that my tone will be a little softer from here on when I debate the Marian doctrines with my Catholic friends.

Thoughts of My Mother's Garden

Evelyn Diephouse   *May-June 1990*

When we bought my parents' home last year, I inherited my mother's garden. It is not an elaborate ornamental garden, nor is it a heavily productive kitchen garden. It is just a nicely designed flower garden, meant to be enjoyed for its own sake. Getting reacquainted with it has brought back memories of the first little patch my mother let me "have," and of my early discovery that one can't simply plant the seeds and then run off and play. Now, as I try to determine the garden's place among many other priorities, I am rediscovering that weekend gardening is not enough: when frost threatens the roses, you can't tell them to wait until Friday. A kind of garden consciousness must be developed — not unlike the consciousness needed for minding young children while working at something else. It requires anticipating their needs, and then keeping an ear open. For a relatively inexperienced gardener like myself, anticipating the needs of those living things already growing in the garden (let alone adding any new ones) is daunting enough. I'm going to have to get to know them better.

One of the commitments competing with my new garden for attention is the work of the Gender Concerns Task Force at Calvin College, on which I serve. Our mandate includes reviewing all the college's activities with respect to the needs of women. This has involved us in inevitable discussions about the effects of gender-distorted language on the growth and development of women, and with inescapable questions about how the church's theology has shaped their self-esteem. We find ourselves talking about the classroom climate (is it too chilly?) and speculating about why male students become leaders so much more easily than female students do. As we struggle to find models of learning environments that will foster leadership qualities in young women, we find ourselves digging all the way back to the images of God that we use and treasure, and debating about how these images (and the ways we select them) have affected our categories of thought about ourselves.

Unfortunately, the discussion of gender issues in our governing synod has been dominated by debates about headship theology as applied to the question of women in church office. The arguments frequently go back to one's interpretation of the creation story, and to what it means that both women and men are created to reflect God's image. No doubt our mental images of the Creator will shape our interpretation of the story. Is it a coincidence that the other major subject of debate that has consumed so much of my denomination's energy of late, namely, the creation-science issue, is rooted in interpretation of the very same story? Perhaps we need to recognize more clearly that not only our hermeneutical principles but also our images of the Creator as role model will shape our thinking about the world as creation and about our role in it.

If we imagine the ruler of the universe to be male (e.g., lord, governor, master), we may have difficulty imagining — and discomfort encountering — women in positions of authority. Think of how usage has diminished the traditional feminine counterparts of these titles: lady, governess, mistress. If our image of the maker of the universe is restricted to the picture of a father, then the categories in which we think about creation are likely to be constrained by the meaning of the verb "to father." The question whether or not God created the world becomes like a paternity suit: Did he or didn't he? It assumes a single event in a limited period of time (a one-week stand!); indeed, in many of the debates one senses a desire for a hidden video camera that might have documented the truth once and for all. If, on the other hand, our image of God as parent of the world is that of a mother, then the questions would shift focus. "To mother" a child involves caring for and protecting as well as giving birth. Mothering is something we usually think of as an ongoing process rather than as an isolated act. The questions we would then wish to ask about creation seem particularly germane to our world today: Is God still alive and active? Does she still care about the world and protect it? Is she making the daffodils come up again? . . .

As we seek to free ourselves of the gender-biased stereotypes that have been captured in our fallen language, it may help us to draw from a broader range of metaphors for God. The Scriptures clearly use a variety of female and male images (as well as inanimate ones) to describe all three persons of the Trinity. Particularly frequent are references to God as giving birth, nursing, mothering, and mid-wifing creation and its creatures. One of my newly discovered favorites, because of its parallel inclusiveness, is from Job 38:

> Who cuts a channel for the torrents of rain,
> and a path for the thunderstorm,
> to water a land where nobody lives,
> a desert with no one in it,
> to satisfy a desolate wasteland
> and make it sprout with grass?
> Does the rain have a father?
> Who fathers the drops of dew?
> From whose womb comes the ice?
> Who gives birth to the frost from the heavens . . . ?
>
> (vv. 25-29, NIV)

Our God-parent is also the gardener of the universe. She is conscious of our needs, attentive, and active in the daily rhythms of our world. Perhaps some imaging of God as gardener can help us to learn what it means to be caretakers of this earth.

A Prophet at Harvard
[On Aleksandr Solzhenitsyn]

Edward E. Ericson, Jr.   *August 1978*

This spring I wrote an article for our local paper entitled "What Ever Happened to Solzhenitsyn?" Four years ago every newspaper in the free world was carrying his name in bold headlines. A Nobel Prize-winning writer was being expelled from his homeland. It was high drama, that struggle between one lone man and a colossal state power: David against Goliath, magnified a million times. What had happened since then?

Here was a Russian who had earned high praise in the West. He was lauded as the greatest living writer, one of the great novelists of all time. Given the extravagance of the adulation, revisionism was bound to set in. Authoritarian, reactionary, obscurantist, nationalistic, anti-democratic — these are some of the adjectives used in more recent years to describe him. . . .

Some have charged that Solzhenitsyn does not understand the West and democracy, and that his remarks about them are thus to be disregarded. Solzhenitsyn himself said that he has loved the West (*worshiped* is his word) and that he is a critic not of the West but only of its current weakness. And even granting that he has less feel for the West than for Russia, one must admit that he seldom criticizes details about the West that are not regular fare for critical columns and editorials in our standard outlets of opinion.

So why, after the early adulation, the sharp turn of opinion against Solzhenitsyn? His vision has been remarkably consistent. But as the secular intelligentsia have come to see more and more of this consistent Christian vision, they have found it alien. Most Western commentators have treated him as a political figure and read *Gulag Archipelago* as a *political* exposé; but he does not see it as the writer's task "to defend or criticize one or another mode of distributing the social product, or to defend or criticize one or another form of government organization."

Rather than being a political writer, Solzhenitsyn is a moral writer. He urges a belief in those "fixed and universal concepts called good and justice." He rivets his vision on the "indivisibility of truth." He writes of "universal and eternal questions, the secrets of the human heart and conscience." These moral matters have meaning for him within the context of his Orthodox Christian beliefs. The centrality of Christianity in his thinking is only gradually coming to be understood. When he attacks Soviet totalitarianism, his protest transcends faulty politics and points to the *immorality* of killing 66,000,000 people. The same principle applies when he attacks details in the West. He fears that the West is losing hold of its spiritual and moral heritage — and has been since the Renaissance and the Enlightenment, when secular ideas began gnawing at the foundations of Christian culture.

This brings us to Solzhenitsyn's Harvard commencement speech this June. Those who were wondering what had happened to him got their answer, loud and clear. The prophetic mood was heavy on him; he let us have it; and we didn't altogether like it. He said we are ill-served by "today's mass living habits, introduced by the revolting invasion of publicity, by TV stupor, and by intolerable music." He decried the heavy dose of pornography in movies. He finds American society excessively litigious. In elections the candidates are often smooth operators ("mechanical, legalistic"). It is not surprising that there is a decline of courage among such leaders, once elected, especially as they confront totalitarian regimes.

As he has done before, he scored Western capitulation in Southeast Asia; the US simply lost the war in Vietnam — cloak it with whatever pieties you wish. Hastiness and superficiality are the psychic disease of the twentieth century. Mired in materialism we risk the suffocation of spiritual life by commercial interests. We may even be verging toward spiritual exhaustion. And all of this stems from our culture's ongoing decline in the belief in a God who rules and overrules in the affairs of men. Whatever else might be wrong in Western society, the greatest danger is from "a despiritualized and irreligious humanistic consciousness."

What should have been overwhelmingly clear is that Solzhenitsyn's specific charges were couched in a religious view of life that compels him to call for spiritual and moral renewal. Judging from many of the rejoinders, a lot of people missed that. Rosalynn Carter, in good Chamber-of-Commerce style, flatly rejected Solzhenitsyn's strictures. Americans, she assures us, have not lost their spirit, are not guilty of "unchecked materialism," are not weak, cowardly, or spiritually exhausted. In place of counter-argument, she offered rhetorical rejoinder: "Solzhenitsyn says he can feel the pressure of evil across our land. Well, I do not feel the pressure of evil at all." (As a matter of fact, his reference to the "forces of evil" was to Communism, not America!) . . .

What shall we make of all this? First, let him be silent ever so long, when Solzhenitsyn speaks the world listens — and not only listens but must speak back. Let him lead with his chin (and surely some of his sentences can hardly help evoking considerable ire); the very mass media he has castigated cannot stay away when he has the platform.

Second and more important, the spiritual foundation of Solzhenitsyn's message is gradually filtering through to the minds of his commentators, including the non-religious ones. To that extent he is returning to the agenda of contemporary cultural conversation issues of cosmic significance which had seemed long since decided. For this achievement Christians — including those who might be offended by his pronouncements about the Vietnam war — should acclaim him. Many Christians have insisted that our society should return to a foundation of religious belief; but when Solzhenitsyn does so, that quintessential Establishment mouthpiece the *New York Times* responds with an editorial in defense of secular humanism. Even while challenging him, they grant him the right to set the questions for discussion.

Solzhenitsyn is a genuine prophet, and one who is listened to in the highest places. There are not many of those around today. And in these hard times we need all the prophets we can get.

Of Prairies and Patriotism

Mary Stewart Van Leeuwen   *December 1987*

This year my husband and I are on leave from our respective academic jobs in Michigan while he pastors a small church in a small city on the edge of the Canadian prairies. Born in Canada myself (as were my two boys, ages nine and eleven), I had my own reasons for wanting to return, at least temporarily. It's not that I don't like teaching at a Christian college in the American Midwest. On the contrary, because American colleges and universities can be certified by independent accrediting agencies rather than all being controlled by state-level governments (as is the case in Canada), Christian higher education has flourished in the U.S. in a way that it has not in Canada. That is a continuing attraction to someone like myself who wants to integrate faith and learning in the classroom but found only limited ways to do so during the ten years I taught at a Canadian university before moving to Michigan and my present post at Calvin College.

But there is another side to the story as well. Because they live in a nation which is a major world power, American evangelicals face . . . the temptation to confuse national loyalty and habit with Christian beliefs. . . . This temptation is often magnified in areas where Christians are concentrated in large numbers, generating a "comfortable-pew" mentality rather than a sense of being a "peculiar people" who must stand apart from the mainstream culture in certain ways, even as they participate in it and are loyal to it. Thus, it becomes easy to assume that "real" Christians would never support socialized medicine, government family allowances, or a nationally owned oil company, simply because these things are not done in America. But Canadian conservatives (and most evangelicals vote conservative in Canada, just as they do in the U.S.) support these practices as part of simple justice and the Canadian way of life. And some American-born members of our Manitoba church are actually relieved to be living in a country where one does not have to face financial destitution to be treated for catastrophic illness.

On the more personal level, I wanted my two sons back in Canada for a year in order for them to sense that what unites Christians is both more basic and more demanding than the lifestyle of a particular Christian community in a particular part of the Midwest. I wanted them to learn that Christians can express regional and national loyalty in different ways and still be united in confessing Christ as the Lord of all of life. I wanted them to begin to figure out both what is nonnegotiable about being Christian, no matter where one lives, and what is open to personal and regional variation as part of the freedom and creativity God gives to individuals and communities.

The resulting culture shock was at first a little hard on them. Suddenly they are learning French in middle elementary school, which they would not have done until tenth grade back home. They are in a city which forbids skate-boarding on the sidewalks, but enthusiastically promotes ice-skating on a dozen or so public rinks. They are in a place where the provincial symbol (the buffalo) is also served up as meat (30% higher in protein than beef, and very much lower in fat, I was told) and where elm trees, virtually wiped out by Dutch elm disease elsewhere, still flourish and are reverently tended by private citizens and public agencies alike. They are in a place where the landscape is flatter but skies are grander than back home, and where the local paper has not only a business but an "agribusiness" section. And instead of being about ten percent black, the local population is about ten percent Native Canadian.

Although I am Canadian, I have lived most of my life near the Great Lakes, so much of this was new for me also. And getting to know and appreciate another region's values and loyalties set me pondering the value and limits of patriotism. Can we bring a biblical analysis to bear on this complex emotion, which at one extreme can weld together millions of diverse individuals, and at the other be used to excuse such things as wars of aggression, genocide, and prideful ignorance about the rest of the world? I think that we can, and especially for American Christians celebrating the 200th anniversary of their constitution, it is essential that we should.

The good news about patriotism is that God has made us irreducibly social creatures whom he expects to form supportive groups. It is no accident (and not just a poetic use of the royal "we") that God says in Genesis 1, "let *us* make humankind in *our* own image, after *our* own likeness." Already at the very beginning of the Bible we have a strong hint about the Trinitarian nature of God; the Godhead is a social unit of three mutually supportive persons; thus we can never fully "image" God as isolated individuals. We were made for community, and for communal interdependence and loyalty. But we are finite and cannot practice equal interdependence with everyone on earth, so it is creationally normal (and intuitively understandable) that we tend to organize primarily in smaller units — families, voluntary associations, local churches, provinces, and nation-states.

Moreover, in the same chapter of Genesis God tells both male and female to "open up" the creation, to "be fruitful and multiply, and fill the earth and subdue it; and have dominion over the fish of the sea and over the birds of the air and over every living thing that moves on the earth" (Gen. 1:28-29). Again, this is something they must do *together,* by implication with the help of their offspring; it would be far too big a task for any one person, even if the fall had never occurred. And the God of the Bible rejoices in diversity. Nothing in this account suggests that opening up creation should result in everyone's doing everything the same way. Our God takes pleasure not just in individual but also in regional, racial, and national variety. And patriotism can be a legitimate expression of all this.

The bad news, of course, is that the fall *did* occur, so that the lovely picture painted above, of groups respecting each other's diversity within a common humanity, went sadly awry. So group loyalty becomes group exclusivity (even in the church); patriotism degenerates into jingoism, civil religion, and prejudice. Even Christians forget that their primary loyalty to Christ must transcend regional and national differences to include people of every nation, tongue, and tribe.

Becoming a world traveler, whether in person or vicariously through books and other learning materials, does not guarantee that we will retain the good aspects of patriotism while at the same time exorcising its demons. In the end, only the transformation and renewal of our minds by Christ's spirit can do this — and never completely in this "time between the times," when even as Christians we continue to struggle against sin. But deliberately cultivating an appreciation of regional and national diversity . . . will certainly help us along this path.

Gradually this is happening in my sons: from complaining about having to learn French, they have gone to being pleasantly smug about returning home more bilingual than their peers in Michigan. From carping about the skate-boarding by-law, they have come to an enthusiasm for local winter sports. From deploring the absence of Mexican food, they have come to sing the praises of buffalo meat. From being homesick for a bigger church and school, they have come to an appreciation of small as beautiful. God willing, this year away will give them a more solidly biblical appreciation of the virtues and limits of patriotism.

Just War and Irony in American History

JAMES C. JUHNKE   *February 1985*

It appears that in the area of just-war theory the climate for dialogue between Anabaptists and Reformed is improving. Interpreters of American history may play a special role by giving fresh attention to the use of traditional just-war theory in evaluating the wars of America.

Anabaptist pacifists in the past have generally dismissed just-war theory out of hand, in part because the theory seemed to be a tool for patriots to justify whatever American war was being discussed. But the context of war/peace dialogue in America has been transformed by the Vietnam War and by apprehensions of a coming nuclear holocaust. There are signs of new Mennonite openness to just-war thinking, not because Mennonites are revising their absolute commitment to refuse participation in any war, but because they see the just-war theory today being used as a tool of restraint rather than of mere rationalization of militarist policy.

Mennonite John Howard Yoder has recently acclaimed the "new look" of the just-war tradition and called churches to the task of teaching members what makes a war unjust. In a forthcoming volume from Herald Press, Duane Friesen, ethics teacher and colleague at Bethel College, has outlined a "realist-pacifist" position which, while critical of the way just-war theory has been misused in the past, argues that the "internal logic" of just-war theory is "appropriate to use when evaluating public policy." . . .

There are doubtless many reasons why American Christian historians have never undertaken a systematic application of just-war criteria to America's wars. The notion that America is a Christian nation has played a part. If America has a divine mandate to establish and extend freedom and democracy, the wars which seem to fulfill this mandate are justified without question or analysis. American wars tend to become righteous crusades, with Christians sprinkling holy water on the troops. Sober Christian historians, looking back on American wars, are more inclined to lament the intolerant excesses of the crusade than to rigorously examine the fundamental issues of justification.

Another inhibiting factor for just-war analysis in recent decades has been the dominance of the ironic mode of historical interpretation. Virtually everyone who studied American history in graduate school since the mid-1950s has been influenced by ideas crystallized in Reinhold Niebuhr's 1952 book, *The Irony of American History*. Niebuhrian irony sees American history on a plane of intention and consequence, observing that the consequences of America's actions have been contrary to our original intentions, and that the cause of the discrepancy is to be found in ourselves. The ironic view sees that America was born in innocence and pretense, in the vain imagination that on these uncorrupted shores we could create a new world unburdened by history. Niebuhrian irony has been especially attractive for Christian historians because it can take account of both human sinfulness and God's grace. America's pretension and arrogance may have been egregious, but God nevertheless has graciously allowed us to play a significant role in fulfilling his purposes.

Niebuhrian irony, as a mode of historical interpretation, stands in tension (though not in absolute contradiction) with just-war theory. Just-war analysis involves us in confrontation with a sovereign God who demands our moral accountability. The focus of attention is upon knowable and achievable standards which our behavior has either met or failed to meet. If America has come grossly short of meeting those standards in waging war, we are guilty and in need of penance. For example, if the War for American Independence was an unjust war (for it was not initiated as a last resort, the rhetoric of cause was delusive, and the killing was disproportionate to the cause), we should name it by its right name and stand accountable before God.

Ironic interpretation, on the other hand, involves us more immediately and directly with God's grace. Despite our sin, God graciously allows America to achieve ends ironically different from her original intentions. The natural response to such irony, said Niebuhr, is laughter. But it can be a celebrative laughter, gratified by our unintended achievements. The danger of such a viewpoint is that it can appropriate grace too cheaply. The historian can too quickly excuse human folly and avoid confrontation with the judgment of God upon those who fail to live by his standards of justice. And so the ironist can easily gloss over the manifest unjustness of the American War for Independence, observing that much good came out of the patriots' misperceptions and bumblings.

Ronald Wells of Calvin College, editor of the provocative volume *The Wars of America: Christian Views* (Eerdmans, 1981), laid upon the eight contributing writers the daunting task of combining *both* just-war theory *and* Niebuhrian irony in their survey of America's wars. Not one of the historians chose to address the task with a systematic assessment of how their assigned war met, or failed to meet, the classical just-war criteria. Meanwhile, nearly all the writers moved quite freely and comfortably within the framework of ironic interpretation. Irony seems to come more naturally than just-war thinking for Christian historians of our generation.

The American War for Independence is a particularly significant test for applied just-war theory, for it not only looms large in national mythology but it also initiated the American habit of conceiving wars as righteous crusades. If we can come to agreement that this war, by clear and coherent Christian moral standards, was an unjust war, we will be well on the way toward a major reinterpretation of American history. George Marsden of Calvin College and Mark Noll of Wheaton have written recent essays on the War for Independence which, without introducing the full range of just-war criteria (in particular omitting the *jus in bello* considerations), make the conclusion almost inescapable that this was not a just war. . . . Marsden shows how revolutionary ideology distorted patriot perceptions so that the patriots mistakenly came to believe in the righteousness of their cause. Noll takes much the same view in the context of a larger argument that America is not, and has never been, a Christian nation. But both historians, at least in these essays, neglect to make an unambiguous, black-on-white statement that this was clearly an unjust war. An Anabaptist-Mennonite critic would probably wonder why.

William O'Brien, a Catholic ethicist from Georgetown University who dissents from the pacifist leanings of some Catholics today, does not shrink from just-war judgments in his book *The Conduct of Just and Limited War* (Praeger, 1981). He models a very explicit definition and weighting of just-war criteria, and applies the criteria to selected twentieth-century American wars. He finds World War II, the Korean War, and the Vietnam War all to have been, on balance, just wars. He is most troubled by the indiscriminate bombings of World War II, a slaughter so unlimited as to nearly tip the balance and make it an unjust war. Any Anabaptist-Mennonite participant in this dialogue will need to meet O'Brien on his terms and respond to his cogent and carefully developed arguments. Many Reformed thinkers would also want to challenge his analysis of the Vietnam War. It will be observed that O'Brien, who is not primarily a historian, does not complicate his analysis with anything like Niebuhrian irony. In addition, O'Brien may be trapped in an anti-Communist ideology as distorting as the Revolutionary-Patriotic misperception of the British empire in the 1770s. But the critique of O'Brien remains to be made. It would seem to have some priority.

Perhaps the next major agenda — for Anabaptists, Reformed, or interested historians of other groups — would be systematically and rigorously to apply the criteria of just-war theory to all the wars of America. This may require a temporary suspension of our ingrained inclinations to ironic interpretations. It may also involve us to some extent in judging past generations by standards they did not hold, at least in the terms we pose them today. Both pacifists and non-pacifists might have to step outside of their normal operating categories for the time being in order to carry on such a task. But the effort, as a limited exercise in historical imagination and judgment, might help us conceive of the American past in fresh and helpful ways.

The results could be surprising — perhaps even an Anabaptist historian admitting that the Korean War did meet the standards of just and limited war. But where the results are more predictable, a discussion around common criteria could nevertheless be eminently worthwhile. It might even prove useful, as historical enterprise sometimes does, in coming to terms with the moral perplexities of our fearful world today.

Black and Reformed: Burden or Challenge?

Allan Boesak   *November-December 1981*

Apartheid in South Africa is unique. But its uniqueness does not lie in the inherent violence of the system, nor in the inevitable brutality without which it cannot survive, nor in its dehumanization of and contempt for black personhood, nor even in the tragic alienation it fosters between people. The uniqueness of apartheid lies in its claim to be based on Christian principles. It is being justified on the basis of the gospel of Jesus Christ. In the name of the Liberator God and his Son Jesus Christ, apartheid is being perpetrated — and it is Reformed people who are doing that. Apartheid is, in a very real sense, the brainchild of the Dutch Reformed Churches. Reformed people have split the church on the basis of race and color and now claim that racially divided churches reflect a truly Reformed understanding of the nature of the Christian church.

It is Reformed people who have spent years working out the details of apartheid, not only as a church policy but also as a political policy, and have presented this policy to the Afrikaner as the only possible solution, as an expression of the will of God for South Africa. Reformed people have created Afrikaner nationalism, equating the Reformed tradition and Afrikaner ideals with the ideals of the kingdom of God. It is they who have devised the theology of apartheid, deliberately distorting the gospel to suit their racist aspirations. In this uniqueness lies the shame of the Christian church in South Africa. Apartheid is the grave of the dignity and credibility of the Reformed tradition.

Many people today, especially black people, believe that racism is an inevitable fruit of the Reformed tradition. In the experience of millions of black people, this tradition is responsible for political oppression, economic exploitation, unbridled capitalism, social discrimination, and a total disregard for human dignity. At the same time, being Reformed is equated with uncritical acceptance of the status quo, silence in the face of human suffering, and manipulation of the Word of God in order to justify oppression. The anomaly has become more acute than ever. For black Reformed people who suffer so much under the totalitarian rule of white Reformed people, the question is fundamental, decisive, and inevitable. Black and Reformed: is it a burden that has to be cast off as soon as possible, or is it a challenge toward renewal of the church and our society? . . .

*   *   *

Let me highlight some especially relevant aspects of the Reformed tradition which need to be redeemed from the quagmire of political ideology and nationalistic propaganda to which they have fallen victim in South Africa.

The first is the principle of the supremacy of the Word of God. In the Reformed tradition it is the Word of God that animates our words, shapes life, and provides the church with a basis on which to stand. Manipulation of the Word of God to suit a particular culture or a specific prejudice or a given ideology is alien to the Reformed tradition. The way Reformed Christians in South Africa use the Bible to justify black oppression and white privilege, the way the gospel has been bypassed in establishing racially divided churches, the way Scripture has been used to produce a nationalistic, racist ideology — these represent a denial of the Reformed belief in the supremacy of Scripture. The Word that gives life cannot at the same time be the justification of that death which comes through oppression and inhumanity. . . .

The kingdom of God is inextricably bound with the lordship of Jesus Christ — another precious principle for people who adhere to the Reformed tradition. Christ is Lord even of those situations in which his lordship is not readily recognized by willful men. We believe passionately with Abraham Kuyper that there is not a single inch of life that does not fall under the lordship of Christ. All of life is indivisible as God is indivisible, and in all of life, personal and public, political and economic, in sports and art, science and liturgy, the Reformed Christian seeks the lordship of Christ.

Here the Reformed tradition comes so close to the African idea of the wholeness of life that these two should combine to renew the thrust brought to Christian life by the followers of Calvin. Reformed piety was never intended to include a withdrawal from the world. The admonitions of politicians and even (Reformed!) churches to black Christians to "keep out of politics" are not only unbiblical; they are also, as Max Warren called them, the "essence of paganism . . . the old polytheism against which the prophets of the Lord waged their great warfare. The real essence of paganism is that it divides the various concerns of man's life into compartments. . . ." This kind of religion is far removed from the faith that characterized Reformed Christians from the very beginning, a faith that said Christians were responsible for their world. That Christianity was what Nicholas Wolterstorff has called a "world-formative Christianity."

As Reformed Christians we see ourselves as human beings responsible for the world in which we find ourselves. It is a world made by us, and we are capable of making it differently. More than that: we *should* make it differently. It *needs* reform. The exercise of that responsibility is an integral part of the discipleship to which the Lord Jesus Christ has called us. Doing what we can to reform the social world in which we live is part of our spiritual life. For us as black Reformed Christians that means that, in following Jesus Christ, the spiritual experience is never separated from the liberation struggle. In the heart of this process God is experienced as a Father to whom every effort and every struggle is offered. Our worship of God is what must give direction and content to our action in the world. From him come bravery and courage, truth and justice. Because God raised our Messiah from the dead to demonstrate the truth of his word, he will also give life to those who, in the path of Jesus, give their lives for others.

In South Africa white Reformed theology has persistently pointed out that we live in the "broken reality" of a fallen world. True enough. But in the theology of apartheid this leads to the acceptance — and indeed the idealization and institutionalization — of that brokenness. The result is a kind of apathy which calls on Christians to accept the sinful realities (like racism) with which we have to live. In true Reformed theology, however, the recognition of the broken, sinful realities of our world becomes the impulse toward reformation and healing. We understand that people do not automatically seek the glory of God or the good of the neighbor. That is why it becomes the Christian's task to work actively for the good of the neighbor in the world.

Allan Boesak

In a fallen world the structures we create, tainted by sin, will not automatically have a liberating, humanizing effect on the lives of people. They will therefore have to be changed so that they may serve the humanization of our world. Reformed Christians are not called to accept the sinful realities of the world, but to challenge, shape, subvert, and humanize history until it conforms to the norm of the kingdom of God. . . .

*   *   *

It is my conviction that the Reformed tradition has a future in South Africa only if black Reformed Christians are willing to take it up, make it truly their own, and let this tradition once again become what it once was: a champion of the cause of the poor and the oppressed, clinging to the confession of the lordship of Jesus Christ and to the supremacy of the Word of God. It will have a future when we show an evangelical openness toward the world and toward the worldwide church, so that we will be able to search with others for the attainment of the goals of the kingdom of God in South Africa. In this I do not mean that we should accept everything in our tradition uncritically, for I indeed believe that black Christians should formulate a Reformed confession for our time and our situation in our own words.

Beginning with our own South African situation, we should accept our special responsibility to salvage this tradition from the grip of the mighty and the powerful who have so shamelessly perverted it for their own ends, and let it speak once again for God's oppressed and suffering people. It is important to declare apartheid as irreconcilable with the gospel of Jesus Christ, a sin which has to be combated on every level of our lives, a denial of the Reformed tradition, a heresy which is to the everlasting shame of the church of Jesus Christ in the world.

To accept the Reformed confession is more than a formal acknowledgment of doctrine. Churches who accept that confession thereby commit themselves to show through their daily witness and service that the gospel has indeed empowered them to live in this world as the people of God. They also commit themselves to accept in their worship and at the table of the Lord the brothers and sisters who accept and proclaim the lordship of Christ in all areas of life and to work ceaselessly for that justice, love, and shalom which are fundamental to the kingdom of God and the kingly rule of his Son. Confessional subscription should lead to concrete manifestation in unity of worship and working together at the common tasks of the church. And in South Africa adherence to the Reformed tradition should be a commitment to combat the evil of apartheid in every area of our lives and to seek liberation, peace, justice, reconciliation, and wholeness for all of God's children in this torn and beloved land.

It is one thing when the rules and laws of unjust and oppressive government make it impossible for the church to carry out its divine task. But it is quite another thing when churches purposely reject this unity and this struggle as the white Reformed churches of South Africa have consistently done. Apartheid is not simply political ideology. Its very existence depends on the theological justification by white Reformed churches. This, too, is part of the burden; in struggling against apartheid, the struggle is for liberation of people, against an oppressive and inhuman ideology, but also for the sake of the gospel and the integrity of the church of Jesus Christ. Those Christians and churches that purport to serve the gospel by justifying apartheid on biblical grounds do so only at the risk of blasphemy.

I am convinced that in this struggle some Reformed expressions of faith — now centuries old and considered redundant by many — can provide us with both prophetic clarity and pastoral comfort. Lord's Day I of the Heidelberg Catechism asks the question: "What is your only comfort in life and death?" To which the answer is: "That I, with body and soul, in life and in death, am not my own, but belong to my Savior Jesus Christ; who with his precious blood has fully satisfied for all my sins, and delivered me from all the power of the devil, and so preserves me that without the will of my heavenly Father not a hair can fall from my head; yea, that all things must be subservient to my salvation, wherefore by his Holy Spirit he also assures me of eternal life, and makes me heartily willing and ready, henceforth, to live unto him."

This is one of the most powerful statements of faith I have ever encountered. For in our situation, in which black personhood is so thoroughly undermined, God-given human dignity trampled on with a heavy soldier's boot, old people uprooted and thrown into the utter desolation of resettlement camps, even the meager shelter of a plastic sheet brutally taken away, so that mothers and babies are exposed to the merciless winter of the Cape, young children terrorized in the early hours of the morning, prophetic voices of our young people are tear-gassed into silence, the blood of our children flows in the streets of our townships — what then is our comfort in life and in death?

When we are so completely at the mercy of people for whom our humanity does not exist, when our powerlessness against their ruthless rule becomes a pain we can no longer bear, when the stench of our decaying hope chokes us half to death, when the broken lives and silent tears of our aged show the endlessness of our struggle, when the power of the oppressor is arrogantly flaunted in the face of all the world — what, then, is my comfort in life and death? That I with body and soul, both in life and death, am not my own, but belong unto my faithful Savior, who is Jesus the Liberator, Christ the Messiah, the Lord. And in this struggle I am inspired by the words of the Belgic Confession: "The faithful and elect shall be crowned with glory and honor; and the Son of God will confess their names before God his Father; . . . all tears shall be wiped from their eyes; *and their cause which is now condemned by many judges and magistrates as heretical and impious will then be known to be the cause of the Son of God.*" This also is our tradition, and it is worth fighting for.

An Evening in Amman

Nicholas Wolterstorff   *July 1982*

My wife and I were part of a group of Americans who visited the Middle East this spring, attempting as Christians to understand the situation of the church there and the conflict of peoples and religions. In Lebanon we talked to the head of the Maronite church, the head of the Armenian church, a bishop of the Melkite church, and representatives of the Middle East Council of Churches; but we also spoke with Muslims, with representatives of the Lebanese government, of the PLO, of the rightist Falangist Party, and of the Syrian Nationalist Party. . . .

During a stay of a few days in Jordan, en route to Israel, my wife and I did have the chance to talk to Father Eliya Khoury, who is a Palestinian Arab. Born and reared in the West Bank, he is now the Assistant Bishop in the Jerusalem diocese of the Anglican Church. Now, in exile from Israel because of his outspoken views, he is serving a small congregation of Palestinians in Amman. . . .

Let me present to you Fr. Khoury's witness. The blend of sorrow, hope, and passion with which he spoke I cannot convey. I can only give his words. I did not take notes while he was speaking. But as soon as we got back to our hotel I jotted some things down. That was hardly necessary. His words were indelible.

Why, he asked, has the church abandoned us Christians here in the Middle East? We are deserted, forgotten by the church of the whole world. Why? Why do the Christians in America support the Zionists instead of supporting us, their brothers and sisters in Christ? I do not understand. They do not even notice us. Perhaps the Palestinian has not known how to cry out.

We are caught between the Israelis and the Muslims. The Muslims see Western Christendom as behind Israel. They see Israel as an outpost of the West — of the *Christian* West. They want no part of it. I tell you, they are becoming fanatic, worse than any time in my memory. And if things continue as they are, they will make martyrs of us. We are willing to become martyrs if that is demanded of us. We shall remain faithful. But you are forcing us to become unworthy martyrs, martyrs in an unworthy cause.

My people, my Christian people, are being destroyed, squeezed between Israel and the Muslims. A few years back 12% of the Palestinians were Christians. Now only 6% are. We are constantly shrinking, constantly getting smaller. What has happened? Have the people abandoned Christ? Have they converted to Islam or Judaism? No, they have not. They are being forced out of Israel by its Zionist policies. Israel is destroying the church in Palestine. Soon, in the land of our Lord, there will be no one left. The old ones have their homes taken from them by the Israelis, confiscated. The young ones, seeing no future, leave — for the United States, for South America, anywhere. Why do you Christians in America support the Zionists, when the Zionists are destroying the church in Palestine? Why do you not support your brothers and sisters in Christ?

And now I am told that conservative Christian groups in the United States are planning to start a radio station aimed at the Muslims. Why do you not speak to us first about such things? Why do you ignore us? Why do you act as if there are no Christians here? We have lived with the Muslims for a thousand years. Why do you not first ask our advice? You say that we have not been successful in evangelizing the Muslims. What do all your Western missionaries have to show for their efforts? I tell you, this will only make the Muslims more nervous, more suspicious, and more fanatic. Our oppression will become worse. It would be easier to convert the devil himself at this point than to convert a Muslim. Today he is not receptive. You will cause Christianity to disappear from the Middle East unless you stop this "American evangelism" — and unless your government settles the Palestinian problem.

I run a small school here in Amman. To this school come both Christians and Muslims. I do not try to convert the Muslim children. I try to show them that Christians and Muslims can live together in peace. Unless the Muslims believe that, and unless the Zionists cease their oppression, the church here in the Middle East will disappear.

What I need for my own congregation is a small place where we can meet during the week. My people must meet so that they can support each other in these difficult days. But we have no money. So I went to Europe, to ask the Christians there for money. Do you know what they told me? They told me that *they* had decided that it was unwise for the church to spend money on buildings. Why do the churches in the rest of the world not trust us? Instead of piping in their Western evangelism, why do they not support us — in building meeting places for our people, and schools, and in holding discussions between Christians and Muslims so that they can learn to live together? Believe me. I love Jesus Christ. I love the gospel. I speak from the standpoint of that love. I say: Trust us. Do not compete with us. Support us. We know the Muslim. We live with him.

Eventually Israel will see that the Palestinians are its only doorway into the Arab world. It will see that its only hope is to form a society in which Jews, Muslims, and Christians live together. The first step to that will be a Palestinian state on the West Bank and in Gaza, with East Jerusalem as its capital. But that won't happen until you Americans help to settle the Palestinian issue — until you see the justice of our cause. You are driving us into the arms of the Russians, where we do not want to be. And you are destroying the church.

God will not desert us. And we will not desert God. Perhaps I sound despairing. But I am not. I live in the hope that our Lord will come. But how much must we suffer? Help us, before it is too late. Unless the baby in its crib cries out, it is not heard. Perhaps we haven't known how to cry out. Please convey this to my Christian brothers and sisters in America. You may use my name.

An Eschatological Moment

Leonard Sweetman   *September 1990*

On Sunday, February 11, 1990, around 3:30 p.m., Nelson Mandela was released from the Victor Verster Prison, which is located in Paarl about 40 miles east of Cape Town. An enormous crowd of black people, sprinkled with an occasional white, awaited the arrival of the Mandela caravan on the Grand Parade in the heart of Cape Town. The police reported that 80,000 people waited for Mr. Mandela; black newspapers reported the number as 500,000; TV reporters used general terms to describe the size of the crowd which assembled to wait for the arrival of this man who had been imprisoned for 27 years along with other leaders of the African National Congress.

While the crowd waited, several people well known in the black community sang songs of struggle and of liberation, songs that are part of the repertoire of the struggle against apartheid in which the black community has been engaged for generations. Groups of young people took turns at toi toi, a celebrative dance that has been a trademark of the young people during the funerals of martyrs in the struggle and at demonstrations everywhere in South Africa. Throughout the afternoon, new groups joined the crowd. Each new group made its presence known by singing one of the popular liberation songs — many of which are hymns — and by dancing through the crowd in skillful maneuvers until it arrived at the center of the celebrating throng. The displaced group then, by equally skillful movements, turned around and retreated from the focal point to the edge of the crowd where it merged into the tens of thousands of singing and dancing celebrants. . . .

Throughout the long oppressively warm February afternoon, the anticipation of Mandela's appearance and address buoyed the waiting throng. The police observed the behavior of the crowd from helicopters drifting along the edges of the crowd like dark clouds. Obviously, we were visitors in a country in which the security apparatus of the state was a foreboding presence everywhere.

Suddenly, we heard a sound that caused the crowd to stir. The police were firing tear-gas canisters on the fringes of the crowd. The evening news report later told the story of the tragedy which occurred shortly after the tear-gas canisters were fired. The police had discovered that while the crowd waited, several young men broke into a liquor store on the edge of the Grand Parade. As the police arrived on the scene in force, one young man began to run away. The police shot and killed him. The sound of the shots echoed and reechoed through the Grand Parade. There is still no unanimity about the young man's participation in the looting. But, in any case, with the shots and with the whiff of tear gas approaching on the evening breezes, people started to leave the Grand Parade. Darkness began to fall. Some people in the crowd faced a drive of many miles before they reached home, and charter buses were scheduled to return to cities sprinkled throughout the Cape Flats area.

Mandela had not yet appeared. Was his appearance merely to be another promise of the government that evaporates like the morning mist as soon as the sun comes out? By 7 o'clock in the evening the crowd had thinned considerably and the sun was disappearing. But what was amazing about this situation is that tens of thousands of black people were still on the street in Cape Town at a time of the day when, six months earlier, riot-control units of the police and army would have rushed to the scene in armored personnel carriers and arrested large numbers of them. The Pass Law had been abrogated late in 1989. And so, on the evening of February 11, 1990, black people had the right to remain on the streets of Cape Town without challenge or harassment.

Finally, at two minutes after eight, a car drove through what remained of the crowd on the Grand Parade. Those faithful who persisted to the end saw a slender, erect figure emerge from the car and walk slowly to the waiting microphone. Mandela had arrived. He needed a flashlight to read his brief message. "Friends, comrades, and fellow South Africans," he began, "I greet you in the name of peace, democracy, and freedom for all. I stand here before you not as a prophet, but as a humble servant of you the people. On this day of my release I extend my sincere and warmest gratitude to the millions of my compatriots and those in every corner of the globe who have campaigned tirelessly for my release."

Mandela's speech warmly recognized all those groups that had been involved in the struggle for liberation from 1964 to the present. These he mentioned by name, one by one. He also outlined, very succinctly, the immediate agenda for relations between the government of President F. W. de Klerk and the ANC. The steps outlined in the Harare Declaration issued by the African National Congress were to be the conditions for discussion with the government concerning "negotiation about the future of our country." He explicitly called for "the immediate ending of the state of emergency and the freeing of all, and not only some, political prisoners." Free political activity, moreover, must characterize the "normalised situation" in which the black people can prepare for negotiations with the government.

The speech ended with a quotation from Mandela's own words during his trial in 1964. "I have fought against white domination and I have fought against black domination. I have carried the ideal of a democratic and free society in which all persons live together in harmony and with equal opportunity. It is an ideal which I hope to live for and achieve. But, if need be, it is an ideal for which I am prepared to die." And then he sent them away, like some ancient patriarch, with these words: "I hope you will disperse with dignity and not a single one of you should do anything which will make other people say that we can't control our own people."

One can only hope, in these days of increasing tension and bloodshed, that the spirit of this benediction will in the end prevail.

The Virgin and the Dynamo

GEORGE M. MARSDEN   *June 1979*

Like most people today I grew up in the shadow of nuclear obliteration, accidental or otherwise. By the time I finished grade school, it
seemed almost inevitable that the Cold War would end in confrontation between the US and Soviet Russia, both armed with atomic weapons. Yet in the same Christian grade school in Middletown, Pennsylvania, I remember learning that atomic energy might be a good thing, an
instance of the progress through science we were then seeing everywhere else. Humanity had hopes that atomic energy would be put to
peaceful uses, as for example to generate electrical power. Since the
Metropolitan Edison plant by the river often spewed heavy black soot
on the town, the prospect of another source of power was attractive.

By the time that dream began to come true in the late 1960s, my
opinion of technological advance had changed markedly. When I
first came back and saw the huge towers of the Three Mile Island
plant looming over my home town, I was reminded of my first
glimpse of Chartres, where one can see the incredible towers of the
cathedral in the sky miles before the town itself comes into view. My
thoughts on the subject had been shaped by Henry Adams' famous
observations in *The Education* on the dynamo and the Virgin. "All the
steam in the world," Adams had remarked, "could not, like the Virgin, build Chartres." The spirit of American civilization had been
captured in the symbol of the dynamo. Now I saw the lesson come
home architecturally.

My resentment, however, was not sharply focused on nuclear
power. I had learned from Jacques Ellul that the deeper danger was the
pervasive force of the technological society — the incessant drive for
rationality and efficiency — rather than the specific engines of that

technology. Though I was living in the era of Vietnam and Richard Nixon and thought I had learned to doubt everything except the ubiquity of human selfishness, the same optimism that keeps me on most days from really expecting a nuclear holocaust kept me from regarding the power plant as particularly sinister.

It did not occur to me, for instance, that the same local company that spewed black soot on the town until forced to stop was now responsible for the environmental effects of the reactor on Three Mile Island. Somehow I vaguely assumed that the plant was managed by disinterested nuclear physicists, chiefly motivated by thoughts of human welfare. My most definite resentment was that they picked Three Mile Island on which to build the plant. The island is on a scenic part of the river — my original model for idyllic spots. Just off the tip of Three Mile was our boat landing, and directly across from it we had had a cabin. I had grown up on that part of the Susquehanna, and my associations with it were altogether romantic. My most specific grievance was aesthetic.

Nonetheless I was assured by everyone in the town that the plant was entirely safe — it would not affect even the fishing. I tended to believe all this, since — despite Vietnam and the like — it seemed inconceivable that if such plants were not entirely safe one would be built so close to anyone's home. Since protesters were protesting almost everything else at the time, and most of the other complaints appeared more substantial, I did not give the opponents of nuclear power much attention. Out of respect for progressive friends who opposed such power plants, I had my suspicions. Still, I never actually looked into the subject. I stayed at the theoretical remove of Henry Adams and Jacques Ellul.

What has struck me most in my reaction now to the near disaster at Three Mile Island is its difference from the reaction of most other people I know in Michigan. Concern here, as elsewhere, grew appreciably; yet my impression is that not many opinions really changed. Anti-nuclear types were confirmed in their worst suspicions and commendably renewed their efforts on behalf of humanity. Others, I think, have moved from disinterest to mild opposition. But the prevailing view remains that nuclear power, like driving a car, involves some risks necessary for progress. Energy is a crucial necessity, so we should simply take that risk. Clearly the principal reason I reacted differently from many I know is that the nuclear accident did not take place in their own back yard. They had no terribly immediate sense of the obliteration of a whole section of the country they knew and loved. They did not have families and friends who lived there.

My plea in writing this is to give the subject a second thought. Unlike rioting in Africa, strife in Iran, or hurricanes in Florida, it is something that apparently we can do something about before the worst happens. Perhaps someday someone will set off the spark and we shall all be blown away. In the meantime, however, there is no sense in proliferating such possibilities. More safety measures are not enough. Despite their obvious merits, they will only be cover-up. What is required is a sense of deeper responsibility to humanity extending beyond government and its industrial allies. For that to come about, support will be needed from those who do not live in the immediate shadow of the dark towers. It will have to come from persons — including, I hope, many Reformed Christians — who can sympathetically imagine their own children playing in such a shadow.

Those of us who seldom get more involved politically than by preaching Adams, Ellul, Calvin, Kuyper, and the Bible can perhaps help in that way too. The issue is the larger one of what counts for progress in our civilization. The power of the Virgin has vanished, save perhaps on Saturday afternoons at South Bend. Yet Protestant civilization has been far too ready to revere the power of the dynamo as a sign of the kingdom. What is the power that shapes our life-styles? How many electronic conveniences are worth the outside chance of losing the state of Pennsylvania? Perhaps even if the lights went out all over America it would not be the end of civilization. Perhaps it would be a harbinger of the kingdom in which, after all, there is only one light.

Re-fighting Jericho

Kathryn Lindskoog   *October 1979*

At a time when the general public is indifferent to biblical exegesis, it comes as a breath of fresh air to open *Newsweek* and notice The Tobacco Institute paying for a two-page, full-color ad based upon an Old Testament miracle and dedicated to putting millions of dollars into scientific research on the causes and cures of disease. I'll buy that.

No, The Tobacco Institute itself has no plans to donate millions of dollars to the cure of cancer, heart disease, asthma, emphysema, wrinkles, or halitosis. It is spending its own millions on fancy magazine ads with clean, white smoke-puffs that look like floating popcorn. But, as these ads explain, if American smokers are allowed freely to enhance the air in which we "work, eat, play, and shop," this will save millions of dollars in antismoking propaganda, which can then be spent on medical research. Somewhere, somehow, millions of research dollars are lost to posterity if we put up No Smoking signs and cautionary billboards. Take it on faith (there's nothing else to take it on).

This is no doomsday ad; it is more of a victory cry against the forces of evil that build walls in the form of unseemly prohibitions. "In the long run, the wall-builders must fail, and the walls will come tumbling down — if not to the sound of a trumpet, then at least to the slower and surer music of common decency. . . ."

So we have a clear moral drama about clean air. The hostile, antismoking residents of Jericho are huddled selfishly inside their city wall. Outside, Joshua and sixty million other smokers, cheered on by The Tobacco Institute and God, circle the city puffing about 1800 million cigarettes a day and trumpeting for freedom of choice and thrift. By a miracle or by common decency, Jericho will fall again and God's chosen will rule the land.

Still, acknowledges The Tobacco Institute, we must recognize virtue even in odd places. "The anti-smoking wall-builders have, to give them their due, helped to make us all more keenly aware of the value of courtesy and of individual freedom of choice." That is called consciousness-raising. As Joseph put it in Genesis 50, "You meant it to me for evil, but God used it for good." That's the breaks.

Where in the World?

Virginia Stem Owens   September 1983

Down in the woods behind the house the ground is littered with last year's leaves. They are wet from an early morning shower and limp and layered after the winter. The floor of the woods is dark with them. The mist of new green starts several feet from the ground, thickening as it rises from twigs to spindly limbs until it solidifies in the full bodies of the trees. The lower levels are made of dogwood, wax myrtle, French mulberry. Higher up are sweet gum, post oak, pine. The green, at this time in April, is such a shade that, if I could tell it to you, it would break your heart. You would be a believer, if nothing else, in green.

I sit down on the crossbeam of a deer stand someone built here last hunting season. It sticks up among the trees maybe twenty feet, looking like a prison guard tower. I look at the green, believe in it, and say my prayers. Then I look at a spider's web, stretched like a stocking between a tree root and the ground. Drops of water hang inside the webbed funnel. A brown spider with a white longitudinal stripe down her back had disappeared when I first sat down. Now she has decided the coast is clear and comes out again. We wait there together in the April green, she for food, I for whatever happens before it's time to go.

Three hours later I am on a plane, crushed between two businessmen. The one on the aisle has dark rippling hair and is reading a paperback copy of Conde's *The Religion*. The last joint of the middle finger on his right hand is missing. The other man has a beard and reads a hardback copy of *The Parsifal Mosaic*. They sit quietly immersed in their vicarious violence, ignoring my existence and that of one another. I watch them silently, like the spider.

Several rows up three other businessmen have loosened their ties and are joking clumsily with the stewardess. They are on their third round of drinks. Alcohol, it seems, is the only socially acceptable excuse for conviviality on an airplane. We are moving through the air that covers Texas, Oklahoma, Kansas, and Iowa. Air that is filled, I know, with moisture, pollen, particulates. A sea of shared respiration.

The stewardess brings us trays of sandwiches. We hunch over our tiny fold-down tables like the embarrassed animals we are. We are so close together, the three of us, that when the man on the aisle salts his salad, the grains spill over onto my tray. Our elbows grate. Eating alone is difficult I have found. But eating in communion-less proximity is even worse. Something essential is being denied here that makes it hard to swallow.

The plane lands. We shuffle off and away. I climb into a van full of strangers who have come here for the same conference I have. When we arrive at our assigned hotel it is dark and raining. A back-lit sign announces the office park as "Corporate West." It is too late for supper; too late for room service. In Corporate West there is only the hotel, the office buildings, and the freeway. No coffee shop, hamburger stands, grocery stores. I go to bed very hungry amid the stark opulence.

The next morning we are shuttled to the campus about eight miles away through a steely drizzle. The road runs between two of the suburbs that are glued together like mosaic chips around Chicago. At the space where the mortar in the mosaic would be is an interlude of fields still studded with a few stalks of last year's corn crop. The fields are dark and sodden. Water stands in the low places.

At the school we are immediately encapsulated in warm vinyl. Vinyl made to look like wood, vinyl made to look like bricks, vinyl made to look like wool. Inside the auditorium people are reading lectures over a sound system that marvelously filters irritating electronic feedback from their voices. The amplification penetrates even to the foyer, where private conversation becomes a salmon-like attempt to swim upstream against the implacable current of speeches. The talkers in the foyer mouth at one another with their unamplified voices like mute fish.

At lunch we escape from the microphones into the clatter of the campus cafeteria, a building more humbly human than the auditorium. Here there are scruffy students, tracked-in mud, wet umbrellas, and the ubiquitous bean sprouts and cherry tomatoes of the salad bar that save the nomadic conference participant from scurvy. I sit down with two scholars from Christian colleges. We plunk our trays on the unclad table. Then suddenly, like two ducks diving, my companions submerge their heads in private prayer for about five seconds. I hold my breath until they come up again, reminded in my sudden isolation of the two businessmen on the plane. What hinders a little convivial spirituality? Why this furtive dunking I observe on every hand into solitary supplication? It is an uncommonly cold dash of water in the face.

Back on the bus that evening, headed toward Corporate West, I watch a pair of ducks flying sideways into a stiff wind. They land on one of the cornfield puddles among a clutch of other ducks harboring there from the gale.

The next morning the sun is shining. Outside the hotel window is a little art-object pond. It sits like a hand mirror held in the evenly shorn grass, unencumbered by cornstalks, briars, or debris. A pair of Canadian geese land and take off again at once. Obviously it's not their kind of neighborhood.

After breakfast I walk out into the parking lot, around the side of the hotel, and into another parking lot. It's Saturday and the office park is deserted of cars. Parking lot trees grow in predictable rows like the light poles, two strips of sod a foot wide skirting each one between its concrete borders. I feel like the geese.

A quarter mile away I finally come upon a neglected lot. Real weeds at last, their brown unsightly leftover stalks sticking up above the tentative green below. And real litter. A few blessed beer cans, plastic sacks, wisps of paper. A redwing blackbird perches on a spindly bough in the middle of this clutter and gives his call. Three others rise to it. They take off laughing.

I had been thinking of a quiz I saw in a magazine a year or so ago titled "Where in the World Are You?" Because ever since I left the woods two mornings ago I haven't known where I am. One American airport is very like another; one conference hotel almost identical to all other members of its genre. Locality, even though this is a history conference and locality is supposedly essential to history, has been of interest to no one. The quiz, as I remember it, asked questions like "Where is north from where you're standing now?" and "Name one species of grass native to the area." Could any of us pass?

Jacques Ellul in his book *The Technological System* maintains that we no longer live in the system of nature, as all past cultures have. Instead, we live in the system of technology. Nature is allowed to continue its existence only in little wayside containment areas like the art-object pond. For the past few years I had been living in Wyoming, one of the larger containment areas. There, people must still live largely in the system of nature. It has not proved cost-efficient to transport the technological system to Wyoming so far. But such a life is not what people at the conference would have called the "normative American experience."

What I want to know is: Did anyone else see the ducks in the cornfield? Was the redwing blackbird's whistle as essential to them as the amplified lectures? How else do you know where you are?

I do not mean these to be moral questions. People are not observably less kind or thoughtful or responsible because of their isolation from the natural world. I cannot see that the percentage of responsible bellboys and scholars has diminished for all their immersion in technology. And I know a fair number of folk who live "close to nature" who are uncommonly coarse and brutal. Sensibilities shaped by vinyl are not necessarily depraved. They simply can't see ducks. Their hearts are not broken by gradations of green or any other color.

If you can't see ducks, can you see people? If redwing blackbirds are irrelevant to the technological system, what about one's fellow diners, whether on airplanes or in Christian cafeterias? Is communion still possible, or even conviviality, if creation becomes de-sacralized by renaming it "the environment," a term that emphasizes our isolation from ducks and cornfields? Is there a correspondence between office parks, art-object ponds, and those furtive cafeteria prayers? If we are alienated from creation, will that not mean finally alienation from even our own flesh?

Fire on My Mind

Lionel Basney   *January 1985*

"Anyone with a fire on his mind is in a sort of trance."

— E. B. WHITE

Three winters ago we installed a wood-burning furnace in the cellar and began to take our heat out of the woods instead of the gas pipe. The pipe is still there; some nights in February are too much for a wood fire, even if I stay up to feed it. Most of the time, however, we have the cheerful bellow of an oak flame, the song of the fan, the slight, woolly pungency in the stairs.

Up to now the wood has been arriving more or less on its own. We sorted, split, and stacked it, and burned it. But we have just added to the system twelve acres of wood lot, on a high, sheltered, west-facing hillside. Now it's our project, stump to ash. It will absorb more time and attention, and mean, in the end, less money and less dependence.

We think we've done a good thing. Trading a non-renewable resource for a constantly self-renewing one has eased our minds a little. We're walking a little lighter on the earth. With the wood, as with the garden, we've drawn closer to our real needs, and occupy our days with them instead of bought satisfactions. We're standing a little straighter, more on our own feet.

The gas bills have shrunk, but that's a complicated issue. Our savings on gas have been more than spent on the wood lot so that, in the short term, the gas company's gloating confidence that my pipe will warm again in a season or two has, from their perspective, some foundation. Self-reliance nowadays is not inexpensive. If you go into it with money in mind you may be disappointed. On the other hand, money to the gas company is money gone for good. Whereas after I've thinned my hillside of oak and hickory for a few years, it will hold more fuel than it does now. Eventually, with patience, I'll be ahead.

There are other more personal gains. Splitting wood is good exercise; it saves me from the fidgets on cluttered days, and sometimes gives back joy. I have become a pupil of axe and wedge. There is grace in that whipping blow, the power of giving in to a larger rhythm. I am watching a larger rhythm, the seasons on the wood lot, with fixed attention and wonder.

I put these pleasures down like numbers in an account book, but that is not how we feel them. The small, pragmatic change, gas to wood, has changed whole sets of other things, whole tracts of feeling — sharpened our eyes to the weather, repunctuated our days and nights, made new skills suddenly urgent, added new confidence, anxiety, and anger. Whole months have a new flavor. Parts of the house have a new use, and new odors, wood smoke, the scent of split oak, like peaches.

The change has posted its evidence all around the property. There is a sense, however, in which none of it is new, only a revelation of something that has been going on all along. One part of life in a northern place has come out of hiding. Some of the cushiony surfaces beneath which American homes hide the process of living have rolled back. We have touched the metabolism of the house. A larger learning is going on, which makes the woodpile, the chip-barrel, and the pails of ash welcome and significant. Seeing them there is important to me — I have been trying, more intently as the years pass, to *see what I am doing.*

There are two parts to this — the seeing, or being willing to see; and doing things which can be seen. I garden, do my own carpentry, burn wood, because the human and natural relations of this work are visible. They fall within the space of my hands. They are not obscured by money. They don't use the world in ways beyond my knowledge and judgment.

People think of this work as going with a "simpler" lifestyle, but they are mistaken. Coming to see what you are doing complicates everything. The actual life you are living is the most complicated thing you can try to know.

Coming to see more clearly what our needs cost the world has sobered us — this is another change in the tone of our lives. Bought pleasures, distractions, are being crowded out by work. We don't want to be distracted. Perhaps we are turning into Puritans — but it is a Puritanism of gratitude, a devotion to the purified, undistracted thing. I don't bring work home from the office these days. My work starts at home; it is home work.

It is hand work and head work at the same time. As I try to see what I am doing, I grow increasingly suspicious of ideas I cannot feel the weight of, ones that claim to leave no residue in the firebox. All ideas leave a residue — though we often don't know what to do with it, or where to hide it from the future.

The text of my attempt to see lies in *Walden:* "Moral reform is the effort to cast off sleep. Why is it that men give so poor an account of their day if they have not been slumbering? . . . I have never yet met a man who was quite awake." Awake to what? To the world, Thoreau would have said, knowing that to see this world clearly and wholly would be to see the other world as well. This distinction between worlds would be hard for a righteous man to see. What would his goodness mean, practically, but freedom to be fully present to what he was doing, unreservedly, without distraction or hiding?

It is an ideal I accept, and try to make my own. Sometimes when I plant two blows in a straight line across the drum of oak, I think I'm almost there. But I know better. Enough of my strokes go foul.

On the threshold of our fourth winter, moreover, I'm learning how much a fire can demand. It is not just a new awareness; it's a preoccupation. There are moments, usually very early or very late, when it is quiet, when the cold surrounds the house like an army, and I find myself bracing to meet it. I nurse such a small fire. I carry it, day after day, in the bowl of my mind. I catch myself signaling back to it, encouraging it, projecting my will to stand off the weather. It is as if, suddenly, I had to remind my heart to beat.

Even this is not just liability. This is what I ought to think about, not the stock market, not my ambitions. It is the life of my immediate and precious obligations. The irony is that the fire itself distracts me. Part of my attention is always stuck in the cellar, not available to people directly, not available to study.

You see what has happened. I have traded one engagement for another. Taking responsibility for one thing, I have had to turn half-away from something else. In the fall air of this fallen world the ideal of presence seems complicated and distant; I make choices in its absence — I was about to say, my own absence.

And this is not the only fire I have in mind. A year or two ago I wrote a short lyric, which began:

Then let the trees depart,
    And the horizon clear.
What will a heart
    Do with its fear?

Vanish the green stand
    In the fire of war. . . .

And so on. When I read it to some of my students, one asked, "Is it about nuclear war?" "Not consciously," I said. "Actually, I dreamt the first two lines and just went on from there." I paused. "But it could be that, too." It wouldn't have been the first time I had dreamt about it.

If I seem absent these days, it is not because I do not see that presence is a duty. If I seem anxious, it's not because I don't know that anxiety is a failing. I have fires on my mind. I share my home with all sorts of unaccountables — the weather, and the health of a stand of trees, and a sudden down draft in the flue; and with greater evils I can do nothing to avert, which I cannot *see*, except in nightmare.

This is why I drive up to the wood lot as the fall lights the oaks and maples, as the small animals burrow toward their cool sleep, and see less than is there to see. This is why I tend my early fires, and write these words, with a divided mind.

An Enviable Satirist [on Peter De Vries]

JOHN J. TIMMERMAN   *August 1983*

Peter De Vries is not forgettable. I met him as a fellow freshman [at Calvin College] on a bus trip to the beach at Grand Haven, sponsored by the college to divert homesickness. His already scintillating wise-cracks sparked the bus and the party at the beach. He was entirely worthy of Chicago. I admired him at once and throughout college for his exuberant presence, his chic clothes, rare brilliance, verbal daring, and winning personality. I sat in various English classes with him, worked with him on the *Chimes,* rooted for him at debates and oratori-cal contests, and participated with him in various bull-sessions. He was exceedingly bright, but chose to reveal it only in carefully selected courses. Calvin was then a very small college and one had to be half-conscious not to know him. He was popular but distant. Very few knew him well; he had a shell of reserve about his deeper convictions. I never knew him well, although we were friends. I saw him three times after graduation, each an occasion I savored and still do. Al-though our perspectives on life differ sharply, I have been enriched by some of his books and the memory of his extraordinary presence. One does not often associate with a genius.

This is not the place and I am not the person to count the ways in which he has enriched American literature. The intellectual smart set on the East Coast do that well and frequently. *Time* loves him and the *New York Times Book Review* celebrates even his failures. He has a so-phisticated British audience. According to Ben Yagoda in the *Times Book Review,* he has an unwavering core of 25,000 devotees. I am not a wholehearted devotee. I would serenely predict that five of his novels and his volume of short stories will have a permanent place in Ameri-can literature. Sometimes I find his subject matter unsavory and his style overbearing, but at his best De Vries is a great comic writer who knows that comedy is often the other side of tragedy and seldom confuses the two.

De Vries' literary gifts are well known: the verbal dazzle, the memorable characterization, the satirical thrust, the good story, and the underlying, serious criticism of life. I have always relished the unexpectedness, the twist with or without the barb. Nowhere, in my judgment, has De Vries exhibited the unexpected better than in the beginning of *The Vale of Laughter,* with its ironic title. The book begins thus: "Call me, Ishmael, feel absolutely free to call me any hour of the day or night at the office or at home." When one thinks of Ishmael in *Moby Dick* hunting a whale in trackless seas, this beginning is hard to beat. The unexpected erupts everywhere, a constant source of surprise, shock, and pleasure.

It is always encouraging to see a long-held personal conviction corroborated by a writer of distinction. In the article by Ben Yagoda, De Vries is quoted as saying "humor deals with that part of our suffering which is exempt from tragedy." I have long believed that. Tragedy stifles humor, and that is why "black humor," which has nothing to do with race, has seldom amused me. That is also why a statement by Flannery O'Connor, a comic writer I admire, has puzzled me. O'Connor says in a letter to "A": "In my experience, everything funny I have written is more terrible than it is funny, or only funny because it is terrible, or only terrible because it is funny." Flannery O'Connor's grotesques can be very funny; they can also be terrible, and then I don't find them funny at all. The Misfit in *A Good Man is Hard to Find* is a terrible man; what he does is bloodcurdling. Certainly, he is not terrible because he is funny. Humor ceases when the terrible strikes. De Vries is entirely right about this, although we all know that sometimes tragedy and comedy are grotesquely related.

Peter De Vries grew up in a parochial society made for a satirist's delight, a bustling, paradoxical community crammed with contrast and opposition. He radiantly exercised the satirist's franchise of exaggeration and dared to risk alienation as well as to enjoy appreciation. I have lived in his early world and remained in it for most of my life, and I have enjoyed the spectacle. It is a fairly tight world with many dimensions, some of which deserve great praise rather than censure. On the one hand I know many stories of outlandish behavior on all its levels. I know and have known paradoxical people memorably gifted

John J. Timmerman

and pitiably vain, savage infighting by saints who celebrate agape, overblown and overpaid pomposities fattening themselves on the idealism of others without practicing it, moneyed men who didn't want their left hand to know what their right hand was doing because it wasn't doing anything, screwballs, and cheats in sacred places. But that is far less than half of the story. I would need many pages to describe the goodness, unwavering integrity, and unstinted sacrifices I have so often observed. The immigrant community in which I grew up has, through uncommon persistence, native ability, and God's grace, become a community that serves many noble causes in many places and provides leaders in almost every walk of life. What a gift it would be to achieve comic distance with intense appreciation, to recreate the complex texture of this society in the light of the convictions it much more frequently honored than betrayed. . . . I envy the talent that could have done it, even when it doesn't.

The Uses of Lewis

KATHRYN LINDSKOOG   *January 1978*

For at least ten years, occasional advertisements have been claiming that this or that new book is "written in the style of C. S. Lewis." A sort of slander, but it sells. Nowadays I see not only Lewis's name but his own words and even his own face in strange places. For example, there is the introductory folder put out by Ralph Blair's organization called Evangelicals Concerned. What they are concerned about is homosexuals. One-fifth of the folder is given to a sketch of C. S. Lewis and his following words:

> Of all tyrannies a tyranny exercised for the good of its victims may be the most oppressive. It may be better to live under robber barons than under omnipotent moral busy-bodies. The robber baron's cruelty may sometimes sleep, his cupidity may at some point be satiated; but those who torment us for our own good will torment us without end, for they do so with the approval of their own conscience. . . .

This statement is in fact from Lewis's essay "The Humanitarian Theory of Punishment," which does not deal directly with homosexuality. Blair understandably does not quote Lewis on homosexuality itself, since Lewis stated clearly that he looked upon homosexuals with bewildered pity. Pity is one of the responses that Evangelicals Concerned does not want to solicit.

A Houston priest named T. Robert Ingram is out ahead of Blair. Ingram has brought out a series of books with titles like *Poison Drops in the Federal Senate, Christian Economics, Essays on Segregation,* and *Essays on the Death Penalty.* His coup was to reprint Lewis's "The Humanitarian Theory of Punishment" *in toto* as the featured essay in his book supporting the death penalty. Ingram devotes the first paragraph of his introduction to identifying C. S. Lewis and attributing to him a belief in "the Christian system of law and order as it rests upon the execution of the death penalty after 'due process' as the chief punishment for crime against God." (Goodness knows if Ingram considers homosexuality a crime against God. If he does, no wonder Evangelicals Concerned are so concerned.)

It happens that Lewis's essay is about crimes against society, not crime against God. It also happens that in the first paragraph Lewis gets capital punishment out of the way by stating that (1) he does not know if it is an indispensable deterrent, (2) he is not deciding if it is morally permissible, and (3) it is not the subject of his essay. He goes on to make a strong case against enforced therapy for criminals. Needless to say, this is by far the best essay in Ingram's collection. It takes up almost one-tenth of the book and says no more about the death penalty than it did about homosexuality. (Incidentally, Ingram snuggled his own name right next to Lewis's on the cover, if you consider exactly one-half a centimeter with a dot in the center to be snuggling distance.)

It's a long way from T. Robert Ingram's publishing ventures in Houston to Norman L. Geisler's Division of Philosophy of Religion at Trinity Evangelical Divinity School in Deerfield, Illinois. In more ways than one. In the May 20, 1977, issue of *Christianity Today* Geisler published an essay "Philosophy: The Roots of Vain Deceit," in which he points to faulty epistemology as a reason for the lack of commitment to biblical inerrancy among many scholarly and godly Christians. Geisler concluded his lengthy essay by stating, "In short, we must show the self-defeating nature of the philosophy that would unerringly eliminate inerrancy. In *The Weight of Glory* C. S. Lewis aptly stated our obligation: 'To be ignorant and simple now — not to be able to meet the enemies on their own ground — would be to throw down our weapons, and to betray our uneducated brethren . . . Good philosophy must exist if for no other reason, because bad philosophy needs to be answered.'"

Aptly stated indeed. Geisler did not bother to mention that these words came from Lewis's essay "Learning in War Time." He also did not bother to mention that the words he left out in the middle were about "the intellectual attacks of the heathen," not about differences within the church. That's all right. Geisler also failed to mention that Lewis himself absolutely rejected biblical inerrancy. Well, a person can't include everything.

If divinity school in Illinois does not suit the needs of the Christian laity, a new venture in theological education in Berkeley may help. "New College for Advanced Christian Studies" is being launched there in 1978. Fully half of the handsome one-page description of the college is filled with C. S. Lewis's photo and the following quotation:

> People say, "the Church ought to give us a lead." That is true if they mean it in the right way, but false if they mean it in the wrong way. By the Church they ought to mean the whole body of practicing Christians. But, of course, when they ask for a lead from the Church most people mean . . . the clergy. . . . That is silly . . . we are asking them to do a quite different job for which they have not been trained. The job is really on us, on the laymen. The application of Christian principles, say, to trade unionism or education, must come from Christian trade unionists and Christian schoolmasters; just as Christian literature comes from Christian novelists and dramatists — not from the bench of bishops getting together and trying to write plays and novels in their spare time.

It is clear that Lewis was so prolific and so quotable that words of his can enhance almost any cause, including schools of theology, schools of thought, and, maybe, schools for scandal. He has become today's man for all reasons.

Robert Lowell (1917-1977)

Jack Ridl   *January 1978*

Plath, Sexton, Berryman, Kees — dead by their own hand. There have been too many. Perhaps Robert Lowell's greatest triumph was that he outlived the Savage God.

We are thankful. We are grateful that he wrenched out and wrote of his struggle that he called a life, that a few might see as bearing a cross with the emotional wreckage of a human, the dignity and transformation of a divine, what many would call self-indulgence in suffering.

The so-called mentally stable, the spiritually complacent often complain that the psychically suffering artists are but a splinter group from the heretical Romantic school. The facile equating of the confessional poet with the self-pitying expresser is a cruel indulgence practiced — and one day perhaps paid for — by those who cannot detect the difference between the versifying diarist, who uses experience to draw attention to self, and the poet, whose priest was Lowell, who draws attention through his experiences to life.

Robert Lowell wrote without evasions. He broke out of what he came to believe were the shackles of New Criticism and, while retaining his Alexandrian mastery, substituted immediacy and vulnerability for impersonality and exquisite irony.

> When the timeless, daily, tedious affair
> was over, his Mother shut
> her Bible; her nose was in the air;
> from her summit
> of righteousness, she could not see the boy:
> his lumpy forehead knotted
> with turmoil, his soul returned to its vomit.

Confronted once by a smug self-righteousness, Robert Lowell did not turn his back, cynically dismissing Christianity as a sweet myth. Though it may have failed him as a placebo for his mental anguish, he did not recoil in anger. Though he fought the false fronts of a Christian complacency, he fought through them to a rarity in Christendom. Lowell looked not for supplication or salvation. He let the Christ confront him. Unable to find solution or ablution, he accepted the challenging Christ, the Christ who comes as a two-edged sword. Lowell's vulnerability was at its most courageous as he allowed the Christian God to remind him of his humanity rather than assure him of his possible divinity. There is little, if any, comfort in a Lowell Christianity. He could accept a crucifixion. His attention to the immediate would have been diverted by the resurrection; if there be such a remarkable reality, he dared not make it any more than a result, a decision of God, not a given based on belief. He feared the distraction of the empty tomb.

When the Lord God formed man from the sea's slime
And breathed into his face the breath of life,
And blue-lung'd combers lumbered to the kill.
The Lord survives the rainbow of His will.

Robert Lowell would that eternal life be life eternal rather than man eternal. And the Kingdom? Did he enter as a little child? I think his poems answer often. He shed the tweed of sophistication, a first step: "But we are old, our fields are running wild: / Till Christ again turn wanderer and child."

Was Robert Lowell a Christian? Was he saved? Did he find it? I think he might not know what to do with such doorbell-ringing queries. He might retort, "Why do you ask?" More than likely he'd shake his head sincerely, wondering. We'll err greatly if we assume that when he left the Roman Catholic Church he renounced his God. And if we do so, we shall miss his challenge to us: his opening, offering himself to the stare of Christ.

Robert Lowell will leap not into heaven; he'll wait in misery to be received, for

I hear
my ill-spirit sob in each blood cell
as if my hand were at its throat. . . .
I myself am hell. . . .

Children of the Living God
[on Toni Morrison, *Beloved*]

SUSAN VAN ZANTEN GALLAGHER   *February 1988*

The slave narrative has long been one of the predominant genres of black American literature. Like its poetic counterpart, the blues, the slave narrative emerged as an artistic response to the unspeakable dehumanization of slavery. . . . Perhaps one of the most significant signs of the vitality of black women's literature is Toni Morrison's fifth and most recent novel, *Beloved*, which, along with Ralph Ellison's *Invisible Man* (1952), represents the culmination of the slave narrative genre in 20th-century black fiction. One of the *New York Times'* "Best Books of 1987," recently nominated for a National Book Critics Circle Award, and a consistent bestseller for the past several months, *Beloved* well deserves its success.

A fictional slave narrative, the story traces, in its account of Sethe, a former slave at the Sweet Home plantation, the psychological trauma, the wounded mind as well as the wounded body, that results from slavery. The novel is set in 1873, when Sethe lives just outside of Cincinnati with her eighteen-year-old daughter Denver and a spiteful ghost who haunts the house, dumping simmering kettles over, hurling the dog against the wall, forming pools of sad, red, undulating light. Everyone has abandoned Sethe: her husband has mysteriously never joined her as they had planned; her two sons have fled the supernaturally inhabited house; her mother-in-law has given up fighting the skirmishes of life and dies; the black community has ostracized her for eighteen years. Sethe stoically accepts the ghost's rampages, while Denver, who has grown up with little contact with the outside world, regards the ghost as a sisterly companion. For indeed the ghost is her sister, whose throat was cut when she was two years old and whose tombstone bears one word: *beloved*. "For a baby she throws a powerful spell," Denver tells her mother. "Not more powerful than the way I loved her," Sethe answers.

The ghost is temporarily exorcized with the arrival of Paul D, another former Sweet Home slave, who has been wandering the country ever since the Civil War. But no sooner does the furniture begin to stay in place than a strange young woman with lineless new skin and a raspy voice arrives. She can answer no questions about her past except to say that her name is Beloved, and she gradually takes over all of Sethe's life, cutting her off from other relationships, demanding ceaseless attention, and physically draining her. Sethe is torn between her overpowering love for the dead child, her concern for the living Denver, and her reawakened emotional and sexual attraction to Paul D. These emotional battles are punctuated with a series of flashbacks that reveal the terrible history of Sweet Home, the fate of Sethe's husband, the circumstances of Denver's birth in the midst of Sethe's flight from slavery, Paul D's brutal life in a Georgia prison, and, most significantly, how and why Beloved died.

Beloved explores the paradoxes of love. Because we all struggle to define the best expressions of love, the novel speaks to us. But the universal theme of the difficulty of love is given a culturally specific expression, as all themes must, by its historical context. The struggle to love is particularly difficult when one is a former slave living in the late 19th century. One of slavery's most devastating consequences is its effect on love. Normal male-female relationships are perverted; families have no stability; husband and wife, mother and child, are cavalierly separated at the whim of the slaveholder. One former slave named Ella, who spent her puberty in a house where she was shared by a father and son, regards love as "a serious disability." "Don't love nothing," she advises Sethe. Paul D, like the tin man in Oz, has a rusty tobacco tin lodged in his chest instead of a red heart. He thinks Sethe's love is dangerous. . . .

Sethe's indomitable love for her children epitomizes her humanity and proves wrong the Southern slaveholders' belief that slaves had no maternal feelings. Yet as Paul D realizes, Sethe's flinty love is also dangerous. "Your love is too thick," he tells her. "Love is or it ain't," she replies. "Thin love ain't love at all." Paul D must learn to give more, to realize that his political freedom is not true freedom until he opens up his tobacco tin, but Sethe must learn to give less to Beloved, to avoid being swallowed up by her own love and guilt. And all the characters must relearn the importance of community, for the ghost does not flee forever until the formerly distant black women come to Sethe's house to save her.

While the plot of *Beloved* may sound melodramatic in summary, Morrison's skillful characterization, narration, and imagery make this novel both complex and satisfying. The treatment of the supernatural is matter-of-fact and nonsensational; the characters are vividly brought to life in their actions and conversations; and the complex narrative structure is rendered clearly and skillfully. Morrison writes lyrical prose. One memorable section presents the inner voices of Sethe, Denver, and Beloved. The dead girl's eerie, disjointed thoughts about her time "on the other side" and her desire to join and eat up Sethe effectively evoke the disturbed kind of love that she represents.

Morrison's lyricism and use of inner voices are characteristic of much contemporary feminine writing. Similarly, some of her image patterns have particularly feminine associations, such as her treatment of food. The escaped slaves celebrate their freedom with a grand banquet of turkey, shortbread, new peas, and mouth-watering blackberry pies. Sethe's love for Paul D blossoms as she plans a special supper of "itty bitty potatoes browned on all sides, snap beans seasoned with rind, and yellow squash sprinkled with vinegar and sugar." Food is associated not only with love, giving, creativity, and life but also with the greatest moments of violation, when its proper function is distorted. Sethe repeatedly dwells on the time when two adolescent white boys hold her down and drink from her breasts the milk that belonged to her baby. And at the end of the novel, Sethe and Denver are starving even as Beloved daily grows larger and larger. . . .

In the traditional slave narrative, three forces help blacks to overcome oppression and achieve identity and freedom: education, community, and Christianity. Morrison has only a little to say about the first and the third; her focus is on the loving relationships between man and woman, mother and daughter, individual and society. When the women converge on Sethe's house to drive Beloved out, their Christianity is lumped together with their superstitious beliefs: "Some brought what they could and what they believed would work, stuffed in apron pockets, strung around their necks, lying in the space between their breasts. Others brought Christian faith — as shield and sword. Most brought a little of both."

Yet the epigraph of *Beloved* is Romans 9:25: "I will call them my people, which were not my people; and her beloved, which was not beloved." While this passage may suggest both the magnitude and the moral ambiguity of Sethe's love for her dead child, it also makes a larger claim for the black race. The "beloved" of the biblical text refers to the Gentiles — once a forsaken race, newly chosen by God. Paul continues in verse 26: "And it shall come to pass, that in the place where it was said unto them, Ye are not my people; there shall they be called the children of the living God." The epigraph thus implies the final theological sanctioning of black personhood and identity.

Grace Notes [On *Tender Mercies*]

Roy M. Anker   *July 1984*

At first glance *Tender Mercies* does not really seem to have much going for it. The plot sounds like pure corn, even for Hollywood: a
boozing country music star, once a noted songwriter and singer,
wakes up from a long drunk in a flatland Texas motel cabin.
Deserted by his buddy and flat broke, Mac Sledge (Robert Duvall)
volunteers to work off what he owes the motel owner (Tess Harper),
a youngish Vietnam widow with a nine-year-old son. A few quick
scenes later we find them married. Unable to leave his music alone,
and wishing to bring in some money, Sledge struggles to put his career back together. Amid setbacks, he resists the bottle and even gets
baptized, for he has married a believing woman. Later tragedy
comes his way, and he holds on still. The love of a woman makes father know and do best after all.

The difference between corn and a jewel, we might say, lies in the
telling. The story comes fast, spare, and direct, especially in the somewhat elliptical opening scenes. The usual Hollywood fascination with
pairing and mating is largely absent. A few compact scenes at the outset serve to evoke the coming together of two people, one stoical and
reticent, the other shy and scared. The filmmakers seem in a hurry to
move on to more important matters — especially how kindness and
hope are mediated and passed between three hard-pressed souls.
Widow Rosalee counts her son and new husband among the "bless-
ings and tender mercies" (Psalm 145:9) for which she nightly thanks
God. Her son has to figure out what a father is. For Sledge, the case is
more difficult. He has more hurts and demons than he can name. Long
a mean and angry guy, he once when drunk tried to kill his former
wife, who is herself no angel. Wealthy and famous from the songs he

wrote for her, she still keeps him from seeing their daughter, who at the time of the story turns eighteen. And when Sledge tries to get his career moving again, the ex-wife impedes him with a vengeance. It is small wonder, then, that Sledge observes near the film's end that he does not "trust happiness."

Such sad turmoil is common enough, both in the movies and in life. But in this film we find movement through the tumult toward an unexpected and beguiling destination. Sledge's predicament and passage gather interest and weight from writer Foote's and director Beresford's handling not only of the story itself but of locale, imagery, and music, all of which imbue Sledge's history with urgency and emotional depth. No small part of the dramatic force of *Tender Mercies* derives from the use of setting. The land lies flat and bare, windswept and empty save for prairie grass and plowed fields. From this rises the blue expanse of the clear and fathomless Texas sky. By consistently framing the characters' hardscrabble lives between endless earth and sky, the film underscores the very tenuousness of their physical fragility. The scene at once aggravates and emboldens their daunting questions about their place and purpose within such vastness. A philosopher might call it a pictorial accentuation of existential self-awareness. In the middle of nowhere live some people in a dumpy two-gas-pump motel on a two-lane rural highway.

Occasional cars pass down the highway, a thin ribbon between the land and the sky. And sometimes the motel family itself travels down it — to church, to cemeteries, to stores, and maybe just to some other place, any place that might hold diversion or escape. The road is tied up with their lives — what they are and what they might be. On the one hand, it is their link with the rudiments of sustenance: worship, groceries, schooling, and mourning; on the other hand, it calls them to make choices about freedom and obligations. In Sledge's case, the road stretches away to other destinations, other opportunities; it provides a persistent temptation to leave the intimacy and quiet richness of the bondedness he has shambled into. As he states near the film's climax, there is no apparent reason for the good new turn in his life. The road inscrutably brought him there, and the road can at any time carry him, if he will let it, back into his boozing protest against life's hurt and chaos.

Together the skyscape and road set off the stark reality, often forgotten, of individual life and the burden of choice. The elements of the setting are as much characters and forces in *Tender Mercies* as are the people. If there is such a thing as a transcendental style in film, as Paul Schrader has suggested, a style that evokes or somehow conjures up a sense of a transcendent or divine pressure upon life, Foote and Beresford flirt with it in *Tender Merices*. With a white motel and a road set amid a limitless land and sky, these filmmakers pare away most of the usual histrionic fluff about life to contemplate its essential contours of meaning and value, assent and despair. If nothing else, *Tender Mercies* depicts the route and significance of an individual life as it grasps in some small way the fact and purpose of its own being.

A few films only capitalize on the special capabilities of the medium to prod the viewer to contemplate the simultaneous travail and glory of life and thereby freshen our grasp of the transient thing we have. *Ordinary People* is such a film, as is *Tender Mercies*. But *Tender Mercies* pushes for still more, achieving something that rallies a specifically Christian response to life's nagging ambiguities. Sledge gets religion, more or less. Its progress, if we can talk about it in those terms, is slow and not all that perceptible — no Damascus roads or healings or tongue-speaking. Always shamed and bewildered by his past, by attitudes he never loses, Sledge is first taken aback and then gladdened by his newfound family. Early on, he sings "Jesus Saves" in church with his wife-to-be in the choir; afterward he meets the minister, and a little later he is baptized with his stepson in the standard-issue Baptist church tub.

Of course, in the middle of this alteration, the question remains whether it is romance or religion that prompts his gratitude and belief. The answer, as it should be, is probably both, given what we are. That enigma, though, comes to the test, so to speak, later on in the story, when Sledge is briefly reunited with his estranged daughter, who has searched him out. Near the end of their first short talk, she asks if he remembers, quoting some of the words, a lullaby he sang to her as a little girl. He denies any memory of it. Then after their goodbyes, Sledge stands by the window and watches her car disappear. With his back to the audience, he quietly sings the song, Hank Williams's "The Wings of a Dove." When he comes to the chorus, his body slowly rocks with a slow, deliberate rhythm that is itself a type of witness to his own new apprehension of the mysterious hope of the song. The words convey only some of the scene's impact:

When Jesus went down to the water that day,
He was baptized in the usual way.
When it was done, God blessed his Son;
He sent him his love on the wings of a dove.

On the wings of a snow white dove,
He sends his pure sweet love,
A sign from above, on the wings of a dove.

Near the end of the film, just as Sledge has a possibility of making it again with his music, the worst thing that can happen to his daughter happens, and he is once again set to the task of figuring out the whyfores of fate. Hacking away in the back garden, he confesses to Rosalee that he has prayed for some understanding of the reasons for tragedy and has received none at all. The hurt and anger and wonder are there, framed as always by the limitless unanswering sky. Puny befuddled man asks for what seems to be none of his business. There is no sign from above, no reassurance.

The closing sequence finds Sledge picking up papers by the roadside, as he had done for hire at the film's beginning. Only now he sings to himself, in the midst of his mourning, "The Wings of a Dove." Again he puts off the bottle and protest; the song becomes benediction, lament, and solace. Somehow love might yet prevail. Maybe this is faith looking for hope, for the evidence of the sway of love. Greeted in the midst of his singing by his stepson home from school, he goes with him to the field across the street to toss a new football. Thereupon a quietly jubilant symphonic piece, the first of its kind in the movie, accompanies the game of catch amid the land and sky. The end.

Now it would be easy to make a procrustean operation of fitting this film to the pattern of Christian redemption. And yet Sledge *has* undeniably come a long way. He is not drinking, and he is nicer, and even though he is not in the arms of his wife, he makes there by the roadside some sort of murmuring gesture of recollection and assent. If the mere fact of life itself is at all a wonder, as the visual style of the film suggests, then the possibility that there might be something like love amid the riddle and the mess, something radical and steadfast, a sign from above, is ample cause for not only wonder but gratitude. Unexpected and undeserved as it might be for Sledge, it has nonetheless taken over his perceptions of the way the world is. And there is enough of it to warrant praise, song, and play, as the music and action of the last scene appropriately suggest.

Amid the overarching mystery of existence, mercy comes in many ways and places, even into the mundane passages of an everyday life tending gas pumps. It is the special gift of *Tender Mercies* that it focuses our attention on such ordinary settings and thus, as Frederick Buechner might put it, on the unexpected inroads of grace into the corners of our days.

Born to Raise the Sons of Earth

MARK A. NOLL   *December 1987*

I am busy, Jesus,
screeching ever faster round and round —
you lie calmly in the manger,
Joseph's patient voice the only sound.

I am selfish, Jesus,
grasping, pulling inward, curved in tight —
you stoop lower, ever lower,
mixing spittle for a poor man's sight.

I am sated, Jesus —
stuffed so full I've almost lost my breath —
you are rasping, breathing labored,
stumbling naked, famished to your death.

I am tired, Jesus,
numb and finished, callous and depressed —
you stand wounded, weeping, dying,
quickened; calling, come to me and rest.

On Having the Grace to Live Contingently

Stanley Hauerwas   July 1988

I still remember the excitement I felt when in my senior year in college I read H. Richard Niebuhr's *The Meaning of Revelation*. Believing as I did that no intellectually compelling account of Christianity could be given, since I could not see how our destiny could be based on a historically contingent fact, I devoured Niebuhr's book. Here not only was an honest mind but one that met, in a constructive and existentially compelling way, what I thought to be the most decisive challenge to the Christian faith. Even though I later came to doubt the distinction between inner and outer history, to be suspicious of Niebuhr's confessionalism, I am forever grateful that at one point in my life I was ready to read that book in a manner that I am sure changed my life.

This was not the first time I had read *The Meaning of Revelation*. I read it when I was a senior in high school well before I had ever heard the names of Lessing, Troeltsch, or Barth. Reading it that first time did little for me, as I had no idea why there was a problem about history. Yet reading the book four years later made me so excited I actually trembled with excitement. I remember I read it straight through in one sitting.

I am sure the experience I describe is not unique to me. We all have moments in our lives when we seem disposed to hear, see, and understand what at another time we would not have noticed. Sometimes it is a novel — perhaps not a very good novel — that says just the words we need to hear; or it may be a painting that helps us see what we had been looking at but failed to see; or, as is often the case, it is another person who comes into our lives at precisely the right moment, helping us to see as well as own the direction of our lives or to even change directions.

What is so unusual about these experiences is how contingent factors converge in a way that gives them the feeling of necessity. It was a matter of chance that I ever got so bent out of shape that the problem of history and in particular the question of the "historical Jesus" ever became a problem for me. If Pleasant Mound Methodist Church in Pleasant Grove, Texas, had not had so many young people called to the ministry during the time I was growing up, the idea that I ought to take all this religious stuff seriously would never have occurred to me. Moreover, if I had just been saved some Sunday night I probably would not have thought it necessary as a substitute to dedicate my life to the ministry — a self-chosen commitment that for the good of God's church I was soon led to disavow and subsequent history has confirmed. If I had not had a girlfriend back in high school, I probably would have gone to Hendrix College in Conway, Arkansas, rather than Southwestern University, where I encountered a teacher who knew, in Buber's characterization of the ultimate act of teaching, "when to raise his finger at the right time." If my girlfriend back in Dallas had not jilted me soon after I left, I probably would not have sublimated my lust into a passion for philosophy. On the other hand, if Niebuhr had not been so possessed by the problem of relativism, *The Meaning of Revelation* would not have been written. If, when he wrote *The Meaning of Revelation*, he had been as critical of Barth's alleged Christomonism as he was to be later, the book would have lacked the theological tension that makes it so exciting.

All this conspired and came together in Georgetown, Texas, sometime in 1962 and had a powerful impact on my life.

*   *   *

Our lives are made up of contingencies. We are the result of lucky accidents. We tell ourselves that what we are is what we have made ourselves — after all, I did decide to read *The Meaning of Revelation* — and yet we know and fear that we are more what happens to us than what we do. Even more, we fear the many lost opportunities we have missed because we were not ready to hear this truthful word or because that word was put in a way we were not ready to hear. In short, we fear that for most of our lives we dwell in darkness and have no means even to know that we so dwell.

I suspect this is the reason, moreover, why we — that is, we Christians of modernity — have such a fascination with John 3:16 — "For God so loved the world that he gave his only Son, that whoever believes in him should not perish but have eternal life." Here it seems we have the gospel — the good news — so succinctly stated that it should be available to anyone no matter what his or her circumstance might be. The gospel, we believe, is a universal truth ready to be appropriated by anyone at any place and at any time.

The universal truth we believe John 3:16 embodies, of course, is that God is love. Moreover, we know this truth involves a bit of unpleasant news — namely, that most of us are not as good or loving as we think we ought to be, again a truth anyone is capable of acknowledging. But the good news is that God does not hold this against us. All we have to do is believe in Jesus, a belief that can take many different forms, and we will have eternal life; or, given our doubts about eternity, at least a meaningful life — which is about as close as we can come to the idea of salvation. After all, if we are going to go to the trouble of believing in God — something had to start all this and finally there is such a mystery about life — then we might as well believe that God is also a God of love. Of course, once the gospel is reduced to the formula of John 3:16, one wonders why we need Jesus at all, and in particular why anyone would ever have bothered to put him to death. Note that this is not the standard catechism question of why Jesus had to die, with its equally standard response, namely, as an expiation for our sins. Rather the question is, Why would anyone ever have gotten upset with Jesus if all he had to tell us is that God loves us and does not want us to perish. You'd think that anyone with so wonderful a message would end up with quite a following. Rather Jesus ended on a cross, abandoned by all his followers except for Mary Magdalene, Mary his mother, her sister, Mary the wife of Clopas, and some mysterious figure without a name called "the blessed disciple." How could someone with the message of "pure and unbounded love" end up in such a sorry state? Some terrible mistake must have been made.

A mistake has been made, of course, but the mistake is our attempt to make John 3:16 into a truth of which Jesus' life and death is only an *illustration.* For God's love is not some generalized attitude that names someone always ready to accept and to forgive, but rather the concrete, fleshy love that comes in the person of Jesus of Nazareth. It is in this person that God's love is revealed. It is in this person that God is glorified — a glory that takes the form of a cross. For as we are told in

John 3:14, just as Moses lifted up the serpent in the wilderness, so must the Son of man be lifted up — a lifting that came in the form of a cross so that God's arms might be spread wide in order that the world might be embraced into the kingdom.

Yet the hard and harsh truth is that a cross-formed love brings judgment. That light which is meant to illumine, which came not to condemn, creates darkness. How can this be? How can a gospel of "pure unbounded love" create darkness? Moreover, it is a darkness more black, more thorough, more complete, because the Son has now come. Just as a light makes the gray recesses of a room all the darker, so the sending of the Son makes the darkness of the world and our lives darker and more complete. An odd result, it would seem, for a God that is supposed to be about the saving of us.

Which should make us think twice about what we mean by salvation. The salvation we want to insure by the abstracting of John 3:16 from the life, death, and resurrection of Jesus is a salvation on our terms — it is a gnostic salvation based on the allegedly universal knowledge that God is love. For we think we know what love is — that we know what it means for God to love the world — and we are very glad indeed to think that what we mean by love is confirmed by God's sending Jesus into the world.

We thus pretend that we are always ready to respond to God, that we are always ready to acknowledge and live in the light cast by the sending of the Son. Salvation is not like the rest of our lives — namely, it is not contingent on our being able to see or hear God's word in the contingent form of Jesus of Nazareth. We may not be ready to understand Niebuhr's *The Meaning of Revelation,* we may not be ready to acknowledge that we hate our mother, we may not be prepared to face the fact we are going to spend all of our lives in ministry, but we think we are always ready to believe that God so loved the world.

We thus use John 3:16 to defeat the terrible knowledge that God's salvation is as contingent as our lives. Put differently, we want to believe that when it comes to salvation, we are always in a position ready to respond to God's grace. Thus almost all contemporary theology has been extraordinarily gracious about God's grace, wanting to insure that all people, even ourselves, have it irrespective of the darkness in which we dwell. In doing so, ironically, such theology attributes to us a status that only God has. Only God lives non-contingently, and that is why only God can save using the contingent — that is, only God can save through the calling of Israel and the life, death, and resurrection of Jesus Christ.

*   *   *

A darkness is created by the sending of the Son — a darkness, moreover, that we love since we believe that darkness to be the light. Even more, we are told we hate the light, not wanting our evil deeds exposed — deeds that are formed by our presumption that we are in control of our existence even to being in control of our salvation. We thus believe ourselves eternally ready to respond to the light, to the knowledge that God is love, finding it impossible to believe that we might really be dwelling in a darkness we cannot even see because we call it light. We thus are not ready to face the truth that this love is almost violent as it comes wrenching us from the world we have come to love.

The good news, however, is that because God has sent the Son we do not have to continue to dwell in the darkness. The good news is that the salvation wrought in Christ allows us to acknowledge that we have loved the darkness without that knowledge of our bent loves destroying us. Because God sent his only Son, we can trust God not to destroy us even though we have killed the very One who would save us. Forgiven, we are able to look back on our sins, confessing them, no longer fearing that without our sins we will not be.

In that sense, confessing our sin is not unlike recognizing that our life is contingently constituted. We have an almost irresistible desire to turn the contingencies of our life into necessity. We therefore say that our missed opportunities really worked out for the best. It is good I did not marry Joe or Mary, as otherwise I would not have had the opportunity to be this or that. In like manner we fear letting go of our sin exactly because we fear we will have no life if we let our life open to the life of this man Jesus. But by opening our life we discover that we have no reason to fear the contingent character of our life, as it has now been made part of God's very life.

This new life is a gift that creates its own response called, as we learn in Ephesians, faith. Faith names the new reality, the new history that has been made possible in Christ. It is, moreover, a history that is cosmic in scope as it insures that all ages are now constituted by the sending of the Son. The love that sends the Son is the selfsame love that moves the sun and the stars.

The cosmic dimension of God's love insures that the love found in this Jesus can never be exhausted. We will find the book that was so significant at one time to be limited, if not just wrong; we will find our enthusiasm for an artist to be inappropriate in light of their later work or our increasing sense of the tragic; we will even find that some people who at one time were decisive for the direction of our lives no longer can be made part of our future. The good news, however, is that the Son of man that God has lifted up is inexhaustible. Contingent though our lives are, God, through the sending of the Son, fits each of us into a life, into a love, that has no limits exactly because it is a life contingent as our own. What could be better news than this — that as creatures we have been given the means to live in the light radiating from the cross of Christ?

As those who desire to live in that light, we have been entrusted by God with this gospel so that the world might know the kind of love that moves the sun and the stars. "We are his workmanship, created in Christ Jesus for good works, which God prepared beforehand, that we should walk in them." We are the significant book, the magnificent painting, the crucial person necessary for the world to see, for the world to smell, for the world to touch the one who has wrought our salvation. For God's salvation is a contingent, fleshy business as real as the bread and wine that we must eat to live; as real as the one next to you whose very body pulls you into communion so that we might together stand in the truth. Therefore let us not hesitate to share this heavenly feast constituted by earthly fare, assured that when we do so, we participate with Christ and all the saints in God's eternal life.

Who Is in Control?

M. Howard Rienstra   *August 1985*

The realization that one is dying comes slowly. Six years ago I was di-
agnosed as having cancer. I have non-Hodgkins lymphoma. I was assured that although it was third stage, it was nonetheless treatable. It
has been, and on two occasions I was in remission. At one point I lost
most of my hair, and I have done an awful lot of vomiting over these
years. Yet I seemed to be in control. I knew that the vomiting was only
temporary, and I could feel the lymph nodes return to normal as the
chemotherapy took effect. I accepted the reality of my cancer, but I denied that I had really lost control over my own life. It seemed, in fact,
as if I were not yet dying.

The beginnings of a change came near midnight this past January
30. My fever had risen to 104, and Mary was driving me to the hospital
for the second time this year. I said to her, "You know, don't you, that
one of these times when I go to the hospital I won't return?" She quietly said, "Yes." Without using the words "death" or "dying," we came
to acknowledge the reality of it and that I was losing control — however reluctant my acknowledgment remained.

Early in April, after [three] hospitalizations had produced no clear
reasons for continuing fever and lung problems . . . [Mary and I de-
cided] that I would not return to the hospital again just to treat my fever and cough. I would rather die at home. We, in other words, were
trying to regain control over my life, and even my death. Later, however, it was proposed that I begin a new kind of chemo. . . . Outpatient
surgery was scheduled the next Monday to install a Port-a-Cath so
that I could receive the chemo quickly. . . .

I was in the operating room promptly at 1 p.m., and after the usual
preliminaries and administering of local anesthesia, the cutting in my

310   *1978-1990*

neck began. The surgeon had externally seen and palpitated a vein which he thought would be appropriate. Upon exposing that vein, however, he discovered it was too small to receive the catheter tubing. He then turned to other deeper veins. Let me anticipate questions by saying that I am an oddity. The veins in my neck, as it turns out, are not positioned as in an anatomy textbook. This structural oddity would soon have profound consequences. The surgeon eventually found a large vein which he assumed to be the external jugular vein. For most people it would have been. But as he put the catheter in that vein it could not be positioned correctly. It ran off either to my left or right arm, but it wouldn't go straight down no matter what he tried. A properly structured external jugular vein would have gone down as far as it had to for the successful operation of the Port-a-Cath. This one wouldn't.

At this point, about two hours into the surgery, some dramatic things began to happen. I began to think that I was going to die. I heard my surgeon call for another surgeon to come to assist him. And the surgeons he named were the big names of Grand Rapids surgeons. At that point I began gasping for breath. In my perception I was panicking in the face of death. I said to Mary the next day, "I couldn't breathe, and they didn't know what to do about it." My whole body shook as I desperately fought for air. I asked for oxygen and was given it, but since I was breathing very shallowly, it took a while for even breathing to return and for my panic in the face of what I then thought was my imminent death to subside.

Before what finally was a four-and-a-half-hour operation was over, I went through two more similar episodes of panic and gasping for breath. I was scared to death and scared to die. I tried to pray, but couldn't. I tried to recite to myself my favorite childhood hymn, "What a Friend We Have in Jesus," but the words seemed empty. I was convinced I was dying, and I recognized more closely than ever before in my life that I was no longer in even apparent control. The loss of control came to me in the crudest of ways, as I voided my urine during each of the three episodes of panic and gasping for breath.

Meanwhile the second surgeon, an open-heart specialist, came in and, having confirmed the oddity of my vein structure, scrubbed and took over the operation. He decided to go after the internal jugular vein, which lies more deeply in the neck. It was not easy, but after about an hour he had the catheter successfully placed and the operation was then finished by the first surgeon. . . .

Reflections

M. Howard Rienstra

After four and a half hours of surgery I obviously was not going to walk out of the hospital that day. In fact, they kept me on six liters of oxygen; my fever continued to flare; and I was coughing up heavy sputum. They ran a culture on that sputum, and remarkably for the first time since January a specific infection was identified. It was pseudomonis, a rather bad infection of the lungs. It is now being treated successfully, but it would not have been had I not stayed in the hospital. . . . In fact, I could not have seen a doctor until Thursday, when the second stage of my new chemo was to be administered through my new Port-a-Cath. Speculation is always dangerous about things that did not happen, but it could be that if the chemo had been administered, the pseudomonis would have advanced to a fatal stage. By trying to stay in control I would in fact have been committing suicide. Thus the experience of dying which I had on the operating room table was really God's way of extending my life and his clear demonstration to me that he and not I was in control.

Paradoxes are always difficult to understand. The paradox of good coming out of bad reminds me of John Milton's paradox of the "Fortunate Fall." Briefly, the fortunate fall argument is that if humankind had not fallen into sin, we would never have known the infinite love and mercy of God in Jesus Christ. In my case paradoxes abound. If when I was born I had a normal structure to my veins, I would now possibly be dying of pseudomonis without treatment. If my veins hadn't collapsed on Thursday I would not have had the Monday surgery with the same consequences. And even during the surgery, if I had not experienced the panic and gasping for breath, I would not have been willing to lose control. I had to be beaten out of my arrogant, selfish, and unbelieving sense of being in charge. Thus the primary benefits — the real good that came out of the apparent evil — is neither physical nor psychological, but spiritual. My belief has been strengthened and my faith deepened as dying seemed so near and God so far away.

Some background explanation is probably appropriate. I have always believed, or so it seems, I have always had a sense of God's leading and directing my life. From the time of my adoption at age ten, there could be no doubt about that. Probability theory would be quite inadequate as an explanation of my life. I have had a strong faith and understanding of God's presence — but that faith and understanding were not, as I learned on the operating table, the full assurance of my salvation. To put it in terms that were popular a few years ago, *I was* still on the throne of my life rather than Christ. Intellectually I affirmed the Reformed faith without doubt and I took great delight in defending it. I have never intellectually doubted in the slightest the doctrines of the incarnation and resurrection of Christ, and I would with only slight provocation explain and defend them. And I have always known and taught the distinction between believing *that* Jesus Christ is God and believing *in* Jesus Christ. Salvation comes only from the latter.

What then went wrong? Knowing all that, teaching all that, and even trying in the practice of life to live justly, I still was trying to keep control. I refused to give myself over to Christ completely. I had to be broken for the comforting assurance of the first question and answer of the Heidelberg Catechism — that I am not my own but belong to my faithful Savior — to become a reality. It had always been real intellectually and even psychologically, but not spiritually, because I wanted to belong to myself — to stay in the driver's seat. Perhaps the best example of that is my never having prayed during these past six years for my own healing. I could pray for others, but not for myself. To pray for healing for myself would be to lose control — and God who knows the secrets of our hearts would surely not receive the prayers of one who was yet resisting him.

My brokenness began on the operating table on Monday and continued on Tuesday as I confessed my resistance in tearful prayer with Mary, and then continued the same with my minister. The assurance of salvation began to become a reality as I experienced God's pursuing grace so vividly. I am not, except in the most common biblical sense, a saint. Nor do I anticipate changes in belief or in the practice of life that will be visible to others. But I have been spiritually transformed by the grace of God coming through these paradoxical experiences. I now know more than intellectually that I am not in control, that I do not belong to myself. I have the comfort of the Heidelberg Catechism and of God's real presence.

And all this because of an odd neck.

Risen Indeed: A Story

LAWRENCE DORR   *March 1990*

Sitting behind his desk, he could see only the top of the palm tree that grew in the courtyard at the corner of Killion Hall, the fronds waving with the exaggerated coquetry of geisha fans in a Gilbert and Sullivan operetta. The telephone receiver, his ancient, implacable foe, was pressing against his ear. He was listening to Corrine Young. He knew her from vestry meetings as a calm, middle-aged woman. She sounded distraught now, as if she were speaking from a sinking ship or reading the last communication of a lost revolution before the radio station shut down. Somebody had sent her a church publication from New Jersey in which the bishop discussed his visit to a Buddhist temple and his prayer before a Buddhist shrine. "I am not a Buddhist and do not expect to become one," the bishop wrote. "I do not believe, however, that the God I worship has been captured solely in my words, my forms, or my concepts." He had experienced only "a Western Christ, an American Christ, a major force in behavior control in the Western world and thus a source of guilt that played such a large part in the Western psyche." He had never met the universal Christ, the risen Christ. Since Christianity was only one of many equally valid world religions, there should be no more going into the world to preach the good news to all creation. The bishop of Newark rescinded the Great Commission. Once again, he thought, Christ crucified was a foolishness and a stumbling block to someone.

"You're not listening," Corrine said.

"I am." Below him the courtyard was silent and clean. He wanted peace, palpable now with the students on their Easter vacation. The telephone cord kept him prisoner.

"Can you imagine Buddhists embarrassed by Buddhism's 'exclusiveness'?" she said.

After the death of her alcoholic husband six years ago, Corrine had gone back to school to get a degree in comparative religions.

"Can you imagine them standing in St. Michael's nave?"

He could. He could imagine a fat Buddha appearing after the announcements, after the little children had come in from Sunday school to join their parents in the Eucharist. The Buddha could sit where Santa Claus usually stood on Saint Nicholas' Day.

With a great clatter, two boys on skateboards bounced down the steps in front of Dobson Hall, the humanities building, then with a loud thud landed in the courtyard. One of them looked up. Skateboards were prohibited in the buildings and courtyards. He waved. The boys waved back.

"What hurts me most," Corrine said, "is that the bishop deliberately wounds us by calling the Resurrection 'physical resuscitation' when he is so sensitive and understanding of everybody else's feelings. He knows exactly the words to use to hurt us most. Why does he do it?"

"To prod us into bellowing nasty and stupid things." He remembered the electric cattle prods the buyers brought to the ranch, the bellowing, terrified cows, the sweet smell of their sweat mixed with the smell of dust and manure. He had been a ranchhand when he first came to America.

"Without the Resurrection I have nothing," Corrine said. "You can't imagine the desolation I feel."

*   *   *

He had reached Salzburg at five in the morning in early April 1947. He was dizzy with hunger. He didn't know what day it was, but he was certain of the time. There were church clocks everywhere. By eleven, he stood on the sidewalk across from the U.S. Military Headquarters watching soldiers going in and out, all dressed in clean, well-pressed uniforms. A detachment of tall military police in shiny helmets glided on rubber-soled boots toward the barrier, demigods returning to Olympus. He had never before encountered marching soldiers without first hearing their hobnailed boots. Two years before, in '45, Salzburg had become part of the U.S. zone. In the distant past it had been a Roman settlement named Juvavum, marked in history by the fact that it was here that Heruli had martyred Saint Maximus. After that came the Goths, Huns, and Charlemagne. When salt was found under the hills, the natives renamed the town Salzburg. From where he was standing he could see the house in which Paracelsus the alchemist had tried to turn lead into gold in the 16th century. The house, painted bluish-grey, was streaked with water marks that made it shabby and scuffed like an old boot. He watched the civilians entering the American Express offices. He decided to hit a civilian instead of a soldier. It would still land him in jail and he had heard it on good authority in Vienna that American prison food was first class. They even had plates divided into sections. In one section there would be sliced Spam, in the next beets, and the third would hold green beans.

He had seen his first American in Vienna last year after his escape from Hungary. In Vienna he had lived in the international zone, and had gone every day to the American Library on Kartner Strasse to look in the slick magazines for the beautiful pictures of food. He liked the Spam advertisement best. In the picture the tin can was partly peeled back, the remaining lower, narrower part forming a pedestal for the naked Spam. It made him think of the rotating pedestal at the nightclub CASINO ORIENTAL, on which he stood three nights a week as THE LIVING CLASSICAL STATUE, striking well-known poses to the accompaniment of classical music. He was covered with either white or bronze paint that clogged his pores and had to be removed after 25 minutes. He lived at the Hotel Wandl, because the management didn't insist on passports. The hotel was a few blocks from St. Stephan's cathedral, just off the Graben, in the international zone, where the MPs of the four occupying powers rotated every three months. When he found out that the Russians' turn was coming, he knew it was time to leave. The Russians were known to make political refugees disappear from the streets, never to be seen again. He decided to go to Salzburg, to the U.S. zone, and spent his last Napoleon gold pieces on a high-quality false passport. The passport turned out to be useless. At the final checkpoint before the U.S. sector, Russian soldiers pulled him off the Arlberg Express and marched him away from the train with a burp gun pressed into his back. At first he couldn't think at all or feel fear or any other emotions he had expected to feel. There was nothing other than the sensation of his legs moving without his consent. The gun that touched his back had become a control rod taking over his life. He smelled the Russians: their filthy uniforms, their cigarettes (mahorka rolled in newsprint), their cooking. Their voices made him shudder: nobody had ever addressed him in Russian without abuse, as if charity and love had been expurgated from the language of Dostoevski, Tolstoi, Chekhov, Turgenev, and all the nameless, martyred saints who, for centuries, praised God extravagantly in Russian. They took him to a dirty-white farmhouse with barred windows and locked him in a large room. There were people lying all over the floor like so many abandoned bundles and suitcases left behind on a station's platform. It was almost a year since he had crossed the Hungarian-Austrian border, had crossed over fences, felt his way around land mines. He began yelling and kicking the solid door, which opened suddenly. He smelled onions, booze, and nicotine. A bowlegged little Mongol in a greasy uniform was standing in the opening, waving his submachine gun as if trying to shoo chickens with a broom. To his amazement, he heard himself laugh because he was thinking that his own ancestors must have looked like this in the 13th century when they were fleeing from Genghis Khan to a walled town in Hungary. He took the gun, twisting it away by its round magazine. Then he heard a sound that was like a watermelon splitting open and he was standing alone. The others watched him walk through the open doorway.

The clock on Salzburg cathedral boomed out the quarter hour. Another clock on another church steeple boomed a second later, swelling the sound; then another joined their combined echo till the last one whirred all alone with the sick, dry sound of a clockwork in a child's abused toy. He looked up at the Monschberg, at the fort crowning its summit surrounded by snowcapped mountains. A young man, wearing ski boots, ski pants, and a Norwegian pullover, came through the door of the American Express office, putting bills into his wallet. He followed him, rehearsing his own moves. It was very simple. He would hit the American and people would call the MPs, stationed right here. He would be taken to their jail to eat off a divided plate. First the slices of Spam . . . He was only two steps behind him when the man turned and looked back. He had a friendly face that smiled at the world in general, even smiled at him. He couldn't hit him.

By nighttime he didn't feel hunger pains anymore, only light-headedness that made his eyes heavy and made him think of himself as a rundown gramophone emitting unintended comic sounds. He needed to lie down to stop the burning in his back, but he had no money for a hotel. The train station was out of the question. The police checked for tickets and identity papers. If they wanted to they could put him back into the Russian zone. The wet sidewalk turned icy gleamed in the glare of the streetlights. The wind blew down from Monschberg shaking the leafless trees, shaking him. The cathedral clock began to strike the hour, counting up slowly so that the other clocks could catch up. He crossed the square and entered the cathedral by a side door. It was already warmer inside the vestibule. He opened the second door. He had expected to see streetlights filtered through the stained glass he remembered from before the war when he had been his mother's companion at the Mozart Festivals, but the stained glass had been replaced by clear glass and he was surrounded by light he remembered reflecting from the snow before the machine guns opened up and he had watched people around him dance in a strange, contemporary ballet, bending their limbs at impossible angles before they whirled away to create a mediaeval tableau on the red snow.

He tried to find the ruby glow that should have been there to guide him toward the altar but the lamp was not lit. The altar was bare. It had been stripped of its linen and candlesticks. The door of the safe behind the altar was open. It was empty like the Parthenon was empty, always had been empty. He was standing in empty space where the sound of weeping and crying would always be heard, where hope had ceased forever. There would never be a new heaven and new earth, a new Jerusalem. He cried with dry sobs as if he had been drained even of his tears. He cried for the empty world, he cried for himself, he cried for his little Mongol great-great grandfather.

*   *   *

The palm fronds stretching toward his window imitated the hands of a narcissistic model in a press-on nail advertisement, and then the March wind transformed the vain hands into the beseeching hands of a drowning person. The courtyard was empty and silent after the departure of the boys with their skateboards. He decided to go home early. It was Maundy Thursday. They would be going to the 7:30 service. His wife had also signed them up for the 3 a.m. to 4 a.m. Friday Vigil.

The streetlight coming through the rose window was the only illumination in the church. The Roberts, the couple they came to relieve, passed them in silence on their way out. The stained glass in the rose window was an abstract design, the reddish-brown color like simmering blood about to come to a boil. By a trick of light or perspective, the image of Christ the King which was suspended from the ceiling appeared to be in the middle of the boiling cauldron. Last night with the lights on at the 7:30 Maundy Thursday the rose window had been a jewelled backdrop to the image of Christ the King. The service had begun with foot-washing and had ended with the dismantling of the altar and extinguishing of the sanctuary lamp. There was no recessional. People simply got up and silently left. Nobody stopped to talk. Outside he had been surprised to see the lit-up neon signs of the shops and fast food places and hear the muted bells as cars drove in and out of service stations as nothing was about to happen.

He knelt down beside his wife in the first pew. He was feeling dizzy. His stomach possessed an independent intelligence that automatically switched on if he was awakened between 2 and 4 a.m., as if between these parameters he had been programmed at some cataclysmic occasion to feel fear. He noticed the prayer books left open for them at the appropriate page and also literature for meditation. It irritated him, just as he was irritated with people who underlined books. He closed his eyes.

He saw his three-year-old granddaughter dressed in a white jogging suit standing with her back to him on a scroll of white clouds and blue sky. She turned and smiled at him. It wasn't his granddaughter, but it was the same smile: teeth even and white, chocolate-brown eyes sparkling. He felt incredible happiness, wholeness, then without warning the child vanished and he saw the soccer fields at his school where, toward the end of the war, the goalposts had been transformed into gibbets. He saw the people again with the boards around their necks, their heads bent, hanging next to each other, moving slowly like pendulums in some monstrous clock. He was a pendulum. He was part of the clock. There was no way to escape.

*   *   *

The smell was a mixture of the Easter lilies on the altar, the wildflowers the children had arranged on a wire frame in the shape of a cross, and the lingering odor of incense from the swinging censer carried in the procession. The daylight coming through the rose window reflected from the fair linen, silver chalice, and ciborium on the altar, and the festive garments of the attending priests, deacons, lay readers, and acolytes. The servers moved as in a slow dance, feeding the people kneeling at the altar rail. Corrine Young was among them. They all lived in an antagonistic world that hated and wounded them constantly with ridicule and hostility reserved exclusively for them that for some reason was perceived as sophistication or even as art.

The line moved closer to the altar. He and his wife were among the last. The ushers were right behind them. Some of the white-robed acolytes smiled at him. He had known many of them since they were babes-in-arms, had seen them at their baptisms. He was home here, home where he was loved with a particular love that went beyond his understanding, that could turn a wooden-tongued stranger into a son. He knelt down and made a cross out of his hands.

"The Body of our Lord Jesus Christ keep you in everlasting life," the server said, pressing the wafer into the palm of his hand.

Like a horseshoe the wooden railing encircled the altar. He was one of the people who had sanded it in '68 when they had built the sanctuary. From where he was kneeling he could look across at some of the other communicants. Their faces were radiant, glowing with an inner light that was unearthly in its beauty.

"The Blood of our Lord Jesus Christ keep you in everlasting life."

He drank, then stood up and followed his wife back to their pew. A solo trumpet began to play Charles Wesley's "Jesus Christ Is Risen Today." Because it was Easter he looked up at the choir loft where his young friend Michael used to play his silver Bach Stradivarius, lifting the whole church heavenward. Michael's trumpet had sounded soft and tender, as if he were incapable of uttering harsh sounds, and there was sometimes a forlorn tone that seemed out of character. He had known Michael since he was nine years old. He knew the whole family. The trumpet player wasn't Michael. Michael was dead, had died at the age of 20, and nothing he could do or say would bring him back into the choir loft this Easter or any other. He couldn't stop himself from crying. He wondered if he should leave now, stop disturbing people, and go outside. Then his name was called and he recognized the voice as all the others who had been called had recognized it. It was the voice of Him Who cooked fish on a charcoal fire for his friends and said: "Come and have breakfast." It was the voice that made them know that beyond chronos was the kairos of everlasting life. He looked at the image of Christ the King, at the Easter lilies on the altar, at the cross made of wildflowers, and he cried out with the instinctive cry of the newborn: "Christ is risen. Christ is risen."

"Risen indeed," the others shouted back.

Reformed Journal *Contributors*

Contributors are identified here as they were when they were writing for the *Journal*.

FOUNDING EDITORS

Harry Boer† was professor of missions at Calvin Theological Seminary and a founder of the Theological College of Northern Nigeria.

James Daane† was a long-serving minister in the Christian Reformed Church and taught theology at Fuller Theological Seminary. He was Associate Editor of *Christianity Today*.

George Stob† was a long-serving minister in the Christian Reformed Church.

Henry Stob† taught philosophy and ethics at Calvin College and at Calvin Theological Seminary.

Henry Zylstra† taught in the English department at Calvin College.

OTHER WRITERS

Roy M. Anker has taught in the English departments at Northwestern College (IA) and Calvin College.

Lionel Basney† taught in the English departments at Houghton College and Calvin College.

Daniel H. Benson, formerly of the Judge Advocate General's Corps of the United States Army, has taught at the Law School of Texas Tech University.

Allan Boesak, a prominent anti-Apartheid activist and a minister in the Uniting Reformed Church of South Africa, has also served as president of the World Alliance of Reformed Churches.

Harold Dekker† was a minister in the Christian Reformed Church and taught missions at Calvin Theological Seminary.

Peter De Jong† was a minister in the Christian Reformed Church who served for a time as a missionary in China.

Lester DeKoster† taught in the Communications department at Calvin College and was editor of *The Banner* and of *The Reformed Journal.*

Karen Helder De Vos has taught in the English department at Calvin College and is a writer.

Bert DeVries has taught in the History department at Calvin College.

Evelyn Diephouse served as Registrar at Calvin College; she is a minister in the Presbyterian Church (USA).

Lawrence Dorr is a Hungarian-American writer living in Florida.

Edward Ericson, Jr., has taught in the English departments at Westmont College and Calvin College.

Susan Van Zanten Gallagher has taught in the English departments at Covenant College (GA), Calvin College, and Seattle Pacific University.

Howard G. Hageman† was a long-serving minister in the Reformed Church in America and was president of New Brunswick Theological Seminary.

George H. Harper has taught in the English department at Calvin College.

Stanley Hauerwas has taught theology at the University of Notre Dame and at Duke Divinity School, where he is the Gilbert T. Rowe Professor of Theological Ethics.

Carl F. H. Henry† was the founding editor of *Christianity Today* and was one of the founding faculty of Fuller Theological Seminary.

R. Dirk Jellema† taught in the English department at Hope College.

Roderick Jellema has taught in the English department at the University of Maryland.

James C. Juhnke has taught in the History department at Bethel College (KS).

Hugh Koops† was a minister in the Christian Reformed Church and taught ethics at Western Theological Seminary and New Brunswick Theological Seminary.

Edson Lewis, Jr., has served as Home Missionary in the Christian Reformed Church.

Kathryn Lindskoog† was a writer of fiction and criticism.

George M. Marsden has taught history at Calvin College, Duke Divinity School, and the University of Notre Dame, where he is the Francis McAnaney Professor of History, emeritus; he was an editor of *The Reformed Journal.*

Richard J. Mouw has taught philosophy at Calvin College and theology at Fuller Theological Seminary, where he later became president; he was an editor of *The Reformed Journal.*

Mark A. Noll has taught in the History departments at Trinity College (IL), Wheaton College (IL), and the University of Notre Dame, where he is the Francis McAnaney Professor of History.

Virginia Stem Owens is an essayist and novelist who served for several years as the director of the Milton Center at Kansas Newman University.

Cornelius Plantinga, Jr., has been a professor at and later served as president of Calvin Theological Seminary; he was an editor of *The Reformed Journal.*

Jon Pott is editor-in-chief at William B. Eerdmans Publishing Company and was editor-in-chief of *The Reformed Journal.*

Bernard Ramm† taught theology at the American Baptist Seminary of the West and at Baylor University.

M. Howard Rienstra† taught in the History department at Calvin College.

Jack Ridl has taught in the English department at Hope College.

Sidney Rooy has been a missionary educator in the USA and Latin America.

Lewis B. Smedes† taught in the Religion department at Calvin College and at Fuller Theological Seminary; he was an editor of *The Reformed Journal.*

Leonard Sweetman has served as a minister in the Christian Reformed Church and taught in the Religion department at Calvin College.

Henrietta Ten Harmsel has taught in the English department at Calvin College.

John J. Timmerman† taught in the English department at Calvin College; he was an editor of *The Reformed Journal.*

Steve J. Van Der Weele has taught in the English department at Calvin College.

Marlin Van Elderen† was editor-in-chief at William B. Eerdmans Publishing Company and of the *Reformed Journal,* and later served as executive editor in the Communications Department of the World Council of Churches.

Mary Stewart Van Leeuwen has taught in the Psychology departments at Calvin College and Eastern College (PA); she was an editor of *The Reformed Journal.*

Bernard Van't Hul has taught in the English departments at Calvin College and the University of Michigan.

Ernest Van Vugt† taught in the Classics department and was Registrar at Calvin College.

Ronald A. Wells has taught in the History department at Calvin College; he was an editor of *The Reformed Journal* and of *Fides et Historia.*

Stanley Wiersma† taught in the English department at Calvin College.

Nicholas Wolterstorff has taught in the Philosophy departments at Calvin College, The Free University of Amsterdam, and Yale University; he was an editor of *The Reformed Journal.*